STEALTHILY BY NIGHT

Crécy Books publications by the same author

The Hunting Submarine
  The Fighting Life of HMS *Tally-Ho*

Operations Most Secret
  S.O.E; Malayan Theatre

STEALTHILY BY NIGHT

The COPPists

Clandestine beach reconnaissance and
operations in World War II

Ian Trenowden

CRÉCY BOOKS

DEDICATION

To the Father of COPP
Captain the late Nigel Clogstoun Willmott DSO, DSC* (RN
Retd) whom the author was privileged to meet, but sadly
only once.

Published by CRÉCY BOOKS LIMITED, 1995

© Ian Trenowden, 1995

ISBN 0 947554 54 8

Typeset by Ace Filmsetting Ltd, Frome, Somerset
Printed and bound by Bookcraft (Bath) Limited,
Midsomer Norton, Avon BA3 2BX

Contents

Foreword

I am honoured to be asked by Ian Trenowden to write a foreword to his book *Stealthily by Night* on the COPPists' clandestine beach reconnaissance and operations in World War II.

He has so rightly dedicated his book to Nigel Clogstoun Willmott whom he correctly designates 'the Father of COPP'. Nigel was an outstanding, independent and innovative naval officer and an exceptional navigator who founded and commanded COPP. I was fortunate to be accepted by him as COPP's first senior army officer in the rank of major, in May 1943, when COPP already had a number of successful operations to its credit and was firmly established. Although he was ten years my senior, we were of equivalent rank until his promotion to commander in January 1944. He was, of course, the Captain of the ship in every respect except for army discipline. At the COPP Depot in the Hayling Island Sailing Club, we shared a cabin; we soon became firm friends and remained so throughout his life. Nigel was a most courteous man, convivial, eloquent, well-read, full of humour, and an inspired and imaginative leader. He was also a strict martinet in all that mattered and fanatical about physical fitness. His thoroughness is illustrated in the many and detailed COPP training instructions, all written by him. In addition to being a very courageous operator, he was a fearless advocate with Admirals and Generals of his views on the organisation, training and higher operational control of COPP – so essential to its success.

Surprisingly nearly all his outstanding achievements were made when he was still a lieutenant commander. He gained the full confidence and vital support of Vice Admiral Lord Louis Mountbatten, Chief of Combined Operations and a member of the Chiefs of Staff Committee. Thus he was able to obtain essential priority support from all three Services and the specialist production agencies in the provision of personnel, training facilities and equipment.

The diverse operations required of COPP in the Mediterranean, North Africa, North West Europe and the South East Asia theatre of war were nearly all 'possible'. To write a comprehensive history of

COPP fifty years or so later was, in my view 'impossible', for many years, at least thirty, security constraints had overshadowed any serious attempt to do so. Some publications over-dramatised and over-personalised, appeared, by authors who worked uninhibited by such constraints. However, these did bring to the public notice the wartime existence of COPP and its purpose. Fatal casualties, premature deaths and normal attrition have dramatically reduced the number of ex-COPPists, particularly of the few army officers who could have contributed to a history. The author over a period of seven years in addition to interviewing available old COPPists has painstakingly discovered and researched many official documents and operational reports, which tend to be single-service orientated, and some illegally kept personal records, adding as they often do, interest and colour to formal histories.

Major the Reverend Alec Colson, MBE, MA, when a young emergency officer joined COPP at the same time as I did. I realised then that he was a determined, brave and persistent man. He was soon operating with courage and distinction in Burma. Later he was granted a permanent commission in the Royal Engineers retiring in 1960 to take Holy Orders. At our occasional small reunions he invariably told me that something must be done over our history. Finding retirement hard work and in view of the difficulties mentioned above, I avoided action. However, he persisted and found through the Imperial War Museum an author, Ian Trenowden, who had in a fascinating book *Operations Most Secret* on SOE in the Malayan Theatre, made reference to COPP; he succeeded in persuading him to take on this history. Alec Colson, our 'COPP Padre', is totally responsible for initiating the writing of this book and deserves full credit for doing so.

The author points out that appalling losses do occur in amphibious operations where adequate knowledge of the navigational, pilotage and beaching conditions, and of the natural and man-made obstacles and enemy dispositions is not available. The primary purpose of COPP was to obtain that vital information not available from any other source. However, the reader may wonder at the diversity of COPP operations in the various campaigns from reconnaissance for the major assaults for North Africa, Sicily, Italy and North West Europe to reconnaissances for numerous minor operations down the Arakan coast and delta areas of Burma. Inevitably for Burma, operational planning and control were devolved to a low level. Although these operations provided valuable support in assisting the 14th Army to defeat the Japanese Field Armies and seize the port of Rangoon before the monsoon, it probably led to an accepted lack of the strict high-level control of planning, briefing and operations needed for the subsequent strategic reconnaissances of Phuket Island and the Malayan beaches, where exceptionally brave COPPists were killed, captured and in some cases, executed, and in two cases evaded capture to link up with SOE in Malaya.

Fortuitously, the invasion of Malaya took place across the planned beaches unopposed as the Japanese had capitulated following the dropping of the two atomic bombs on Hiroshima and Nagasaki.

Many who landed on those beaches said that owing to their very poor bearing capacity, the operation was a complete shambles in many areas. If the landings had occurred against the usual ferocious Japanese opposition, the outcome might have been disastrous. COPP could have received some unjustified blame.

COPP evolved in the Mediterranean with many successes but inevitably at a cost in lives as expertise was developing. In North West Europe the proximity of all headquarters enabled the very highest level of control to be exercised, and the availability of every conceivable support ensured that it was correctly, effectively and sparingly used without the loss of a single casualty. Owing to the completely different circumstances and vast distances in South East Asia, it had many tactical successes to its credit, but the strategic missions, although they made a contribution, were not sufficiently effective and were too costly in casualties.

Nigel Wilmott did more than any other man has done to improve beach reconnaissance and evolve the means of minimising the inherent risks of amphibious assault.

Ian Trenowden has from much depleted sources masterfully collated an historic account which will stand as an authentic record of Beach Reconnaissance in World War II.

Logan Scott-Bowden

Major General L. Scott-Bowden, CBE, DSO, MC*
COPPist May 1943 to June 1944

Major General Scott-Bowden was one of two COPP personnel, who landed on the Normandy beaches to reconnoitre, months prior to the D-Day landings.

Notes on Photographs

Sadly no collection of photographs of COPP in wartime can ever be complete. The illustrations for this book are mainly from the collections of former COPPists: many prints are enlargements of tiny wartime snapshots. Wartime COPPists who have seen them, are surprised how many contemporary photographs were taken and survived.

Where ascertainable, copyright holders have been approached for their permission to reproduce them. Pictures of the 1977 Reunion appear courtesy of Martyn Hayhow Photography, Hayling Island.

The photographs of Nicholas Hastings, Paul Clark, Peter Wild (with dog), and Prue Wright appeared in John Bull, in 1957. The author has tried but has been unable to trace the photographers.

Acknowledgements

All Copyright material quoted appears courtesy of the Copyright holders.

In addition to the late Nigel Clogstoun Willmott, DSO, DSC*, RN (retd) – 'The Founder of COPP' – and Major General Logan Scott-Bowden, CBE, DSO, MC*, the author wishes to acknowledge help from the following, listed alphabetically:

COPPists and SBS, and COPP personnel
Commander Frank Berncastle, DSC*, RN (retd), FRICS
James Booth, C de G
John Bowden, DSM
Terence Burke
Major, the Reverend Alec Colson, MBE, MA
Colonel G. B. Courtney, MBE, MC
Captain Basil Eckhard
Alexander Fullerton
Richard Fyson, DSC
Geoffrey Galwey
Nick Goodyear
Rear Admiral Geoffrey Hall, CB, DSC, DL
Peter Hamilton
John Hashim
Alastair Henderson
Commander Ken Hudspeth, DSC**, RANR (retd)
Commander George Honour, DSC, VRD, RNVR (retd)
The late Lt-Cdr Alex Hughes, DSC, RNR
David Kay
Douglas Kent, DSC*
Hugh Maynard
Ruari McLean, CBE, DSC, C de G
Captain Neville McHarg, DSO, RN (retd)
Francis McNally

Kim Patterson
Mike Peacock
Mike Pearson
Jack Phillis
Major Jack Powell, MBE, MM
The late Arthur Ruberry
James Sherwood, MM
Don Slater
Commander Ralph Stanbury, DSC, RN (retd)
The late Lt-Cdr Peter West, DSC, RNVR
Ronnie Williamson

Others, all of whom helped
Daphne Bancroft
Gus Britton, Research archivist RN Submarine Museum
David Brown, Naval Historian, Ministry of Defence
Peter Elliott, RAF Museum, Hendon
The late Admiral Sir Royer Dick
The late John Milverton
Sally Mitchell
John Pierce Williams
Roderick Suddaby, Philip Reed and Ron Markie of the Imperial War
Museum, Lambeth and Duxford

Introduction

ORIGIN OF COPP

'During 1941 and 1942, shortage of equipment restricted our amphibious operations to a series of small scale raids. These were carried out both in conjunction with the Libyan campaign and from the United Kingdom. As a result of experience gained in these operations it became clear that the information on beaches that could be obtained from charts, PRU (Photo Reconnaissance Unit – aerial photography) and existing intelligence sources would not give sufficient details on which to plan larger operations. Information would be required by the navy about the approaches and the beach to seaward; the army would require details of the texture of the beach, beach exits, defences etc. Accordingly a specialist party of sailors and soldiers under a qualified navigating officer was collected. This party was first used in connection with large scale landings in North Africa and, as a result of information obtained, approval was given to the formation of a number of these parties. Owing to the nature of their work the Chief of Combined Operations was made responsible for their training, the personnel being supplied through the Admiralty and the War Office.'*

Every word of the forgoing official account is true, but it is not the whole story. This is the first attempt to produce a history of the whole of COPP, based on official documents.

Combined Operations became a stratagem identified with the Second World War, but the principles of amphibious warfare and of inter-services co-operation had been established between the wars:

1. Seaborne landings to pre-empt long land campaigns.
2. No seaborne landings, without prior reconnaissance of invasion beaches.

COPP (Combined Operations Pilotage Parties) were established for

---

* Combined Operations Headquarters, Bulletin T/18, dated June 1945, *COPP: Combined Operations Pilotage Parties* (Courtesy Imperial War Museum).

these purposes – allied to the equally important task of guiding the invasion fleets in to the right beaches – established by the strenuous efforts of Lt-Cdr Nigel Clogstoun Willmott DSO, DSC*, RN. His uncle 'Cloggy' had served with the ANZAC forces at Gallipoli – with 'up the sharp end' experience.

In 1911, Captain H. O. Clogstoun, RE, had founded one of the first field companies of Royal Australian Engineers. Thereafter he'd served with them during the fierce fighting at Gallipoli and later in France. Captain Clogstoun was badly wounded. Nigel Willmott knew that at Gallipoli, seaborne attacks had been hampered by under-water, barbed-wire defences, unsuspected and untouched by the naval bombardment. . . . Something that – had there been beach surveys, prior to the attack – would have been discovered and means devised of breaching the obstacle. Heavy losses were incurred through difficulty of coordinating the flat-trajectory naval bombardment with troop movements. If the bombardment ceased for fear of hitting our own troops; the Turks reoccupied trenches that the shellfire had forced them to evacuate. It was clear evidence of a need for naval and military co-operation.

Nigel Willmott was well aware that in proposing to form COPP he was batting on a sticky wicket: the SBS (The Special Boat Section) was already established and its remit included beach reconnaissance; but SBS was busy on other things. There would be other problems, too, besides demarcation. The units had to be commanded by lieutenants RN, who had done the 'Long-N', Navigator course or the Hydrographer course. Such personnel were at a premium, and generally ear-marked for orthodox general service. They were after all capable of cruisers or aircraft carriers.

Logistically, Willmott's task would be, principally to obtain or develop the right kind of craft and equipment for reconnaissance surveys. A first thought was the pre-war commercially marketed *folbot*, but the company was thought to have gone out of business. . . . In any case the commercially produced article was a two-seat, sports canoe – built for calm seas, lakes, rivers and inland waterways – a puff of wind or a choppy sea and it would probably turn turtle . . . or so it was thought.

SOURCES

COURTNEY, B. G., *SBS in World War Two*. The story of the original Special Boat Section of the Army Commandos, Robert Hale, 1983.

SMYTH, Brigadier Sir John Bart, VC, MC, *Leadership in Battle 1914–1918*, David and Charles, Newton Abbott, 1975.

CHAPTER ONE

The Evolution of Beach Reconnaissance

S ome thirty years after the end of the war Nigel Willmott set down his own recollections of the evolution of COPP in an aide memoire, composed in his yacht, in Chichester harbour; he presented them to the late Earl Mounbatten of Burma, who had consented to be patron of the 1977 COPP reunion. Willmott began by stating that the *Admiralty Seamanship Manual* Vol II, edition circa 1920 regarded previous reconnaissance for all landing parties as a sine qua non. His uncle Clogstoun had been badly wounded at Gallipoli, so that Nigel Willmott felt he had a personal interest in this chapter regarded as recondite in 1939. His own reconnaissance reports for the first projected major amphibious assault of the war, at Rhodes, scheduled for early spring 1941, seemed to have disappeared without trace; no-one seemed to remember reading them, nor were the officers who'd seen them taken with the idea. Willmott had experienced at Narvik guerrilla and commando service; though the Boer word Commando was not used at that time. So that as Navigator on the Naval Force Commander's staff he persisted in pressing for prior reconnaissance before strategic landings; forseeing danger in raids where the troops mis-landed – just as they had done at Suvla Bay in 1915.

He succeeeded in converting the Force Commander, Rear Admiral Baillie-Grohman, and found Brigadier 'Bob' Laycock, who had arrived with the newly-raised Special Service Brigade, sympathetic to his ideas. It was Laycock who had introduced him to Roger Courtney. The Courtney-Willmott friendship became a long-standing alliance. Sadly after their successful reconnaissance the assault of Rhodes was postponed sine die, because of the need to evacuate Greece. The Assault Staff successfully acting as beachmasters to assist that evacuation. Throughout his time in this theatre he kept in touch with Roger Courtney.

In May 1942 Willmott was shipped home to the Navigation School and at the request of the new Chief of Combined Operations (Vice-Admiral Lord Louis Mountbatten), was transferred to the Combined Training Staff in Scotland, under Admiral Theodore Hallet and later Admiral Sir Wilfred Wood. Here he got a Beach Pilotage school for junior RNVR officers started – HMS *James Cook*, intending that beach intelligence might be transferred into sailing directions.

In mid-September 1942 he was suddenly asked to collect, organise, equip and train a team of navigators and SBS to act as reconnoitrers and assault pilots for Operation *Torch*, the forthcoming invasion of Vichy French North Africa. This will be described in detail in Chapter 6.

*

Anticipating somewhat, one of the lessons learned as a result of the North African Assault Pilotage experience was that landing craft who missed or ignored the Party Inhuman pilots or advice landed their soldiery up to 12-miles away from their proper designated landing beaches. But all pilots required were on station and got their first flights in to the correct beaches.

As a result of the experience in North Africa in December 1942 Willmott found pressure put on him to put his ideas for reconnaissance and assault pilotage on a permanent basis. Naval and Army force Commanders understood now the need for such teams – being faced with real plans but having few charts available. Charts in any case were generally intended to keep ships away from beaches. So that beach reconnaissance intelligence was needed at the early planning stage. Fortunately Combined Operations were well aware that such information gathering was a skilled operation, but whilst it was a high priority one, half-trained teams employed ill-advisedly might well blow vital strategic secrets; because of this Willmott was well aware of the need for watertight cover stories.

Willmott's first opportunity to demonstrate his theories in practice came – as will be seen – in November 1942, when he had personally participated in beach reconnaissance from a submarine and later acted as a pilot to the first assault waves of Operation *Torch*, the Allied invasion of North Africa, supported by teams he had instructed doing similar tasks on other beaches.

*

Willmott's ideas were far from popular but as a professional naval officer he realised that intelligence brought back at high cost in submarine-time and security risk, must inspire confidence in force commanders and even the Chiefs-of-Staff Committee. So that officers in command of teams must be Navigators – i.e. RN officers who had done the long-N course – or be Hydrographers. The sort of officers, one might say, who were capable of being navigators in cruisers. And he was keen to hazard them in folbot canoes off defended enemy beaches.

Willmott was also pragmatic enough to see that the co-operation of military and naval personnel which had characterised the Rhodes recce and the Party Inhuman ones was essential to their permanent establishment. Naval personnel could take soundings and do the offshore reconnaissance: onshore reconnaissance must be done by military personnel. Each COPP team – the term had now been adopted, though it was absolutely top secret – must have a Royal Engineers captain or senior subaltern, commando trained. All COPP personnel would require Combined Operations training – including stalking and unarmed combat – in case of enemy defender interference. The teams would also need much endurance and physical hardening and toughening would be an essential. It would all take time and corners could not be cut.

Around May 1943 a signal was received from the Commander-in-Chief Mediterranean, Admiral Andrew B. Cunningham, calling for the despatch of two more trained teams within a fortnight, and for the eventual provision of fifty trained teams. Willmott was not prepared to cut quality for quantity. He decided that ten teams would be a tall order, but was one that might eventually be achieved . . . . in time it *was*. Sad to relate that signal seems to have disappeared.

The Naval Historian was unable to suggest where it might be found. He advised the author to contact Admiral Sir Royer Dick, who might remember. The author looked Sir Royer Dick up in *Who's Who* and wrote to him. Next day the admiral telephoned the author's office and suggested it might be easiest if he gave his answers to the questions in the letter over the telephone.

Briefly his answers were as follows: he could not remember the precise text of the signal – that would have been the province of Staff Officer (Signals). Nevertheless he was in no way surprised that 'Andrew B' should have been in favour of setting-up beach reconnaissance teams; because he'd always favoured the principle of using the sea – amphibious operations – to avoid long land campaigns.

At the same time he doubted if Admiral Cunningham would have approved in detail of the principles by which COPP military personnel were attached to SBS, but trained by Combined Operations Headquarters. The reason behind this was that Special Forces units comprise people of high character, full of 'derring do'; so that they have to be kept on a tight rein and prevented from making attacks on objectives for which strategic offensives are scheduled. Personally Royer Dick had, he said, always favoured inter-services co-operation; as early as 1925 he had participated in inter-services Staff co-operation at Quetta, now in West Pakistan. He also mentioned that in 1942 both he and Cunningham had felt the Dieppe landing had been botched. In his autobiography Cunningham had praised the work of COPP parties after the Operation *Torch* landings. Plainly he could see the potential of COPP: an early important convert to Willmott's ideas.

SOURCES

NIGEL CLOGSTOUN-WILLMOTT: aide memoire prepared for Earl Mountbatten of Burma, dated 18 March 1977
Conversation with Admiral the Late Sir Royer Dick, 24 April 1989.
CUNNINGHAM, Viscount Andrew B. of Hyndhope, *A Sailor's Odyssey* (autobiography).
STRUTTON and PEARSON, *The Secret Invaders*, Hodder and Stoughton, 1958.
Imperial War Museum, Lieutenant-Commander A.I. Hughes DSC, RD, RNR. (Retd) Archive.

CHAPTER TWO

Reconnaissance Intelligence

This can most simply be explained by considering the requirements of naval and military force commanders.

Pilotage directions were the most important aspect from the point of view of the naval planning staff: both in general principles and detailed requirements. A prime consideration was that assault convoys should reach their lowering position, so as to release their landing craft at the correct time. They therefore required coastal silhouettes – from sketches or periscope photography – to assist in pin-pointing their position. Periscope photos could be developed inside the submarine. Naval force commanders also needed all natural land marks and navigational aids carefully checked, charted and verified. As depth can be used to provide a check on position they also needed echo sounding trace results, on a suitable course. To this one might add: recommendations for suitable positions for submarine markers or sonic buoys; precise fixes for navigational dangers and location of any sheltered anchorages.

For detailed assault pilotage directions: sailing directions and approach courses for the run-in; including time charts landing marks, bearings and approaches for dog-leg approaches: detailed enough for time-charts to be prepared. Silhouettes of beaches not only from the lowering position, but also from closer inshore, where landing marks will have altered.

Natural obstructions, such as rocks, bars, sand-banks, shoals; and man-made, such as seamines, nets, wrecks and scaffolding – would all have to be noted in sufficient detail for them to be charted.

In addition, COPP would have to have observed the strength of tidal sets close inshore; have established beach gradients by soundings; have observed surf conditions; have ascertained the geological nature of the beach itself and prepared beach plans to assist landing craft, shore parties and beachmasters, with suggested sites for piers and breakwaters.

Military force commanders would require to know beach gradients from low-water mark to beach exits; beach samples to determine bearing strength and assessments of the necessity for beach roadways. Beach obstructions natural and manmade would have to be listed as well as defences and the defensive nature of the ground. Detailed information on beach exits and an assessment of the equipment necessary to implement them.

*

In order to ascertain such beach intelligence it would be necessary for the folbot, once launched from its carrier vessel, to paddle perhaps two miles from a submarine anchored on the ten-fathom line, to a point about two-hundred yards from the water's edge. At this point the naval or military reconnaissance officer would go over the side and swim ashore. The paddler in the folbot canoe would then drop anchor and await his return. Canoe paddlers wore camouflaged, water-resistant clothing, designed to protect them from rain, wind and weather; though not designed to swim in.

The officer, on the other hand wore a swimsuit, designed to give him positive buoyancy and to protect him from cold, abrasions, fish stings etc. These suits were made of rubberised fabric, they had tight-fitting cuffs, ankles and hood. The suit embodied a life-jacket, inflated by mouth. The swimmer could adjust his trim by raising his hood's face mask to release air trapped in the suit. In the tropics a light-weight version of the suit was adopted. It was in two pieces: jacket and trousers. On both suits, leather patches protected elbows and knees. The jacket had an inflatable stole and built-in kapok buoyancy.

Naval beach reconnaissance officers did not swim unencumbered: they carried arms – a .38 pistol and ammunition, which might or might not fire after immersion – and a fighting knife. Later Major L. Scott-Bowden would prove that the best operational handgun for COPP operatives was the 0.45" Colt Automatic: it had superior stopping power and would fire after immersion, provided it was stripped-down after every sortie.

COPPists also carried equipment: a sounding lead and line, beach-gradient reel, wrist watch (in water-tight container), under-water writing tablet and Chinagraph pencil, an army oil-immersed prismatic compass and two water-proofed torches for homing on the canoe. Also carried would be survival and evasion equipment: copper acetate fish scares, 24-hour emergency ration and a brandy flask.

The E/COPP military reconnaissance officer would carry all the equipment previously described, except for the sounding lead and line and he might well also carry an augur for taking beach samples, rubber protectives to store them in and a bandolier designed to receive and hold the samples in the order taken.

Nigel Willmott's experience had already established that sentries onshore unless they are expecting an attack are not particularly vigilant and can be readily avoided. In all cases, however, the exception proves the rule. So that whilst onshore or in the shallows, both naval and military reconnaissance officers would have to be particularly vigilant.

The military E/COPP would not have time to sweep for buried anti-personnel mines. The presence of footmarks might reassure him that no mines had been laid, but only at low tide would he be likely to see such foot marks. The amount of time available on shore might well determine to what extent he would be able to use his specialist equipment. If unable to embed his beach-gradient reel's spike at waterline and pay it out behind him as he crawled up the beach, taking samples with the augur every time he encountered a bead on the line – he might instead have to rely on his own assessment of the beach's bearing strength based on whether his feet sank in. Always bearing in mind a minimum requirement of 14-inches of compacted sand.

Trenches, barbed-wire entanglements, defensive positions, fox-holes and weapon pit positions would all have to be noted. Above all – if possible without capture and compromise – beach exits had to be examined from a distance, or preferably from as close as possible. There could be no point in landing an army on a suitable beach, only for it to be pinned-down there, at the mercy of enemy fire, and unable to make a push inland. Ideally he should sketch the coastal silhouette to indicate the exit's position.

Whilst the military E/COPP was so engaged, his naval counterpart would be involved in taking soundings by a process similar to the use of the beach-gradient reel, save that having anchored the spike on the end of his line he would swim out taking soundings every time he encountered a marker bead. He would also have to swim through shallows – and quite possibly surf – to measure the limits of offshore obstructions. Both naval and military officers would have to keep a careful watch on the time they were taking in order to rendezvous with his folbot and paddler and, eventually, with their carrier vessel.

Information both reconnaissance officers had gained from prior examination of navigational charts – rarely accurate as regards beach approaches – their intention is to keep mariners safely offshore . . . would enable a beach plan to be drawn up.

SOURCES

Transcript Report of Operation David, Part 4 (Alec Colson collection).

LADD, James, *The Invisible Raiders*, David and Charles, Newton Abbott, 1958.

Combined Operations Headquarters, Bulletin T/18, date June 1945, *COPP: Combined Operations Pilotage Parties.*

Discussions with COPPists.

CHAPTER THREE

Early Beginnings

I n January and February 1941 – when the London Blitzes and the Battle of the Atlantic had become depressingly intense, a strategic attack on the Dodecanese was planned, to be mounted from the Middle East. The navigating officer responsible for planning was one of the first two to be appointed to the Staff of the Admiral who was flying out as Force Commander. Rear Admiral H. T. Baillie-Grohman had had Combined Operations experience in the 1940 Norwegian operations. Subsequently he was to help found the Raiding Craft base HMS *Tormentor*, at Warsash. His navigation officer, Lieutenant-Commander Nigel Clogstoun Willmott DSC RN, was already in the Middle East, on loan to GHQME, for special services. He had some knowledge of the islands.

Nigel Willmott was well aware that existing hydrographic information and pilotage information of the islands would be insufficient to enable landing-craft carrier ships to fix their position four miles off-shore at night, to provide a reasonably accurate release point for troop-laden landing craft.

In particular nothing was known of the background to the proposed landing beaches, nor were there defined landmarks for the landing craft to pick up as they made their run in. So it seemed there would be little likelihood of the landing craft finding their correct beaches even if released at the correct location. In any case, even if the correct beaches were pin-pointed no-one could say they were not barred, or rocky nor if they had steep gradients. If they were: troops, vehicles and naval beach parties* would be pinned-down in stranded craft, well off-shore and at the mercy of the defence.

Aerial photographs existed, of course, but these did not show such

* Later to be known as RN Beach Commandos: their duties were certainly no picnic party.

essential military information as bearing capacity of beaches, height of anti-tank obstacles like sea walls and ledges, nor did they show whether beaches were mined.

Willmott was acutely conscious that there was no naval beach organization and that landing craft officers were untrained for pilotage duties. In addition the vast majority of craft had no magnetic compasses, or none that were of practical use. All-metal landing craft are not a good compass platform. None the less planning was going ahead for a landing of at least a division in strength.

Willmott decided on his own initiative that it was essential to obtain pilotage and beach information: or the operation would be doomed to failure. It was known that the intended invasion beaches were guarded, so that any attempt at reconnaissance must be made circumspectly.

He therefore proposed to conduct his own reconnaissance from a submarine, then by dinghy – provided a dinghy could be carried by a submarine.

Despite considerable opposition – chiefly because it could lead to loss of a submarine, or compromise of the offensive – Willmott began an early morning programme of swimming training in Cairo . . . not something he enjoyed. In 1989 he was to tell the author: 'I didn't enjoy swimming – I don't even now, when I live in Cyprus!'

*

Eventually Willmott was allowed to sail, in March 1941, in HMS/M *Rorqual* (Commander Dewhurst RN) to do a preliminary reconnaissance and to report on the possibilities of a proper one. First of all parts of the islands of Kasos and Scarpantos were investigated and night pilotage directions for landing craft compiled, as well as silhouette sketches and as much beach information as could be gleaned by periscope observation. This proved that a skillfully handled submarine could approach beaches close enough to observe the essentials, including military defences. Willmott couldn't pick and choose: *Rorqual* was a minelayer and he might have fared better in a smaller, more manoeuvrable S- or T-Class boat – that could have got closer inshore.

The Rhodes Recce
At this stage the strategic plan was changed in favour of an assault on Rhodes: to pinch off the city and the north end of the island. Tank landing craft were to be used and beach pilotage information was *urgently* required as well as military intelligence: could tanks get into the

town? The value of Willmott's researches had evidently been realised.

Fortuitously Willmott now met Lieutenant Roger Courtney, King's Royal Rifle Corps, of the Special Service Brigade – part of Layforce – recently arrived. Courtney had two two-men folbot canoes and some trained men. The folbots were of the peacetime commercial pattern. In England Courtney had used them to make audacious dummy attacks on warships in the Clyde. Folbots were collapsible but hitherto had been carried by MTBs. Experiments proved they could be carried by submarines.

*

The craft had their disadvantages: they were still as produced prewar, with seats for two in an open well. Lacking spray canopies they could be readily swamped and were unseaworthy in a wind approaching a Force 2 or-so. None the less, with the assistance of Captain (S) 1st Submarine Flotilla (Captain S. M. Raw RN), Willmott and Courtney practised launching, canoeing, swimming and recovery, camouflage and infra-red torch visibility trials. They bought privately most of the gear required and succeeded in getting two of the first Infra-red transmitters and receivers in existence loaned to them. These had been produced for the RAF. Their principle is identical to the modern high-technology Infra-red light beacons, used by downed Tornado pilots in the Gulf War. Infra-red emissions, invisible to the naked eye; though visible to the pilot of a CSAR (Combat Search and Rescue helicopter) wearing night glasses. Or in the Case of the COPP RG ('Red-Green') seen through the glass of the receiver.

All their equipment had to be water-tight, pressure tested to a depth of five-feet. The military Assault Division gave them assistance but pressed them to hurry.

The swimming reconnaissance was to be done wearing longjohn' underpants and submarine sweater, both well soaked in 'crab fat' (periscope-grease), with a Gieves-waistcoat for buoyancy. Interestingly in the midst of doing their planning the pair realised the need for a cover story: this was to be that their recce was from an MTB, preparatory to a raid on the south-east part of Rhodes Island. Their MTB had struck a drifting mine – there was no shortage of those – and sunk. The pair were to be armed: the canoe paddler with a Tommy gun; the swimmer with a 0.38-inch revolver – waterproofed inside a cellophane envelope – at that time considered the best method.

Willmott and Courtney set sail towards the end of March 1941 aboard
HMS/M *Triumph* (Lieutenant-Commander S. Woods RN). They were
accompanied by Lance-Corporal J. B. B. Sherwood RASC (later captain
J. B. B. Sherwood MM, Royal Ulster Rifles). Sherwood had joined up
as a driver RASC, but it was not inappropriate that he should have
reached the original Folbot Troop, in September 1940, at Sannox, north
of Corrie, on the east coast of the Isle of Arran. Before the war Jimmy
Sherwood had bought himself a two-seater folbot – it had cost £15 –
and he had sailed it in Eire, where he was living, in Kingstown harbour
(now Dun Laoghaire). Before the sailing gear arrived he had got in
plenty of paddling experience which proved useful once he joined the
folbot troop. For sailing his folbot did not have a drop keel, or centre
board. Instead there were pivoting side, or barge boards, as with a
Thames barge. All that now seemed long ago.

The first Folbot Troop – fifteen strong, with ten canoes – survived
because Courtney had the ear of Admiral Sir Roger Keyes, then Head
of Combined Operations.

Experience to date had convinced Courtney that submarines were far
better carrier vessels than MTBs. Willmott and Courtney thought alike
on most important issues; though probably not on the importance of
physical exercise. During the voyage to the operational area the weather
was bad by day, but calmed miraculously by night. Several notional
enemy minefields were penetrated; and appeared to be bogus. The
necessity to cover the Battle of Matapan reduced the number of nights
available for the reconnaissance of the five designated beaches to five.
The waters were mercifully free of enemy surface patrols, though there
was much air activity by German and Italian aircraft from Maritza etc.

First periscope surveys were made of all the target beaches from
about a mile offshore. The method was soon established: the submarine
surfaced by night and charged batteries, then proceeded to about one-
and-a-quarter miles from shore and launched the canoe from the casing.
Lieutenant-Commander Willmott and Lieutenant Courtney would then
go in by canoe and confirm Inner Pilotage marks and investigate the
beaches above and below water. The swimmer, swimming the last 150
yards and spending two-to-three hours on shore before returning to the
canoe. They had made some practice runs at Kabrit beforehand.

The first sortie was made on a calm, moonless night in early April
1941; the objective to reconnoitre a beach north of Rhodes harbour.
Sherwood remembers vividly coming up on to the wet casing of the
newly-surfaced *Triumph*. It was a velvet-dark, still night and he could
smell the sea. He helped manhandle the canoe up through the torpedo-

loading hatch, which was then clipped shut against the need for a rapid dive, should enemy action necessitate this. The folbot was lowered over the side and drawn up alongside the starboard fore hydroplane, which was lowered to provide a flat platform on which he knelt to hold the canoe steady, whilst Willmott and Courtney slid into it. On the dark distant, silent coastline not a light was visible. Seconds later the pair cast-off and vanished shorewards, into the night.

It proved bitterly cold in the water. Willmott swam ashore, investigated the bar, rocks and seawall, noting the presence of barbed wire and taking soundings. He penetrated to within sixty yards of the large Axis HQ, in the Hôtel des Roses – some accounts have him crawling about its lawn – it is perfectly possible that he did. He had already concluded that enemy sentries, who are not expecting an attack, keep a pretty poor watch. At times sentries came within thirty yards of him. He discovered that moving with wave breaks muffled noise on a shingle beach.

Next night, launched once again by Sherwood, the pair made a recce on a beach south of Rhodes city, Willmott penetrated through wire onto a street. Sentries flashed torches on the beach ten minutes after his departure. Perhaps something was suspected – it was an exceptionally calm night – but no alarm was sounded. Next day periscope observation would be used to check the information gained.

After a night off, Courtney swam ashore to recce a beach 20-miles down the east coast. Willmott investigated another beach before returning to pick-up Courtney. Because Courtney's torch failed and he suffered cramp, Willmott had to go in and pick him up from the beach itself, homing in on his sound signal. A dog followed Courtney on the far side of barbed wire, growling at him but not barking . . . that had been a tense moment. The 'carrier' submarine had closed to within one-and-three-quarter miles of shore, by bearings. The canoe then paddled to within half a mile of it or-so and flashed her Infra-red beacon. The submarine did likewise for the canoe to home on to. In theory it worked very well, provided the weather didn't suddenly worsen. Operational necessity meant that it was a risk that had to be taken.

The following day, in the small hours, *Triumph* struck an uncharted shoal, close inshore and surfaced several times, under the eyes of defence forts. Little apparent notice seemed to be taken, though in worsening weather and with reports of a worsening situation in the Western Desert, when an urgent recall signal was received *Triumph* sailed for Alexandria forthwith.

Useful information had been gained: charts of the area had been shown to be wildly inaccurate. Willmott considered that he and Courtney had been very lucky. It was apparent that the job required a high degree of toughness and daring; first-class seamanship and navigational skills and, a well maintained canoe. Thanks to Sherwood there were no worries on that score. If reconnaissance was to be done continuously, improved equipment special gear and facilities would be required. Despite some necessary improvisation the operation had been a success.

Both Nigel Willmott and Roger Courtney were decorated for their exploit. Willmott received the DSO and Roger Courtney the MC. In addition Courtney was promoted captain and returned to Britain to form and train the No. 2 Special Boat Section. A unit that would use canoes mainly for sabotage and demolition, although military beach reconnaissance was part of their unit's designated role. Roger Courtney would probably have agreed they could achieve few of those objectives without a highly-skilled naval wing. In fact No. 2 Special Boat Section were to work mainly from Malta, and were destined to annoy the enemy considerably.

Sadly Willmott and Courtney's reconnaissance findings were never put to good use, because by the end of the month the Royal Navy was concerned not with invading Rhodes; but with evacuating Greece. Nothing had been done to put Nigel Willmott's proposals on an organized basis.

Willmott and Roger Courtney continued to keep in touch on an unofficial basis.

Willmott was then employed as a Principal Beach Master in Greece. He was to organize other operations – including a survey of Cyprus – in case of invasion and recapture. Thereafter he organized landing craft Pilotage parties at Kabrit, with practical courses in the Red Sea. Willmott had by now convinced himself that in the future naval reconnaissance should be done by naval officers: he began training naval personnel in beach reconnaissance and pilotage. Before the course was a week old, however, he had been enrolled as a desert navigator with the RAF's Long Range Intelligence Unit of the Long Range Desert Group. He had earlier served as a desert navigator with the Long Range Desert Group, using astro and stellar navigation in a featureless desert. LRDG files and private information indicate that SBS and RAF personnel went on LRDG patrols deep into enemy occupied territory.

*

PRO DEFE2 740
There follow Courtney's recommendations for folbot operations:
FOLBOT OPERATIONS Landing Special Boat Section
A few hints are here enumerated for the guidance of those who have
not yet had the opportunity of carrying out one of these operations.

1 Have a rehearsal in harbour, *in the dark*, with the same men and the
same gear you intend to work with, so as to acquaint everyone with
the conditions.
2 Preliminary reconnaissance through the periscope of the area of
operations is essential. Remember the unusual angle of sight when
examining a coast through the periscope e.g. "dead ground" is much
exaggerated. Enemy is clever at camouflage. Note every possible
hiding place for gun-positions and patrol posts.
3 If you have choice of locality important points are: -
(a) A good landing beach,
(b) Deep water close inshore,
(c) Easy access from beach to hinterland, steep cliffs are undesirable
for men carrying infernal machines.
(d) Remote from focal points therefore unlikelihood of efficient
patrols and coast watchers,
(e) A good natural mark on the coast which is easily recognised at
night i.e. a conspicuous hill to give Submarine and folbot a good
"landfall" and to give the the folbot a good "departure" for return
journeys.
4 Think out carefully any special requirement. A few are:
(a) A wooden mallet for knocking off external butterfly nuts on Fore
Hatch to prevent noise.
(b) Carefully test casing for loose sections which rattle, before
leaving harbour. Securing beams should be parcelled with canvas
and casing securely battened down to ensure silence when
trodden on.
(c) Casing party should wear thick socks over their boots. Rubber
soles prohibited, they slip on wet steel.
(d) Provide a number of white wooden chips or crumpled balls of
white [plain] paper on the bridge to throw over the side to
ascertain which way is off ship.
(e) Have a password and single letter recognition signal for boat
party to flash to identify themselves returning alongside.
Practice diving astern: keep screws in deep water.

Procedure

4–5 miles seaward trim up-for'ard, get boat and gear up and lightly secure on for'ard casing. Trim down using inboard vents to avoid noise. Go in on main motors at low speed. Asdic watch closed up throughout.

Recommended distance to shore 300–400 yards and calm water conditions. Italians are later in bed than most British, so pick a time after midnight. In Italy 17 is more unlucky than 13 – this could be a two-edged sword.

For the latter stages of approach have leader SBS with you on the beach so he can accustom himself to the "lie of the land" and recognise salient features. Stop ship as close to shore as possible, folbots are not designed for long distances. Before getting SBS on deck make them synchronise watches with the control room clock. After sending folbot in, withdraw a little keeping the bows heading for the beach. Reverse procedure holds good for re-embarkation.

Folbot operations are not practical except in calm weather. 1,000 yards is a long trip in a small canoe, when encumbered by heavy gear and explosives – 300–500 yards is the ideal distance depending on light conditions, given suitable depth of water. 100 yards per minute is fast canoeing. Carry out the enterprise on a moonless night.

Crown copyright: reproduced with permission Controller HM Stationery Office.

SOURCES

COURTNEY, G. B., *The SBS in World War II*, Robert Hale, 1983
PETERS, John and NICHOL, John, *Tornado Down*, Michael Joseph, 1992.
STRUTTON, Bill and PEARSON, Michael, *The Secret Invaders*, Hodder and Stoughton, 1958.
Public Record Office
DEFE2 1116 – COPP reports and history
WO24/939 – Long Range Desert Group
WO2/8/89 – Long Range Desert Group
DEFE2 740 – SBS

CHAPTER FOUR

Gap in the Development of COPP

Nigel Willmott's own account speaks of a gap in the development of COPP. Just how big a gap? one might ask. In fact, if one takes the date of the Battle of Matapan as the date on which Operation *Cordite* – the Rhodes reconnaissance – finished, it was over eighteen-months, from that date, before Nigel Willmott was asked to lay on another party for beach reconnaissance, and pilotage marking for a major offensive. Those eighteen months included at least three landings for which COPP facilities as envisaged by Nigel Willmott could usefully have been deployed.

By the time Willmott joined the planners at Combined Operations Headquarters he was no doubt aware of the background of the three principal operations involved. On the night of 22 April 1942, Operation *Abercrombie* was mounted. This involved one-hundred men of Lord Lovat's No. 4 Commando, together with fifty Canadians, who were landed from six Landing Craft Assault at Le Hardelot, near Boulogne. It was a reconnaissance in force. Naval forces supporting the landing crippled two German armed trawlers. The landing succeeded in its objectives, and the troops were re-embarked with few casualties. Lord Lovat, who led in person, as was his wont, modestly dismissed the opposition as half-trained and said its success was not due to skill on the raiders part, but the defenders' unpreparedness. None the less the enemy probably were scared, one month after the extremely successful St Nazaire raid. Sub-Lieutenant D. T. Kent RNVR – later with COPP5 – was a Beachmaster on the Hardelot raid, for which he was decorated with a DSC. Interestingly Lord Lovat's Commando raiding force was required to bring back beach intelligence of the sort Willmott might have requested: a questionnaire, no doubt memorised by Lord Lovat before going ashore, read as follows:

a. Nature of beach: width, composition, texture, surf etc
b. What is its gradient? (he couldn't assess this)
c. Width at time of landing
d. Obstacles on beach
e. Conditions of tide
f. Tidal stream experienced
g. Communications: exits available for infantry, tracked or wheeled
   vehicles.

In the absence of any implementation of Willmott's ideas, no special equipment or method had been devised: beach-gradient reels had still to come.

*

Another two amphibious operations: *Ironclad* and *Streamline Jane*, were mounted in the Far Eastern Theatre and involved the fourth largest island in the world: Madagascar. Nowadays it is known as the Malagassy Republic. In the spring of 1942, Japan's successful invasion of Malaya, followed by capture of the Dutch East Indies and finally of Burma had radically altered the balance of power in the Far East. Great Britain, having lost *Prince of Wales* and *Repulse* found it necessary to maintain strong naval forces in the Indian Ocean – to counter further Japanese expansion towards the West. It was vital to secure the Vichy French naval base at Diego Suarez before the Japs did.

The offensive was mounted by a British naval squadron, consisting of the battleship *Ramillies*, the aircraft carriers *Indomitable* and *Illustrious*, the light cruiser *Hermione* and the Dutch cruiser *Van Heemskerk*, under the overall command of Rear Admiral Syfret CB, RN. The first landing in strength of a mixed force, led by No. 5 Commando, took place, at Courrier Bay, on the north-west of the island, on 5 May 1942. Two days later the ports of Diego Suarez and Antisarene were taken over. The United States duly approved Britain's action and warned Vichy against serious resistance. Local garrisons, though loyal to Vichy offered little more than token resistance. Diego Suarez was soon converted into a big air and naval base of considerable help against Japan.

The attacking force had gained surprise – the garrison believed Courrier Bay secure from attack because of its defensive minefield, which the attackers' minesweepers had swept. The attacking force's landing craft, however, were hampered by heavy swell and it was possible to land vehicles and stores on only one beach – instead of the intended three. Everything that got ashore was drenched in spray. Landing of artillery had to be delayed. By contrast Adolf Hitler did place some credence in beach intelligence, on 7 May 1942 – having landed clandestine beach reconnaissance troops on some Maltese beaches – abandoned his plans to invade that island. In fact, two German parties were landed: one was captured and the other achieved nothing. Operation *Herkule*, the projected invasion, had envisaged preliminary parachute landings by German forces and a seaborne landing by Italian forces, using captured Russian tanks.

Returning to Madagascar, it is clear that the offensive, though swift and successful, could have benefited from prior beach reconnaissance and prior knowledge of defences and sea conditions likely to be encountered. The same was true of the September offensive when it became necessary to extend British control over the whole of the island.

*

On 19 August 1942, the Dieppe, reconnaissance in force was enacted. This involved a frontal attack on the port by all three services, with the intention of taking the port over for some time, capturing landing craft in the port and landing armour and capturing an airfield inland. The whole frontal assault being supported by commando landings on both flanks to neutralise coastal artillery batteries. It is well known that although the commando attacks on the flanks succeeded, the armour could never be adequately deployed, partly because tanks were landed in deep water and, above all, because they were unable to get off the shingle beach, surmount the sea wall and get on to the esplanade. As the late Earl Mountbatten of Burma – then Chief of Combined Operations – has pointed out: valuable lessons were learned at Dieppe, ones that saved lives on D-day, in Normandy. None the less beach intelligence could have saved lives on the Dieppe beaches. Beach surveys at ground level could tell more than aerial photographs.

It is perhaps a glib over simplification there were many other factors involved: a frontal assault, without prior saturation bombing or bombardment by capital ships, despite effective air cover, seems difficult to justify. Certainly beach intelligence could have helped. For Nigel Willmott, involved in planning at Combined Operations Headquarters, this knowledge must have been galling.

Sub-Lieutenant T. M. Burke – later to join the reconstituted COPP1, in the Far East – commanded a flotilla of Landing Craft at Dieppe, Pourville (Green Beach). He also had to make a detour to Varengeville (Orange 1 Beach) to pick up Lord Lovat.

SOURCES

DEFE2 1116 COPP Reports, History
DEFE2 63 Operation *Abercrombie*
ELLIOTT, Peter, *The Cross and the Ensign*, A Naval History of Malta 1798-1979, published by Patrick Stephens, 1980.
ANON, *Combined Operations 1940-1943*, HMSO 1943

CHAPTER FIVE

Development of COPP Resumed

The Rhodes reconnaissance had been a success and the information brought back considered valuable. Nigel Willmott felt that was in part because luck had been with the pioneers of the art. He was quite definite that it would not be possible to do such work continuously – precisely as would become necessary – without better gear and special facilities being organised.

Despite the proposals he put forward nothing was done by the Royal Navy to put the matter on an organised basis. The Army, on the other hand, started No. 1 Section of the Special Service Brigade under Lieutenant Courtney, promoted captain. No. 1 Section SS Brigade – perhaps an unfortunate title – used canoes mainly for sabotage and demolition purposes, though of course they were capable of military beach reconnaissance. Willmott felt strongly that a highly-skilled naval wing was essential. Meanwhile Courtney's No. 2 Section worked mainly from submarines, in the Malta area, becoming a thorn in the enemy's flesh.

When Courtney returned to the United Kingdom to start No. 2 Special Boat Section, Nigel Willmott after the evacuation of Greece, had sailed home through the islands, and whilst organising one or two other operations carried out a beach survey of Cyprus – against the risk of invasion and recapture. He had also organised Landing Craft Pilotage courses at Kabrit, with practical instruction in the Red Sea, and was Principal Beachmaster Middle East for some while. In November 1941 he began to train one RN and two RNVR officers in beach pilotage and reconnaissance, in cooperation with No. 2 Special Boat Section.

After the retreat from Msus, when the LRDG was disbanded, appointed Principal Beachmaster once again and Navigation Instructor,

Willmott took part in operations which did not come off and in a raid on Crete.

He was by now convinced that to be of value, naval reconnaissance should be undertaken by officers who were skilled, both in Navigation and Combined Operations – so that they could interpret what they saw without waste of time on the beach, which he saw as worth several guineas a minute. In that way their opinions would be of value to the staffs.

Back in Britain he was employed on Chief of Combined Operations staff organising provision of special navigational equipment (then almost non-existent) for Landing Craft and starting a Beach Pilotage School, later called HMS *James Cook* and to a degree in advising on Naval Beach Party training and equipment.

As his duties were full time there could be no reconnaissance training or development. He thought bitterly that reconnaissance intelligence is very little use if neither personnel nor craft are trained to use it.

In fact he was to be called upon to assemble operational parties far sooner than he anticipated.

SOURCES
Public Record Office
DEFE2 1116

CHAPTER SIX

Party Inhuman

In August 1942, to Willmott's chagrin – only two months before the projected North African landings were due to take place – he was told it was considered necessary to have detailed information of the beaches to be used in the Oran and Algiers sectors.

Invoking the strongest priorities Willmott assembled a party – code-named *Party Koodoo-Inhuman*. It comprised four qualified Navigation officers, with a dozen RNVR and RNR assistants, five SBS Commando officers and maintenance party etc was collected at HMS *Dolphin* in mid-September 1942.

They were hastily and partially trained and equipped with improvised stores and craft and were finally sent out to Gibraltar. The reconnaissance officer, Lieutenant-Commander Willmott and the three untrained ones (Lieutenant(N) Teacher RN, Lieutenant(N) McHarg RN and Lieutenant Amer RNR) were told just before departure that only periscope reconnaissance could be considered because Vice Admiral Gibraltar considered risk of compromise too great. However on arrival at Gibraltar by air, having left all their special gear behind, the Gibraltar authorities reversed this decision on hearing the method proposed and asked if onshore reconnaissance was still possible. A desperate search of Army and RAF stores in Oran, revealed four canoes and various other gear; the canoes were patched up and other gear improvised once again. Every assistance was received from Captain(S) 'Barney' Fawkes.

However as the submarines (*P219* (Lieutenant Jewell RN) Algiers; *P222* (Lieutenant-Commander Mackenzie) Oran) were sailing the prospect of a full reconnaissance was finally quashed by signal from the UK and only periscope surveys were done. Perhaps under the unsatisfactory circumstances this was as well.

*

The remaining personnel (Assault Markers etc) came out by slow convoy, so training time was lost. However by intensive training in Gibraltar a certain level of efficiency was reached. During this time three of the SBS officers were lent to land General Mark Clark and later helped collect General Giraud.

In order to ensure finding their beaches on a rather featureless coast the Assault Markers had to have a 'night run' near to their beach before the assault. This entailed five marking submarines being in their area to allow for bad weather, interruptions by patrols etc, four days before the assault. These Assault Markers went in submarines with an (N) reconnaissance officer to show them their beaches before D-day and finally meet the convoy in the submarine and act as an Assault Pilot to Landing Craft.

*

Operation *Torch* was the first major offensive to use prior beach reconnaissance and assault pilotage. Those facts were not made public at the time. No doubt, their cover story that they were Combined Operations Police Parties helped. Certainly nothing was mentioned in the papers, or in the wireless news bulletins, at the time. COPP remained secret throughout the war: its cover was blown by the Americans in postwar years. This account is based on an unofficial *Party Inhuman* Log kept by Basil Eckhard. *Party Inhuman* was their code name.

Captain Basil Eckhard, the Buffs and Special Boat Section, was one of those who travelled to Gibraltar by slow trawler for Operation *Torch* marking. He had been summoned to Fort Blockhouse to meet Lieutenant-Commander Willmott, in August 1942. Other SBS members arrived there too, and days were spent at Portsmouth dockyard trying to recover their canoes, collecting kit and wondering what it could all be about. All they were told was that their advanced base was code-named *Picton*. On 1 October 1942 the party left by train for Glasgow. Their journey was to take 24-hours in a second-class carriage, personnel victualled mainly on pork pies, bought at the stations they passed through. At Greenock there was no one to meet them. By now the popular rumour was that they were going to Gibraltar by trawler. Last time Basil Eckhard had made the journey he'd gone on a Q-ship: small but nothing like as small as a trawler. He found himself wondering why he always travelled in such small vessels. Eckhard, Thomas, and Cooper of SBS found themselves allocated to HMT *Rousay* (Lieutenant Mayford RNR). They met the officers, enjoyed an extremely good dinner and were taken down to the wardroom. It was very comfortable but they still had to sail.

They sailed on 3 October 1942, steamed round the Clyde, then took on the captain. Then left Gourock, knowing they were two-hours late to catch up with the convoy they were escorting. By nightfall they were in the company of HMT *Ruskholm* and *Stronsay* and some merchantmen. There was a tanker in the group and some brightspark promptly exclaimed 'Target for Tonight'. That could mean they'd be left alone . . . but all their stores were in the tanker; and they'd be no use without them. The weather worsened and Eckhard found himself sea sick. If he stayed on deck he was unaffected; but if he went down to the wardroom . . . .

Three corvettes joined them, together with HMS *Ibis*, a sloop, and they settled down to convoy routine: watching, waiting to be attacked and hoping to catch an unsuspecting U-Boat on the surface. Their passage proved uneventful, they passed a convoy from America taking troops to England – a most impressive sight – and no doubt attractive to a U-boat or Focke Wulf pilot. Even the weather calmed down. This lasted the five or so days it took them to reach Gibraltar. About half-way across some of their escort left to join a homeward-bound convoy. Once a submarine was sighted, but it dived. Twice aircraft were reported in the vicinity. The AA guns crews were closed up, but none came in sight.

They approached the Rock in late evening: the Straits were an impressive sight. One could pick out Tangiers, Tarifa, Ape Hill. To Basil Eckhard little seemed to have changed: he'd been in Gibraltar before, as part of a unit of fluent Spanish speakers and wireless operators trained at Lochailort, sent there to counter the threat of a pro-Axis take-over by Franco. There were very few big ships in the harbour; only trawlers, MLs, minesweepers and tugs. This sparked off a rumour that their destination might be Dakar. If so would it be a raid or an invasion? Unlikely, or a rumour deliberately put about.

Food was good in Gibraltar. Eckhard ran into someone who said he owed him £3.0.0, Gibraltarian money – Basil didn't argue – it paid for several dinners. The party lived on the submarine depot ship *Maidstone*, but she was very full and cabins hard to come by. Eckhard slung a hammock and found it agreeably comfortable. The party began training: coffee and teeth-breaker ship's biscuit at 0600, followed by a run up the Rock before breakfast. When that started to seem easy they did it in full kit. There were conferences in the forenoon; followed by canoe building practice, after lunch: canoe-building trials after dinner; and after tea night exercises, that could last till 2300. Eckhard's mornings were kept busy trying to corner supplies of ammunition and arranging for firing time on the ranges. He put the whole party through grenade-throwing practice; making every officer and man throw two. For his pains he had to pick up one that bounced back into the strongpoint: tricky but possible even with a four-second fuse. He had cautioned all concerned, that if a grenade was dropped it was to be left to him: there was no point in bumping heads and having an unnecessary number of people killed. He was congratulated by the CO and subsequently awarded a King's Commendation.

Tommy gun practice was accident free: single shots, automatic fire, from the shoulder, from the hip, even on the move: nothing was left to chance.

One evening SBS put on a much-appreciated demonstration of unarmed combat and fieldcraft, followed by a night stalk. Use of RG was practised and signals exercises held. Individual NCOs practised navigation. Soon beach sectors were allocated.

Eckhard allocated himself Algiers C Sector: he'd have with him Noel Cooper – also from Buenos Aires. Eckhard's and his parents were friends there. Cooper was to be lost on the Sicily operation. Each party had two canoes and both had to be up to operational standard. There were a great many stores to be sorted out. Cooper and Eckhard sat in their stored canoe and they topped 650 lbs. Cut Mae West lifejackets fitted around the canoe coaming gave it positive buoyancy.

They found they had been allocated submarines. Eckhard found himself lucky enough to be given *P-45*, HMS/M *Unrivalled* (Lieutenant H. B. 'Mossy' Turner RN), with whom he'd practised on the Clyde. In the fore ends two torpedoes were cleared out to make room for the two stored canoes. Nigel Willmott would be travelling with them.

Launching procedures were worked out. Basically the Torpedo Gunner's Mate was in charge in the fore ends: the SBS officers directed the canoe through the torpedo-loading hatch; with a casing party of six seaman, under the torpedo officer. That was good: each canoe had a seaman at bow and stern and two at each sling. It was all practised in harbour by day and night: the canoe would have operational stores embarked; its sides had been soft-soaped to facilitate passage through the hatch; the casing party had their lifelines secured to the gun platform; and the boat was trimmed down to facilitate launching.

They sailed at 0800 and after three hours passage dived, still in sight of Gibraltar. They stayed at periscope depth all day and surfaced at night. Adopting typical submarine routine they turned day into night. That meant lunch at midnight, diving at dawn and surfacing once it was dark again. Eckhard was glad to spend a few hours on the bridge once the vessel was surfaced. It was marvellous to breathe fresh air after the stuffy atmosphere down below. He found his ears clicked several times after the conning tower hatch was first opened. Willmott slept in the ward room; Cooper in the ERAs mess: Eckhard himself, in the passage between the control room and engine room. Sleep was only possible when dived and running on electric motors, not on diesel engines. The officers and crew were particularly good to *Party Inhuman*; that was their code name. Food was good: frozen meat, dehydrated or tinned vegetables and white bread and butter. Once when they ran short, bread was baked over night.

The first night from the bridge one could clearly see the lights of Spanish Morocco to the north and those of the Alborian Islands to the south. With a following wind and only slight swell, *P-45* was making 12 knots. It was agreeable for once not to have the fear of being torpedoed: to be the hunter not the hunted.

On the second night out Willmott and Cooper did a practice launching, homing back on the submarine using RG. Eckhard and Cooper went next. An alarming pink light suddenly appeared on the horizon, but it was only the moon. They were only about twenty miles off shore and one could see the lights of Oran.

3 November 1942 – Eckhard's father's birthday – the plans have finally been unfolded: it was to be an invasion of Morocco and Algeria by British and American forces. Later to be known to the world as Operation *Torch*. The landings at Oran and Casablanca will need to be simultaneous. During daylight they examined the Oran beaches through the periscope, knowing that much would depend on them there. When darkness fell they closed to within about a mile-and-a-half and used night glasses. Three would require reconnaissance: Red Beach by Surcouf: Green Beach by Ain Taya; Blue Beach by Ain Beide. Bordellaise Rock, one mile from the shore, was a good landmark for all three.

4 November 1942, Nigel Willmott and Cooper went inshore for a reconnaissance and were picked up again about 2½ hours later with the news that they had found an anchorage for Eckhard. The pilotage plan was that Salisbury and Eckhard would be dropped on the night of D–1 i.e: 7th November and they would flash the morse code letter C seaward – using RG if fishing boats or patrols were about, or white light if the coast was clear. Willmott would pilot in the Commando to Beer Beach and Cooper would pilot in the first flight of landing craft to Blue Beach. Once they'd picked up Eckhard's light or RG, they'd set their course for their beach on a bearing.

On the night of 5–6th November they closed the beach for a further recce. All lights were still on; so plainly the Vichy French did not expect an invasion at Algiers. During the day they spotted two trawlers – unarmed and engaged in fishing. Then to everyone's astonishment a man rowing near the rock, in a dinghy. Amazingly he didn't see them. They looked at the lights of the city. Algiers, the Paris of North Africa, how long would it be before they set foot in it?

November 7–8th: D–1 they had been wakened by explosions; either the invasion convoy was being bombed or their own destroyers were dropping depth charges. Packs and duffel coats were loaded into the canoe. Eckhard and Cooper would wear oilskins over battledress. 0715 from the bridge the sky was starlit, the lighthouse at Cape Matifou was still flashing, but the sea was far from calm. An east wind meant that they were on the weather side of the Cape. The swell would make launching difficult.

Their time table had been worked out: canoe to be launched 1930; then paddle to Bordellaise Rock and anchor. At midnight they'd begin flashing C-for-Charlie, covering the arc: 60° west of north to 90° east and not stop until 0100. Two hours later they were to proceed ashore and report to the Beachmaster and, hopefully, meet the rest of their party at the eastern extremity of Blue Beach and thereafter carry out the Beachmaster's instructions as required. Should the scheme be cancelled or the landing be made elsewhere on a lee shore the submarine would endeavour to pick them up by 0300. If that didn't happen they were to paddle to the Aguelli Islands and lie up there for a day. After that the CO would try and get them picked up. Failing that they were to make for Algiers as soon as they thought they could make it. We were on no account to be captured and the use of RG signals was intended to prevent this. Three miles from Bordellaise Rock the canoe was launched not without difficulty.

*

The canoe was several times smashed up against the submarine's ballast tanks, breaking the coaming support by the after cockpit. Nor was it calm near to Bordellaise Rock, waves were breaking over it. Eckhard decided against attempting to land on it: there seemed every chance of losing their gear and the canoe if they attempted it: the tidal stream was running east-west at an estimated 2 knots. It was impossible to keep the canoe still long enough to check bearings. At 2230 they managed to anchor close to the rock on its leeward side. At midnight Eckhard began flashing on a white torch. By now the submarine would have met the convoy transferred the pilots and Leading Seaman Greenwood to a landing craft and ML and returned to a position two-miles north of them. Shore lights were still alight and the invasion convoy was an estimated six miles away. Elsewhere along the coast other marker canoes would be waiting. Rollo Mangnall's canoe attracting unwelcome attention from a porpoise in the process. . . . Precisely at 0330 there was a sound like a squadron of aircraft: the arrival of the first flight of landing craft. They sped past within about twenty yards, Eckhard spotted Cooper aboard *ML 273* which struck the rock a glancing blow, but wasn't seriously damaged. Now with landing craft twixt the shore and marker canoe. Eckhard observed the shore lights still shining. A slight mist formed. Feeling cold he found they were both sitting in about two-inches of water – not enough to sink them, but uncomfortable.

A burst of Tommy gun fire sounded from the beach and bright flashes and loud reports told them that the ships and shore batteries were exchanging shot for shot. Searchlights came on and they could see a destroyer blazing away at the fort. The shore batteries suddenly ceased fire but the destroyers kept up their barrage. Eckhard was still busily flashing the torch and avoiding being run down by returning landing craft.

*

At 0400 Eckhard decided to go in to the beach. He grounded in alarming surf, with the canoe full of water and both occupants soaked by the time they'd beached it. On the beach were troops, wrecked landing craft, three jeeps and an armoured car – facing a six-foot cliff: the price of not letting the parties land to make their surveys. There was no Beachmaster. They hid the canoe under the cliff's overhang and waited for the Stukas to attack.

8 November 1942, the day had now dawned, having laid out wet clothing to dry and changed into their dryest they opened a 48-hour ration tin, hoping for something to cook. All there was was biscuits, chocolate and sweets. Still there were plenty of American rations lying about, including coffee. To date no sign of Stuka dive bombers. The invasion fleet out to sea was a fine sight. Much firing was going on on land. They learned that Fort Matefon had not been taken – the Commando had arrived four-hours late on the beach, when it was almost light.

Offshore two destroyers were bombarding what was probably the

Fort de L'Eau, finally after closing the shore they went steaming out at speed making smoke. They tried to salvage landing craft; the weather was worsening. The Americans seemed unbothered. Aircraft patrolled overhead and ships came close inshore to anchor.

The beaches were suddenly invaded by Frenchmen and arabs: friendly and on the scrounge for food, clothing, cigarettes. Their clothes were tattered.

Just before dusk the Stukas did come. The ships put up a terrific barrage. Seeing tracer going up at a low angle they realised the attack included torpedo bombers. USS *Yorktown*, a large liner was hit but stayed afloat. Aircraft survived some near misses. A Ju 87 flew right overhead at 100-feet and they wished they had their Tommy guns. The range seemed quite close enough. By the time it was dark the attack was over and they settled down for the night wearing everything possible, plus their blankets and duffel coats. The wind had risen to Force 4 or 5. More bombs fell in the night and the beaches were machine gunned and flares dropped. Eckhard slept through it all! He had been tired.

9 November 1942, a dawn air attack but without observable damage. Salisbury and Eckhard walked the length of Red Beach counting thirty wrecked landing craft; some quite large and ships moving into the Bay of Algiers, all except *Leedstown*. Commandeering three rooms in a house that had been an art gallery they lived on American rations, supplemented by oranges. That afternoon a bomb hit the *Leedstown* and they heard the crew were abandoning ship. The sea was rough and they saw about a hundred rafts full of men drifting helplessly towards the beach. They shouted to them to take off their tin hats and use them as paddles. On the whole the survivors were shocked and cold. The crowd on the beach saved many of them though some drowned and others were injured, through rafts crashing down on them, or smashed against rocks. Some very plucky arabs went into the sea many times. Eckhard was dragged out once by one. They found their art gallery billet invaded by survivors. Eckhard's duffel coat and blankets were on a negro soldier who'd somehow got ashore with his leg in a plaster cast. A housekeeper, the owner and his wife rendered aid and provided a drink just after another air raid, in which an aircraft was brought down in flames. Its crew were packed off to Algiers. Then Eckhard got his best night's sleep since Gibraltar.

10 November: Eckhard and Willmott went off to contact a unit that might give them some motor transport. They needed to get their canoes and stores into Algiers. They walked six miles to La Perouse, bought a bottle of wine and ate rations, regarding the shipping in the bay:

hundreds of ships of all sizes. Two American Ranger sergeants said there was no motor transport. They also met two British officers – paymasters – survivors from the *Leedstown*. Whilst chatting to them and changing some money for francs, a convoy of jeeps passed. They hitched a lift back to Ain Taya, in time to watch the nightly air raid.

They saw two planes shot down by Spitfires or Hurricanes. About to turn in Eckhard heard a commotion outside. He found an injured Frenchman, seriously wounded, in a pool of his own blood, breathing his last; he'd been riding a bicycle and had been knocked down by a jeep which had not stopped. The villa owner went off for a doctor and reappeared with a handcart. They got the injured man onto a stretcher left behind by the Americans but he died a few minutes later.

11 November 1942 – Armistice day – Nigel Willmott and Noel Cooper set off in search of transport. About 1400 they were back with a six-tonner and some boxes of army rations, given them by the RAF, at the airfield. They loaded on all their stores and drove around trying to obtain accommodation and stores for their gear. Everything was disorganised and they were told no rooms were to be had in Algiers. Cooper contacted the ML for cigarettes and Eckhard went off to HMS *Bulolo*, the HQ ship (Captain R. L. Hamer RN). On the quarter deck, grubby and dishevilled, he asked for Captain Hamer – he'd stayed with his family, before the war, whilst working in London. The officer of the watch was most disbelieving, but did take him to see Captain Hamer. Hamer, glad to see Eckhard gave him a couple of much-needed gins. Later, with difficulty Willmott and Eckhard obtained rooms at the Grand Hôtel de Nice: comfortable, reasonably priced, but no food provided.

12 November 1942 a day spent getting themselves organised and hearing one another's stories. Lieutenant L. G. Lyne RN and Lieutenant P. D. Thomas RNR – assault markers at a beach near Algiers – had been captured and had a tale to tell of French prison life. They had been paraded through the streets of Algiers, in chains, and had expected to be shot. They had been picked up exhausted, by a Vichy French trawler, but were able to sink their folbot, however, together with all their equipment – and their cover story, that they were downed aviators, had held and the operation had in no way been compromised. After a good natter they took a look at the town and tried to get acclimatised to their new surroundings.

November 21st Willmott, Hastings, Tongue, Hayden, Corporal Thompson and some ratings left for Gibraltar, leaving the remainder with two good canoes and one not-so-good, a fair amount of stores and nothing to do. Frequent nightly air raids still occurred. The population divided between the calm and the panic-stricken. In the morning they found broken glass everywhere. A few bombs had fallen in the town, some in the docks, but most in the sea. The AA barrage was still like a solid wall of steel. They drew rations for breakfast which Eckhard cooked on a Tommy Cooker, but ate their other meals out. The hotel had hot water on Saturday and Sunday only; and they made the most of it for baths. The town was generally full of drunks in the evening.

Despite the fiercest AA barrage Eckhard had seen, air activity by night continued, often with recce planes in the morning. They learned their art gallery billet had suffered a direct hit. Eckhard's party were uninjured; their blankets had stopped the broken glass.

*

November 24 to 2 December 1942: days spent with little to do, trying to relieve boredom. A signal to return to England via Gibraltar was most welcome. On December 5th troops and one naval officer embarked aboard HMS *Rochester*, whilst Lieutenant Ayton SBS and Eckhard sailed in HMS *Erle*, with other officers aboard other ships, escorting a convoy to Gibraltar. It was an unexciting journey: the water calm as a millpond and no serious alarms beyond gunnery practice. By December 8th they were at Gibraltar, but *Maidstone* had already sailed.

Basil Eckhard subsequently found himself posted to COPP Depot as military training instructor, attached 'on loan' from SBS. That loan was to prove a very long one indeed.

POSTMORTEM

At the time of the assault all markers and pilots were in station and as far as Party Inhuman was concerned the Assault Operation was a great success.

Some officers with beach experience helped to survey and work beaches after the assault.

Many Landing Craft were lost by using unsuitable beaches due to lack of reconnaissance and this might have jeopardised the whole invasion had the enemy not been known to be on the point of surrendering.

After the initial landings certain officers were used mainly on Pilotage duties etc on further landings (Djedjelli) etc. The parties gradually assembled in Algiers and Gibraltar.

*

There were many lessons learnt from this operation: it is essential for Officer-in-Charge Reconnaissance and Marking to be in closest touch with staff. It was not known till the last moment which beaches required which marking; and the question of whether this was feasible or navigationally needed or not could not be discussed with staff. In some cases the party was told to survey one part of a beach while final plans envisaged another.

Use of improvised gear, canoes etc was a waste of valuable officers, and that high degree of training and gear maintenance were required.

*

As no further operations in the Mediterranean were then likely it was suggested two (N) officers with naval and military assistants should be left out there to continue training. As this was not agreed by the Commander in Chief, the whole of *Party Koodoo Inhuman* disbanded and was sent home in driblets.

On return to UK at the end of November 1942, Willmott was asked to form a proper Combined Operations Beach and Reconnaissance Organisation. Subsidiary roles were for Assault Piloting and Marking duties, Royal Engineer assault and minefield guides and beach survey work during and after the assault. As a result of many conferences basic requirements for teams of ten were established (later an M/COPP : a lieutenant, sub-lieutenant or Midshipman, was added). In addition a pool of Sailmakers, Supply and Writer staff. All Combined Operations personnel were to be kept at COPP Depot for loan to units operating.

A TITLE FOR THE UNIT
Combined Operations Beach and Pilotage Reconnaissance Party: cover to be Combined Operations Police Patrol, Naval and Ordinary Commandos etc.

Depot staff (non-existent) were required. The military side was largely technical, Royal Engineers matters and the establishment of No. 2 SBS, Special Service Brigade (under Major Roger Courtney MC, KRRC) was enlarged so as to carry extra personnel for COPP as a Sapper Reconnaissance Section of Special Boat Section and major beach recces were taken out of the role of normal SBS.

Teacher and McHarg (ex *Koodoo Inhuman*) appointed to ships in the meanwhile had to be recalled to Combined Operations.

Taut-line gradient lines were invented. No winter operations having been previously attempted, essential protective swimwear had to be obtained. Hasty trials resulted in somewhat inefficient and uncomfort-able kit; as soon as possible a suit was put into production at Siebe Gorman Ltd. It was apparent by now that operational Parties could not rely on bases abroad for stores or equipment – and must in future bring all their own.

SOURCES
Party Inhuman Log: a contemporary record compiled by Basil Eckhard
Public Record Office
DEFE2 1116 COPP reports and history

CHAPTER SEVEN

COPP Established and Official

As Nigel Willmott has since said:
'By December 1942 the pressure was on to put recce pilots on a sound permanent basis. Naval and Army Force commanders understood the need when faced with real plans but had almost no charts etc (charts are mostly made to facilitate keeping shipping AWAY from beaches!). But this was too late, they needed the information at the early-planning stage. Since the Highest Level was usually distracted by other important business, it was fortunate that Chief of Combined Operations realised this, for without his foresight and backing recce-pilotage would never have succeeded and might well, if employed ill-advisedly, have blown vital secrets. There were risks enough of this as it was. Some felt *Party Inhuman* had been well named.'

Nigel Willmott was well aware that having convinced the Highest Level of the necessity of having beach survey and landing force pilotage teams, he would have difficulty having the teams constituted as he wished. He was far-sighted enough to realise that the end result must be that the team leader would be asked – probably by someone at Chiefs-of-Staff level – if he felt the beaches surveyed were fit for a large scale invasion. The COPP team's CO's assessment of whether troops and tank landing craft could land would be the one the strategic planners accepted, or ignored at their peril. He was convinced that the only person who could make such an assessment must be a navigator or hydrographer: he set his sights on 'Dagger Navigators': those whose special proficiency is recognised by a printer's dagger mark in the Navy List. He also felt COPP operational party CO's needed lieutenant-commander's rank. Inevitably such highly-qualified officers would be straight-lace regular, career Royal Navy officers – capable of navigating capital ships, cruisers or aircraft carriers* – and he was asking for their services to take soundings off mined enemy-defended beaches, from vulnerable small canoes and, in an emergency, killing interfering enemy sentries in hand-to-hand combat . . . plainly it would be a tough task.

Nigel Willmott's first committee room battles began at Combined Operations Headquarters. Major General J. C. Haydon VCCO (Vice Chief of Combined Operations) called for a meeting to get those concerned together. He suggested the date of 4 January 1943, because Brigadier R. E. Laycock would be in London that day. That only gave two days to lay on the meeting. In the event it was held on 5 January 1943: twenty-one months after Courtney and Willmott's Rhodes recce.

Brigadier Laycock, who had been on the Rommelhaus raid when Geoffrey Keyes had won his posthumous VC, was head of Layforce; and SBS (the Special Boat Section) had operated in the Mediterranean under his aegis. There could well be problems in terms of demarcation. Military aspects of beach reconnaissance had always been considered the SBS's province; indeed that had been one of the original reasons for their formation.

On 31 December 1942 Laycock had minuted the Chief of Combined Operations to the effect that Captain Basil Eckhard – who had been one of the principal assault markers for Operation *Torch* – must be considered purely to be loaned, on temporary attachment to Lieutenant-Commander Willmott and COPP1: that Eckhard must be returned to the Special Boat Section, and in the future other officers would not be spared. On the credit side Willmott's establishment was already being referred to as COPP1. Otherwise he seemed figuratively to be under fire from all sides.

Laycock went on to point out that, if military officers for COPP were not to be found in the Special Services Brigade, the War Office must be asked to pass establishment for a new unit, the personnel of which would not count against the Special Service Brigade.

As regards the naval aspects Willmott had at least one highly-placed ally, influenced, no doubt, by the original COPP1 (*Party Inhuman's*) successes in Operation *Torch*. Admiral Andrew B. Cunningham was supporting Willmott to the extent of having convinced the Admiralty of the need for highly-qualified naval officers in COPP teams.

The discussion veered back towards the military component. They would have to be Royal Engineers, it was generally agreed, and draughtsmen must be found among other ranks. For draughtsmen no

* Previously stated but worth repeating.

special skill in boatwork would be required; but it must not be forgotten that the allocation of military personnel to Combined Operations had already reached its ceiling. It must have seemed very petty to Willmott especially when one panel member stated that the needs of COPP were insufficiently important to justify further demand. It was, however, agreed that Willmott should draft a letter to the War Office setting out fully the arguments for his demands. That this letter in draft should be submitted to the VCCO for signature by CCO (Chief of Combined Operations). A recommendation was passed that the Directorate of Manpower Organisation and Personnel should be informed in advance. It was agreed that no decision should be made until Willmott's paper had been produced. Willmott, who was no mean staff officer was undismayed: he could and *would* prepare a convincing paper and the resolution could be interpreted that once it had been prepared a decision would be made.

He did produce his paper and it foresaw a draughtsmanship component for up to ten COPPs: *preferably* Commando SBS, Willmott had his own ideas. His paper also pointed out the need for a cover for the COPP teams. COPPs would always be referred to as Combined Operations Police Patrols. That could well cover the activities of such a party near booms, gangways, off beaches in an assault etc. In fact, the approved title for the scheme was CO Pilotage Party, that meant that the compromising word reconnaissance had been dropped from the title: he preferred that to the originally proposed *Combined Operations Beach and Pilotage Reconnaissance Party*. In practice, usage would determine that the parties were referred to simply as Naval Parties.

*

As regards each party's composition Nigel Willmott was sure from the start: as soon as he had committed his ideas to paper, he fought any suggestion to vary them. The teams were to be as follows, each COPP to consist of:
1 Lieutenant-Commander (Navigator) or (Hydrographer) i/c
1 Lieutenant RNR or RNVR, Assistant
1 Captain Royal Engineers, Commando SBS 2 i/c
1 Lieutenant RNVR, Maintenance and Intelligence
2 Seamen Ratings (up to PO) Leadsmen/Paddlers/Coxswains
1 Seamen Rating spare ditto and Maintenance Mate
1 Electrical Mechanic/Maintenance Petty Officer
1 Cpl or Sergeant (SBS Commando) – paddler guard
1 Draughtsman Royal Engineers (Commando SBS)
1 Writer Royal Navy (on occasions).

Willmott, far-sighted as ever, pointed out that the size of the team would be limited by the size of the 'carrier' craft, whether it be a submarine or other vessel. He had taken the trouble to make his own point that even the draughtsman should be SBS trained. Also that, once a team had been set-up, it was essential it remain as a team after its long cohesive training. If they had to be rested, the officers could act as training instructors. They could not be expected to operate for long stretches without rest periods. Nor could COPPists be trained over-night. His paper outlined the necessary syllabus for training. In a further paper dated 24 February 1943, he spelled out the detail, it should include: Combined Operations, Landing Craft pilotage capabilities, secret navigational radio aids, beach gradient and tide limitations of Landing Craft and Landing Ships (Tanks), submarine periscope work, launching canoes from submarines, sketching, photographic inter-pretation, beach organisation (military and naval), beach seamanship, canoe and swim surveying, fin swimming, physical hardening, stalking and a close-combat commando course. As if this were not enough he added: invasion obstacles and how they could be overcome, strategic planning and intelligence, forms of reconnaissance reporting, military considerations and hydrographic and topographical work and General Staff organisation.

Electrical mechanics and maintenance mates, would need to be trained in joinery and repair of rubberised fabric (swimsuits, canoes etc) and making equipment water-tight.

Importantly, by then he could report progress; COPP1 was already training at Hayling Island; COPP2 a special all-naval team, differently composed under Lieutenant (H) H. M. F. Berncastle RN, would be working in the Channel; COPP3 under Lieutenant-Commander N. M. J. Teacher DSO, RN was at Malta; COPP4 Lieutenant (N) McHarg RN was at Algiers.

COPP5, 6 and 7 were already in training. COPPs 8, 9 and 10 should complete training – they would start round about June. Unless the navy could release any further suitable or qualified (N), (H), or the army qualified RE officers, no further teams would be formed, Nigel Willmott said firmly. COPP teams were Combined Operations personnel, they should be based and messed separately from other (General Services) personnel and their teams once formed should not be split up.

SOURCES

Nigel Willmott Aide Memoire prepared for Earl Mountbatten of Burma, prior
    to 18 July 1977 COPP reunion, held at Hayling Island Sailing Club House.
Public Record Office
DEFE2 971

CHAPTER EIGHT

COPP Depot at Hayling Island

In the chapter outlining the setting up of COPP reference is made to the fact that the COPP Depot had been set-up at Hayling Island Sailing Club. Hayling Island is off the south-east coast of Hampshire, connected by a bridge with Havant on the mainland. The people even today still consider themselves islanders. Hayling Island, is roughly triangular in shape, measures about four miles from north to south and has a seaboard, to the English Channel of about four-and-a-half miles. Before the war it had been prime yachting country, being midway between Langstone and Chichester harbours. It was certainly sufficiently remote for secret activities, and it had its fair share of featureless beaches like the Normandy ones and the Beaulieu River and other waterways not unlike the chaungs of Burma, Malaya and Sarawak were not far distant.

More than one account of the setting-up of the COPP Depot on Hayling Island has been written, all pay tribute to Geoffrey Galwey's part in the enterprise. So that it seems fairest to lean heavily on his own account.

Before that, one should consider Nigel Willmott's brief version, in which he says, that the small Hayling Island Sailing Club, on its sand spit, called Sandy Point, seemed an excellent choice for its setting, facilities and security. It was in fact in a remote spot and could only be approached by one narrow, chalk road. It was arguably too small. This was not too serious a problem: many buildings requisitioned during the war were extended by the simple expedient of building nissen huts around them. Nigel Willmott makes no bones that COPP owed much of its success to its two excellent maintenance officers. These were, in fact, Lieutenant-Commander Nicholas Hastings DSC, RNVR, at COHQ: and Geoffrey Galwey RNVR, once RN and an ex-Flag Lieutenant, at Sandy Point.

In 1942 Geoffrey Galwey had indeed been appointed Flag Lieutenant to Admiral Theodore Hallett, Vice Admiral Combined Training. Hallett was based at Largs. It was here that Galwey met Nicholas Hastings, the son of Sir Patrick Hastings KC. Nick had not long before won a DSC commanding a flotilla of landing craft in the Commando attack on Vaagso. Nick introduced Geoff to some influential friends, because of medical down-grading Geoffrey had been relegated to Home Shore and Harbour Service. Through Hastings and his influential friends, and with the connivance of Admiral Hallett, Geoffrey became a beachmaster and did a Commando course. After this it was through Nicholas Hastings that Geoffrey met Nigel Willmott. Geoffrey knew a little of Nigel's technique for enabling landing craft to find their right beaches – at the right time, under guidance of pilots who had taken up station, under cover of darkness, as markers in canoes launched from submarines, from which they had surveyed and sketched coastlines: working through the periscope by day and from the submarine's conning tower by night. Nigel Willmott had as has been related personally carried out reconnaissance and marking, with his *Party Inhuman* teams, for Operation *Torch*.

Geoffrey Galwey discussed the subject with Nigel Willmott and derived some idea of the urgency involved. The establishment would have to be naval. Geoffrey pondered this and decided the soldiers would appreciate being victualled by the Andrew [Royal Navy], especially if he could arrange for attached soldiers to draw their tot of rum.

*

Soon after their first meeting Geoffrey found himself appointed M/COPP of COPP1 of which, of course, Nigel Willmott was S/COPP. His first task was to find and equip a suitable base for training COPPs for the Mediterranean; one that could accommodate COPPs and their instructors. It would be a welcome change from a flag lieutenant's or a beachmaster's duties.

He discovered that Lieutenant-Commander L. H. 'Gaffer' Moorhouse RNR had already done a preliminary survey. Geoffrey rejected HMS *James Cook*, on the Kyles of Bute – it was already full to capacity. The second possibility was Hayling Island Sailing Club: it seemed ideal. Geoffrey accepted that it was already occupied by a military unit. Undeterred by that fact Geoffrey thought it would be suitable for COPP. The Clubhouse building was modern, flat-roofed and with large plate-glass windows; it has been described as resembling an aerodrome control tower. It was owned by Ivan J. Snell MC a Marylebone Stipendiary Magistrate – who although he had been a soldier himself – Snell said that he preferred his property commandeered by the Royal Navy rather than by the soldiery. He agreed to take the many 14-foot International and Sharpie sailing dinghies that remained around the Club House building and store them in Mengeham Rithe and on the lawn by his swimming bath. Geoffrey Galwey's account of how he became a 'marauding COPP', and scrounged furniture and fittings is a fascinating one.

Nigel Willmott having decided the COPP operational parties constitution, Geoffrey Galwey decided what crew he would need to run a happy ship. This resolved itself into a Coxswain, Chief Regulating Petty Officer, to look after discipline: a Leading Seaman as Bosun, two cooks and two officers stewards; one who would act as wardroom messman. He also indented for a Petty officer to run the Ship's office. Stoker Reavell, who Geoffrey entrusted with the task of keeping the boiler going for central heating and hot water, never let him down. Hot water for showers was always available; and Ivan Snell was the first to admit that Stoker Reavell had succeeded where prewar civilian staff had failed. Geoffrey's efforts to cope with sewage problems are a saga in themselves. A triumph, one might say of the san' wallah, over the security officer. The story of the sentry box is quite remarkable too. Anyway the essentials were that boathouses, workshops, a wardroom and lecture room were all fitted in. For motor transport the COPP Depot had its own vehicles and four WRNS drivers, who in time were accommodated in their own duty room 'The Temple of Beautiiful Thoughts,' of which more later.

A part of the courtyard was designated the quarter-deck and a mast was erected here, on a tabernacle, and the White ensign flown from a cocked yard.

Dannert wire laid to restrict entry by the single chalk road access to the Club House, built itself into a groyne to protect the Winner Shingle Bank from erosion. Geoffrey was quite pleased and felt it compensated Ivan Snell for his displeasure when they'd tried to treat the septic tank as a soakaway. Basil Eckhard succeeded in constructing an assault course. Sporadic attempts by depot ratings to garden petered out in the face of more urgent matters.

All in all the Club House at Sandy Point was a comfortable billet and this compensated those quartered there for the rigours of their training. Of course Sandy Point was also a windy point and the tidal flow of 4-6 knots out of Chichester Harbour and Bosham Creek could easily be whipped up into very nasty steep seas. It was a chilly place to go swimming, especially in winter and without trunks but, as will be seen, that was all part of the training scheme. As in all remote places on the island birdlife abounded; there were waders, ducks and waterfowl, if anyone had had time to look at them.

SOURCES

GALWEY, Geoffrey Valentine, *Geoff's Opus* A Record of Survival, one way or the other, privately printed,1991.

STRUTTON, Bill and PEARSON, Michael, *The Secret Invaders*, Hodder and Stoughton. 1958.

CHAPTER NINE

Folbots and X-Craft

I mmediately prior to their joint Rhodes reconnaissance Willmott had been glad to back Roger Courtney's judgement on folbots. Courtney had lots of experience of them prewar: he had stalked rhino in them, on rivers as a white hunter. He'd paddled one down the Nile, with all his possessions on board. Courtney and his bride, Dorrice, had even paddled the folbot *Buttercup* down the Danube, in June 1938, on Honeymoon. Courtney was adept at handling a folbot, whatever the conditions. Even so, for their use in choppy seas – with COPP personnel – Willmott was convinced they could and must be improved.

Who made them? That was the first question for consideration. Prewar they had been manufactured and marketed by the Folbot Folding Boats Ltd. That prompted other questions did the company still exist? If so, were they still trading?

There were problems: one day a messenger couldn't get through to the firm's last-known address because of an unexploded bomb. In spite of everything the company produced photographs of all variants. One was twin-masted, with a centre-board drop keel, rigged like a cutter, with jib, mainsail and staysail. Unlike the standard two-man model, it had a rudder. It was picturesque but one doubts its potential seaworthiness.

Various assessments were made. As early as 14 October 1940 2/ Lieutenant Roger Courtney KRRC, was supervising trials. Some fascinating items survive in the Public Record Office. An Admiralty view was that the folbot was more efficient than the RAF Type 'D' dinghy: this came from Sir Max Horton, Flag Officer of Submarines. It made sense: a folboat wasn't pneumatic or round: it had a bow and a stern and could be navigated. Inevitably, someone else commented that the RAF rubber dinghy could be easier to rig: one simply inflated it with a cylinder of gas.

There were problems: on 20 November 1940, Folbot Folding Boats Ltd promised delivery. A year later they were reported to be out of business, but to have ten boats in stock. The same month Brigadier J. C. Haydon from the HQ Special Service Brigade reported that an excellent folbot might be obtained from Tyne Folding Boats, Richmond on Thames. Goatley of Cowes were also recommended as being able to produce the craft. On 29 July 1941 an order was signed for thirty folbots. Did it matter who made them?

The folbot by anyone's standards appeared admirable for special operations: it could carry two men and a payload of 200-400 lbs. If one equated that to a two-man sabotage team, that could mean 160-320 one-and-three-quarter-pound demolition charges. And the folbot had the advantages of complete silence, a low silhouette and easy manoeuvrability – unlike a circular rubber dinghy – what's more a man in training could propel it at four-knots, certainly for a good hour.

Folbot was German; it meant a boat that folded. It had a wooden frame with a rubberised covering. When collapsed there seemed no doubt a folbot, or folbots could be stored in a submarine, taken up through the torpedo-loading hatch and launched from the casing. The boat could be trimmed low in the water to facilitate launching the canoe. The canoe was just too broad beamed to go through the hatch: another problem to be solved.

For military purposes it was soon agreed that it was desirable to improve the craft's stability perhaps with an annular skirt. This idea was discarded in favour of inflated tubes along the gunwales: these would make it harder to roll or turn over. Two air tubes 6-feet long and 4-inches in diameter kept the craft upright and didn't slow it down. Some of the SBS disagreed and preferring their folbots without the buoyant tubes – cut them off.

It was a hard problem to develop the most satisfactory military model and maintain security. And there were supply problems: good timber was in short supply, as was the right sort of fabric for a covering. It had to be light, thin and durable enough not to tear on contact with rocks.

On the credit side it was said that in four to six-weeks a man could be made thoroughly proficient in the use of folbots. Modern sophisticated warm-when-wet fabrics were not available to folbot canoeists, but they acquired water-resistant anoraks and wore sweaters under them. On the debit side Roger Courtney reported cases of struts, spars and ribs broken when boats were delivered. Timber used was cheap and inferior: wood from sugar boxes, still with printed lettering on its surface. Often unit maintenance staff had to strengthen the ribs of their timber framework. The important thing was that the SBS had already proved they could be used as weapons of war.

Using a Mark 1 folbot Major Gerald Montanaro RE and Trooper F. A. Preece RAC, of 101 Troop SBS mounted a daring attack on Boulogne harbour, on the night of 11/12 April 1942, three weeks after the St Nazaire raid. Both men wore kapok-filled Tropal suits, designed to protect downed airmen from exposure and keep them warm. It's said any equipment Montanaro couldn't requisition he patriotically purchased at his own expense. Dropped a mile from Boulogne by a Royal Navy MTB, the pair entered the harbour undetected and attached limpets to an enemy merchantship, carrying 5,000 tons of Copper ore. It sank and Montanaro and Preece just made it back to their carrier MTB before their waterlogged folbot sank beneath them. Montanaro was awarded a DSO and Preece a DCM. Their security was so good that the Germans, believing it sabotage, it is said shot one-hundred Frenchmen. A sad postscript to the brilliant exploit of the two SBS personnel. After this Montanaro, a regular sapper, became a Lieutenant-Commander RN – he was a professional, and declined an RNVR commission – thereafter, on secondment, he did valuable development, amphibious work for three years.

Major Hasler of the RMBPD – then planning the 'Cockleshell Heroes' raid was interested to see Montanaro's placing rods: used to attach limpets to the enemy ship, but rejected the folbot for Operation *Frankton*, at Bordeaux later that year. He wanted a craft with a half-inch plywood bottom that could be dragged over shingle.

Nigel Willmott produced a report dated 19 April 1943 on a batch of the latest improved Models 1*: they had been taken to the Clyde for operational use in a sea trial with HMS/M *Seraph* between 13 and 16th April. They'd undergone four day and night launching and stowing exercises. After that two full-dress operational exercises. One canoe had filled completely with water and capsized; the other returned half-full of water despite baling, on both exercises. One buoyancy sausage had partially torn off and a stern piece was carried away from the skin.

Nigel wasn't pleased; these craft had been well maintained and treated with a care one couldn't guarantee on operations. One canoe had a tally of 29 leaks or porous abrasions. Experience had shown that patches could only be put on when the pressure in a submarine was atmospheric. This factor could mean postponement of operations or exercises.

This proved conclusively, to Nigel's mind, that folbots with a second-rate, sackcloth-based skin were non-operational and unfit for training purposes. Had the canoe that capsized not been close to the carrier submarine – it could have meant the loss of two valuable officers, in training – as heavy and thick weather was coming on. Valuable stores had also been lost or damaged and the value of the exercise spoilt for the personnel concerned.

Plainly the problems were not licked yet but Nigel was prepared to go on fighting personally, in the committee room, with the manufacturers – if necessary even with his superiors until his personnel had the best equipment possible. He cut red tape and short-circuited channels, making direct contact with suppliers, invoking top priorities, even at the risk of offending his superior officers. In time the Mark 1** appeared and proved satisfactory for COPP reconnaissance work.

*

At a COPP Association a former COPPist remarked that the X-Craft might have looked a bit odd, but it worked superbly for COPP work. It was no accident that it did. Nigel Willmott had already assessed the Welfreighter submarine and discarded it as unsuitable.

The Welfreighter was a two-man development of the Welman midget submarine; intended for use by SOE (Special Operations Executive) in clandestine landings. The one-man Welman midget submarine had a fat, cigar-shaped hull and was propelled by a pair of 5-horse-power electric motors. Her pilot sat with his head in a raised, round cupola with small, glass observation scuttles at his eye level. There was no periscope: so visibility was limited to a range of a few feet. The Wellman was controlled by a joy-stick like a fighter aircraft's one. Instrumentation was limited to a magnetic compass and depth gauge. On the surface, at night it was preferable to manoeuvre with the hatch open. Submerged speed was around 3 knots and surfaced speed 4 knots. A cylinder of oxygen was carried, to be cracked open to facilitate the pilot's breathing when submerged. Another, larger cylinder: of compressed air controlled the craft's buoyancy. Lord Louis Mountbatten got a ducking testing one.

*

Nigel Willmott produced detailed specifications how the X-Craft, midget submarine should be adapted for COPP. They are appended to this chapter. Having once had a good idea he was prepared to follow it through, whatever it took. No doubt the W and D (wet and dry compartment) by which a swimmer might leave the craft appealed as a good idea for a start.

What was it like in an X-Craft? Nigel Willmott had the answer: 'Like living under a billiard table – that leaks!' Conditions were very cramped and condensation formed continually: it never stopped. COPP1 decided to use the X-Craft for the Normandy beaches reconnaissance. So far so good, but even with the right equipment they'd need training to operate it.

Geoffrey Galwey who was present during the training and the operational sortie has described it very amusingly in his own autobiography *Geoff's Opus* which interested parties should read. Without spoiling their enjoyment it is possible to summarise that account. No one could stand upright in an X-Craft. The wet-and-dry flooded up through the 'heads': a 'Baby Blake' yacht type water closet. All cooking had to be done in a glue-pot. When surfaced the watchkeeper clipped a safety harness to the snorkel ventilating trunk; but it doesn't end there. This is what Nigel Willmott had to say about it:

'It was found desirable for the officer on watch on the casing to lift his head above water for breathing purposes. He is strapped to the induction pipe, and has a bar to which he clings with fervour, while floating on his front like a paper streamer on the bottom of the ocean . . . . Legs are liable to considerable injury. There is a vacancy in the complement for an intelligent merman to fulfil this rôle!'*

The continual condensation meant that the labels of all tinned food peeled off, so that the comestibles had to be identified by painting direct on to the tin can. Geoffrey Galwey has eloquently described the problems of BO after a submergence of any duration and the problems of voiding the stale air. Willmott's specification called for a cover on the chart table to prevent condensation falling on the chart. It also called for stowage for equipment, this could only be provided by slinging netting, like hammocks.

SOURCES

Public Record Office
DEFE2 842 Folbot Historical File 1940-43
DEFE2 1059
GALWEY, Geoffrey, *Geoff's Opus*
ROSKILL, Captain S. W. DSC, RN, *The War at Sea*, the Official History, Vol III, The Offensive, Part II, HMSO.

* Roskill op cit pp110-111.

DEFE2 1059

SBU DO387/C/43 MOST SECRET   4 NOV 1943
FROM: OIC COPP DEPOT. C/o GPO HAYLING ISLAND
DATE: 27 Oct 43 No. 23/4
To: CAPT SBU
Copy to O.C.(COHQ) Ref: ISRB s DMN/5829 of 1st Oct 1943

SUBJECT RECONNAISSANCE SUBMARINE

Opportunity was taken four weeks ago at the request of Colonel
Neville RM of COHQ, to visit ISRB to view the Welfreighter and
various other products.
2. The Welfreighter was found quite unsuitable for normal recce
work, but the actual requirements for a CO Recce Submarine were
discussed. These are not fulfilled by the X-Craft which will be
a difficult craft to work with, from the point of view of exhaustion
and various other reasons.
3. It was thought it might be necessary to design a modified
Submarine or X-Craft or Welfreighter (say) type for recce purposes.
For this reason the requirements have been put on record and are
forwarded herewith (Enclosure No.1). They have with the exception
of No. 17 and No.18 been discussed with ISRB. No. 17 and 18 were
thought of since the meeting there.
4. ISRB state that the Admiralty Small Craft Committee are the
deciding authority to whom such requirements are normally
forwarded for preliminary consideration.
                                (Signed) N. Willmott.
                                Lieutenant-Commander.

Enclosure No1
Outline requirements for a COPP Submarine.
        Enclosure No.1 to COPP Depot s No. 23/4 dated
                    27 October 1943
                                        MOST SECRET

OUTLINE REQUIREMENTS FOR COPP SUBMARINE

1.   1,000 miles endurance, more if possible. Speed? Engines?
2.   Good accommodation for 5 man, suits etc. Human endurance
at least 10 days, 14 days if required, cooking etc.
3.   Room for 3 canoes Mark III** (free-flooding with
Kingstons in each compartment if necessary) must be protected
by casing from sea.
4.   Good seawater seaworthiness.
5.   Low silhouette, no high conning tower.
6.   Able to dive for whole of daylight with a good margin of
safety. Protosorb etc.
6a.   Battery charging if necessary.
7.   Suggest round section hull with free-flooding flair etc.
8.   Navigational and survey fittings as for X-Craft
(list attached — Appendix 1)
9.   Accessibility of diesel motors and batteries for maintenance)

10.   Simple as possible to operate, dive etc (Part of crew will be RE)
11.   Non-magnetic material in way of compass is required. At least one magnetic compass is essential.
12.   Browns or Sperry gyroscope compass and Submarine pressure type repeater required in conning tower.
13.   Good astern power.
14.   Draught as shallow as possible.
15.   Craft must be towable.
16.   Craft must be capable of being hoisted.
17.   W and D [Wet and Dry] compartment in conning tower compartment for going on deck in swell (as for X-Craft principle).
18.   Remote control of steering and motors from conning tower.

Appendix 1 to Enclosure 1 of COPP DEPOT S NO. 23/4 dated 27/10/43
                    SECRET
                                        MOST SECRET
          COPP FITTINGS REQUIRED FOR X-CRAFT
       Agree with Captain S. 12 on 16 September 1943

(a)   Large 2-power telescope with sky search to be capable of being raised and lowered. This will vastly improve efficiency and safety from detection.
(b)   E/S [Echo sounder] (Recorder Type) to be usable on surface i.e. consider aeration.
(c)   Receiver QH Size 10"x 10"x18" plus small alternators
  Gee   (2) Total weight with aerial 105 lbs
Expert: Sub Lt Graham Weston, AEE Haslemere
(d)   Improved chart table fittings. Book and chart stowages etc (anti-drip screens above table).
(e)   Bearing compasses on desk before the W and D compartment hatch.
(f)   Anchor gear wire or better rope cable (not chain). Small cable winch and fairleads for using fore and aft alternative. Spare anchor CQR type anchors preferred.
(g)   Taut-wire measuring gear. 20 mile drum preferred. If feasible and gear will stand up to it, to be fitted on casing aft. Free flooding (illuminated by ultra-violet torch).
(h)   Propeller guard to prevent anchor cable fouling).
(i)   Telephone or Voice Pipe from Conning position at W-and-D compartment hatch to controls. This will be main conning position by deck compass.
(j)   Steering control on wandering lead from W and D.
(k)   Chamfering off after corner of rudder.
(l)   Sounding pole and clips on casing.
(m)   Cheernikeef Log as fitted, but not if possible on lowest part of keel (to avoid injury on beaching). To be easily hoistable.
(n)   R/T reception.
(o)   Stowages for special gear, arms, and accommodation to be provided.

Crown copyright: reproduced with permission of Controller HM Stationery Office.

The late Captain Nigel Clogstoun-Willmott DSO, DSC*, RN. Father of COPP.

Top: Hayling Island Sailing Club in prewar days, below in wartime days.

Two more views of COPP dépôt in wartime days, in lower picture Jemima Puddle-dukw on left.

Ralph Stanbury's COPP5 on completion of training, at the Dépôt.
Back Row: Simpson, Goodyear, Smith, Matterson, Sykes. Middle Row: Nichol, Stanbury, Kent.
Front Row: Williamson, Thomas, Hatton.

Geoffrey Hall's COPP7 on completion of training.
Back Row: Hall, Lucas, McLean, Jennings, Gimson. Front Row: Nichol, Kennedy, Morrison,
Alexander, Owen Kennedy, Witham.

Donald Amer's COPP6 on completion of training.
Back Row: Watson, (Mackenzie), Hunter, Amer, Wild. Middle Row: Plummer, Sayce, Palmer.
Front Row: Bowden, Manning, Phillips, Gray.

Freddy Ponsonby's COPP8 on completion of training.
Back Row: Richards, Crafer, Ponsonby, Peacock, Colson. Front Row: Spence, Gascoigne, Rourke,
Pond, Duffy. Note: Spence was not part of COPP8, but HQ Back-up for Cocanada. Cumberland is
absent (in hospital: tonsilitis).

Tanker' Townson's COPP10, photographed overseas.
Back Row: Brown, Lemont, Casey, Harding, Carter, Parker. Front Row: Stanley, Lamb, Townson,
Talbot, Maynard.

Some of Alex Hughes's COPP3(1) at Hammenheil.
Back Row: Thomas, White, Hughes, Sowter, Young. Font Row: Cockram, Ruberry, Turner,
'Canada' Alcock.

'Alex Hughes's COPP3(1). Photographed by Arthur Ruberry at Hammenheil, Jaffna, Ceylon. Back Row: Turner, Cockram, Cammidge, White. Front Row: Thomas, Sowter, Hughes, Johns, Alcock, Young, Hood.

Jack stirs the Polenta – Amasino, December 1943. Sketch by the late Kim Patterson.

COPP9(1) personnel, 'Ian' Morison with pipe, and Albergo Savoia, Cassonichila, Ischia Island, where they were based.

CHAPTER TEN

Folbot Technique for COPP Reconnaissances

I t was initially envisaged that the carrier vessel for COPP reconnaissance parties would be a submarine. In which case T-Boats, being larger than S-boats were regarded as the most comfortable. Submarines had been designed to carry their wartime patrol crews, so that in many cases the best accommodation supernumerary special forces personnel could hope for was a 'hot bunk' i.e. one recently vacated by someone else: there simply weren't any spares.

During the patrol, en route to the zone of operations the COPP party's folbots would be stowed for'ard, in the fore-ends, where re-load torpedoes are kept, just abaft of the torpedo tubes.

Before launching all operational stores would have to be loaded in. They would need to be stowed in custom-made pockets, attached to the craft's wooden frame by a depot sailmaker; they would be arranged so as not to cause trim irregularities when the boat was in the water.

In principle COPP canoes were expected to operate in pairs. The naval personnel canoe doing the sea reconnaissance and the army personnel canoe the onshore military reconnaissance. In either case, the officer would be accommodated in one cockpit; his paddler in the other. A P8 aircraft compass was provided for navigation purposes. This could be 'swung' for accurate adjustment, just as in an aircraft, because the canoes contained so many metal stores to affect the compass. This had been done prior to Montanaro's Boulogne raid.

Once the submarine had reached the zone of operations and the exact position and bearing checked: the submarine would be trimmed low in the water so that the canoe might be floated off its free-flooding casing. Ideal working conditions were considered no moon and a slight lop on the water – its surface broken by short lumpy waves: not quite a slight chop.

The laden canoe would be taken up onto the casing. The Mark 1** folbot measured 17 feet long and 30 inches beam. It was brought up on to the casing through the angled torpedo-loading hatch with the buoyancy 'sausages' along its gunwales inflated.

*

A word of explanation: whilsts COPPists talk of flipping a capsized folbot keel upwards, strictly speaking it had a wooden kelson, rather than a weighted keel to keep it upright. In fact, it was possible to navigate a folboat because it had positive buoyancy – inflated bags, fore and aft – and inboard ballast: in the shape of the stores and the two occupants. Add to that the fact that both its crew wielded double-ended paddles, with elliptical blades, and the buoyancy sausages along its gunwales helped to prevent it turning turtle. The SBS considered double-bladed paddles noisy and often preferred to 'break' them into single-bladed ones for more silent travel . . . the COPPists, feathering their paddles considered that they were silent.

To launch the canoe off the trimmed-down casing would require two ratings to hold the canoe's bow-line or painter, at the bow, and its stern line. As 'Jumbo' Courtney has pointed out it is essential for the canoe to float free with the sea's swell. If both ropes are pulled tight, the canoe will certainly capsize. Once the canoe is floating satisfactorily, with the paddler in say the for'ard seat, the other crew member had to board the canoe over her stern. In fact he had to be pretty quick: the paddler steadying the canoe, as it bobbed up and down, in the swell. Even at this stage there is a strong risk of being swept against the submarine and stove in – in time the folbot would carry a No. 82 Gammon bomb, with a sensitive detonator and this increased launching risks. In any case, without the risk of touching-off one's No. 82, there was always a chance of being swept under the for'ard hydroplanes and smashed to pieces.

Having avoided both these pitfalls and cast-off the folbot had to be paddled near enough to the enemy coast for the swimmer to go over the side. The folbot, being only a timber framework, with rubberised fabric covering was fast and silent, although fragile. It had an undeniably low silhouette and could be propelled fast: up to 4 knots. At the same time it could be easily swamped or capsized. It had to be held bow-on to wind or waves or it was likely to broach-to and turn turtle.

If it did capsize, it had to be rolled-over, into the keel-up position, to trap the air inside it, before it filled with water. Thereafter, once both its crew had retrieved their paddles – their first priority – the canoe had to be righted and baled out. Once this was done No.2 climbed in, over the stern: and No. 1 climbed in over the bow: unless they'd worked out their own, even better system. All COPP members practised the drill, usually in daylight and certainly not in enemy waters. With a heavy swell and a strong sea running it could well be tricky to right a capsized canoe, especially on the way-in to a sortie.

Once successfully launched – probably about two miles from shore – and hopefully not having capsized, the canoe would paddle on a previously memorised bearing close enough to the shore for the swimmer to go over the side. To do this the swimmer might use the technique originally perfected by Roger Courtney. He'd ship his paddle, bring his legs out of the cockpit to straddle athwart the rear cockpit, then flip over face-downwards and lower himself into the water. In the process he had to avoid upsetting or swamping the canoe. Alternatively, if a soldier, he might simply say: 'Going out left!' and the paddler would lean out to the right.

The paddler would now drop the non-magnetic, brass single-fluke CQR ('Secure')anchor. Check his position and await the return of the swimmer on completion of his tasks. The paddler alone in the anchored canoe, perhaps a two-to-three-hundred yards offshore, had the satisfaction of knowing that he was probably invisible from the shore, but that could pose problems for the swimmer, who had to find him, if necessary using a hand-held compass then swim out to him without any exchange of signals.

*

Had one posed the question: 'What was it like to paddle a folbot, with a pair of Double-ended paddles, in enemy waters?' One might have come up with the following quotation from a fiction work:

'The blades bit the water without a sound, without the slightest splash as the two men's arms rose circled and fell and the dark, sweeping paddles circled as an extensions to them; the only sounds were the swishing of the sea along the canoe's sides and the heavy drips of water which flying from the paddles during their upward swing, plopped like rain on the rubberised canvas of which the craft was made. Neither of the men was breathing hard or even audibly yet; it was barely ten minutes since they'd climbed down over the submarine's casing into the canoe and pushed off, wordlessly, into the night. Now, almost halfway to the shore they'd already forgotten the submarine in which they'd been passengers for more than a week; the coast ahead, that wide crescent of Malayan beach – in particular the southern end of it – claimed all their concentration. None was needed for the act of driving the canoe; they were so well trained to it through months of practice that it required no conscious thought or effort.'*

SOURCES

COURTNEY, G. B., *SBS in World War Two* The Story of the original Special Boat Section of the Army Commandos, Robert Hale, 1983.

LUCAS PHILLIPS, C. E. OBE, MC, *The Cockleshell Heroes*, William Heinemann, 1956.

Conversations with COPPists

---

* *Soldier from the Sea* by Alexander Fullerton, published by Peter Davies Ltd 1962 (Granada Publishing Limited Edition, 1975, pp 5-6). Fullerton served as an officer of the RNVR, in HMS/M *Seadog* in the Far East. He witnessed launch and recovery of folbots on operations.

CHAPTER ELEVEN

Services of a COPP – command responsibilities

'COPP are under the control of the Chief of Combined Operations who trains them in the UK at their Depot at Hayling Island. As and when the services of a COPP are required by supreme commanders, they will be allocated to that authority, if available by the Chief of Combined Operations. A COPP is sent out with all its equipment and stores unless these are known to be readily available on the station to which it is proceding. Once on that station the personnel come under the administrative control of CCO (Chief of Combined Operations). When not actually employed in an operational role, intensive training, which includes night exercises and swimming practice is undertaken.'[1]

A TYPICAL OPERATION
'The CO of a COPP, known as S/COPP is able to advise on the functioning of any projected operation and to work out the required details. Experience has shown that when a COPP is used in conjunction with an intended amphibious operation, it is best to allocate the party or parties to the naval force commander. When this is done the party is normally placed under direct control of the force navigation officer, who is the individual best fitted to establish mutual confidence between staff and the party.'[2]

SECURITY
'In the training of COPP, the security problem has been carefully considered since it is of paramount importance not to reveal to the enemy the area in which we are interested. Providing a suitable carrier is available, there is little risk of the loss of surprise in the employment of COPP, especially if no actual landing is made. Individuals are highly trained to look after themselves and to leave no trace of their investigations; their method of approach from the carrier by canoe to an off-shore position and thence by swimming and wading to the shore allows the minimum risk of detection.'[3]

All three passages are quoted from a Combined Operations Bulletin dated June 1945 and therefore written with the advantage of hindsight. The bulletin is also classified secret. The facts under command responsibilities were by no means widely known. Had they been the problems of an S/COPP arriving with his Naval Party would have been greatly simplified.

Lord Mountbatten, as Chief of Combined Operations had on 2 August 1943, sent out a most secret paper to Commanders in Chief explaining the function of COPP. There can be no doubt, however, that many officers below Commander-in-Chief or Chief-of-Staff remained ignorant of its existence. And undoubtedly there were cases where S/COPPs had difficulty obtaining facilities, equipment, priorities for carrier vessels, and even persuading the competent authorities to take them seriously.

Nigel Willmott who had experienced similar problems as one of the first in an extremely restricted field was fully aware of the problem. He had proposed unsuccessfully that the mnemonic should be used to designate absolute priority. He was unsuccessful in so doing, but one might argue that it could have spelt bad security had he done so. He also tried unsuccessfully to have all S/COPPs promoted lieutenant-commander. The standard Admiralty argument against this was that submarine commanders bore heavier responsibilities without this privilege until having acquired eight years seniority.

Mindful of the responsibility that the Royal Engineer officer E/COPPs bore and that they too – like the S/COPPs had to talk direct to high-ranking staff officers – he considered having them all made GSO 3's. This would have been perfectly possible: they all had captain's rank, but the wartime staff course, though its length had been halved, was still of six-months duration. So that it is probable Nigel abandoned this idea; not wishing to delay the deployment of operational parties.

SOURCES

[1], [2] and [3]: Combined Operations Headquarters, Bulletin T/18, dated June 1945, *COPP: Combined Operations Pilotage Parties.*

CHAPTER TWELVE

Sicily – the First Serious Losses

C OPP3 Teacher/ Capt Burbidge RCE and COPP4 McHarg/ Capt Parsons RE despatched to the Mediterranean, on 8 January 1943. Both Officers in command and some of their teams had North African experience, but insufficient to call them trained; nor was gear (canoes and RG) adequate for winter conditions: teams suffered colds, ill-health, and strain. The position improved when Captain S (8) had time to look after the Malta-based COPP. Captain S (10) Captain Simpson gave every assistance. Some unequipped and partly untrained Middle East Reconnaissance Party officers were attached to COPP3 and a great deal of training and organisation time was spent at Algiers.

Three parties sailed from Algiers in three submarines the end of the dark, moon period to recce the southern end of Sicily.

*

The first news to arrive at the COPP depot, indicating that the Sicily reconnaissances had not gone as planned was a signal reporting that Lieutenant-Commander N. J. M. Teacher RN, Lieutenant N. W. Cooper RNVR and Captain G. W. Burbidge R Canadian Engineers were missing from COPP3. The eventual balance sheet was to prove far worse. Of sixteen operational personnel who had left carrier submarines in Folbots; at that time three only were known to be safe: all of them were COPP4 personnel – Lieutenant McHarg, Lieutenant Sinclair and AB Harris.

In time more facts became known: Lieutenant P. R. G. Smith RN, the senior officer of the COPP Middle East Party had reached Malta, together with Lieutenant D. Brand RNVR, also from the Middle East COPP party, unable to regain their carrier submarine, *P-44 United*, the pair had paddled a distance of at least 75 miles to Malta. They had made the journey successfully despite heavy weather and with a single paddle – it was a considerable feat of endurance. Brand was on the point of collapse when they arrived, but 'Bob' Smith was still able to paddle his canoe to the submarine base at Sliema Creek. It's said he was asked what he'd done with HMS/M *United*.

Bob Smith produced an extremely frank report in which he attempted to account for all the losses. The Middle East Beach Reconnaissance Party had arrived in Malta, from Algiers on 8 February 1943, he related. The party which consisted of seven officers (including its CO) was constituted on a completely different basis to Norman Teacher's UK-trained COPP party. In the not-quite three-week period, before they sailed every effort was made to bring the Middle East party on to a footing in line with COPP3. Two SBS privates were borrowed from a local commando base and equipment loaned from COPP3. As a result COPP ME (Middle East) 1, under Bob Smith, was able to sail on 27 February 1943 aboard *P-44 United* (Lieutenant J. C. Y. Roxburgh DSC, RN). COPP ME 2, under Lieutenant De Koch SANF sailed in *Unrivalled* (Lieutenant H. B. 'Mossy' Turner RN). From the very first sortie things went badly: Lieutenant-Commander Teacher, S/COPP3, failed to return to the carrier submarine *P-37 Unbending* (Lieutenant E. Stanley DSC, RN). Teacher's paddler, Lieutenant Noel Cooper – who had marked for the Operation *Torch* landings, with Basil Eckhard – was completely exhausted when he arrived back at the carrier submarine, without Teacher.

The following night Smith and Brand missed their submarine rendez-vous and began their epic paddle to Malta. On 4 March 1943, Cooper and Captain Burbidge missed *their* rendezvous with *Unrivalled*. They were never seen again. On 6 March 1943, Lieutenant Hart and Sub-Lieutenant Folder failed to contact *United*. And they were never seen again.

The following night Lieutenant De Kock and Sub-Lieutenant Crossley went ashore for their first night's reconnaissance, but failed to return. On 8 March 1943 Lieutenant Davies went to search for them but did not return.

It has been suggested that Norman Teacher and the other three COPP3 officers deliberately swam out to sea to preserve security. However there seems no evidence for this conclusion. The canoe teams were operating in the height of winter, in bad weather, in suits that fitted poorly and sometimes leaked. Whilst training to use X-Craft, at HMS *Varbel*, a year or so later, Nigel Willmott snagged his suit on barbed wire and got into difficulties when his suit flooded up and became uncontrollable. In fact, Willmott was saved by Geoffrey Galwey letting off a Two-star Red distress signal – something that could not have been done on operations – but could be in the Kyles of Bute. Therefore it seems more likely that Norman Teacher, possibly exhausted by his battles with officialdom – there had been many, in his untiring efforts to secure his COPP proper facilities and equipment – and his unflagging efforts, training the Middle East COPPists, was the victim of extreme fatigue and faulty equipment. His death by drowning could have been an act of self immolation, but could equally have been accidental: there is no evidence either way. As a strong character, cheerful and irrepressible, a career naval officer, already decorated for gallantry – one might say that evidence of character is against the notion of suicide. He was an experienced COPPist and had been brought back from general service for this operation. In any case, all COPP3 team members had cover stories, so that it is unlikely to have been an act born of desperation. The paralysing cold of a flooding suit and a torch that wouldn't light could have put paid to Teacher only yards from his folbot.

Smith reported the results that had been achieved to date – the survey of Beach 38W, had been almost completed, the beach was unsuitable for LCTs, three-quarters of a mile to the west was a beach apparently suitable for LSTs and other types of landing craft; Beach 23 survey had been almost completed – it was useless at its west end; and Beaches 13 and 14 had been partially sketched, but not closely examined. The results gained, he felt, did not justify the losses in personnel.

In both cases where canoes had failed to rendezvous with *P-44*, explosions of SUEs (Signals Underwater Explosive) had been heard, but the submarine had been unable to locate the folbot. Smith suggested that RG technique could be at fault, that the answer might be to use RG in circular, continuously-lit, 'lighthouse' sweep, not flashing morse code letter O (- - -) intermittently. Willmott noted on his copy of the report that this point should be checked with the Admiralty Signal Establishment, Haslemere, to check whether this was likely to make the transmitter's screen melt.

Smith pointed out that the beaches that he had seen were exceptionally well guarded, with sentries spaced every seventy-five or one-hundred yards. Smith was unable to report COPP4's results, as he was unaware that Neville T. McHarg, operating from HMS/M *Safari* (Lieutenant-Commander Ben Bryant) had successfully completed his reconnaissance at the north-west tip of Sicily, for the loss of Captain Edward Parsons RE and L/Sea Irvine, captured.

*

In an annexe to his patrol report Lieutenant H. B. 'Mossy' Turner, Commanding Officer of *P-45 Unrivalled*, deeply regretted that two folbots should have been lost in the preliminary reconnaissance of 13 and 14 Beaches. *Unrivalled* had been the carrier vessel concerned with Nigel Willmott's part in the Operation *Torch* beach pilotage. Her commanding officer, Lieutenant H. B. Turner RN, expressed the view that De Kock's team had been keen and well-trained in what he saw as the secondary side of their work – the beach surveys, pilotage and chart preparation; he did not feel he had been taken into their confidence as regards aspects of the operation where his advice could have helped: he even said it was not the same as working with Willmott: he didn't think De Kock's party was experienced at working with a submarine. He had deliberately waited – foregoing battery-charging, in the hope of recovering the canoe teams, for as long as he could prudently do so without hazarding the submarine or jeopardising the whole operation.

An unofficial conference was held at HMS *Talbot* – the Sliema Creek, Malta, submarine base – chaired by Lieutenant Commander L. H. Moorhouse RNR, it was found that no homing exercises had been held and that only Teacher and Cooper had experience of this procedure. The majority of the party were relatively untrained: some parties had left their beaches before the agreed time; and none of the canoes carried Very pistols or lights. It was considered that homing practice must be included in the training syllabus and the procedure perfected before leaving on a sortie; that RG should be used in an all-round lighthouse sweep; that bad-weather work should be avoided; that each team preferably should have a leader with operational experience: Cooper should have been the leader of the team in *P-45 Unrivalled*.

An attempt was made to thrash out emergency procedures: if a folbot failed to contact her carrier submarine she should proceed inshore, fix her position and come out again on the pre-arranged bearing and fire an SUE to indicate she is going to make another run. That charges fired before Rendezvous time should be a signal for the submarine to surface. Charges fired after zero, the time when the submarine must leave, be taken to indicate that the folbot is still searching and will proceed seawards on the pre-arranged bearing. Folbots need not carry RG transmitters, if unable to pick up the submarine's RG, the folbot can display a white light. It was also suggested that a small-moon period might be used rather than a no-moon period. An observer in an RAF-type dinghy, tethered to the submarine when it was on the bottom was also suggested. Geoffrey Galwey did subsequently experiment being towed in a folbot by a submerged submarine.

On firmer ground the conference agreed that only one team should be away from the submarine at a time. That carrier submarines should go in closer than ten fathoms; and canoes be released in 6-7 fathoms. It was for consideration that canoes might carry an SOE-type attaché case W/T transceiver, or an R/T transceiver. Very pistol signals could be used when ordered by the submarine by RT.

*

Nigel Willmott had the last word, as was his right: he conceded that losses had been heavy – 70% including those captured. Despite the losses in personnel missing or captured, Operation *Husky* – the invasion of Sicily had not been compromised, nor had any of the specialised secret equipment been captured by the enemy. And useful intelligence *had* been obtained.

COPP4 teams, with slightly more experience, did a successful reconnaissance of north-west Sicily. It was bad for morale that COPP3 should have lost their leader and the experienced Noel Cooper, as well as their half-trained military officer – Burbidge. Willmott was quick to point out that it proved his view that training could not be rushed; that teams could not be expected to operate continually through all types of weather. That the equipment used, including canoes had been known to be unsuitable at the time.

Lieutenant N. T. McHarg RN, S/COPP4, was awarded the DSO. Lieutenant P. R. G Smith RN and Lieutenant D. Brand RNVR were both awarded DSCs. Able Seaman James McGuire – one of those taken prisoner by an armed fishing vessel – was awarded a BEM, for his escape from captivity.

List of those lost on the Sicily Reconnaisssance and who have no known grave
Lieutenant-Commander Norman Joseph Macdonald Teacher, DSO, RN
Lieutenant Noel Wilson Cooper, RNVR
Captain George Wheelock Burbidge, Royal Canadian Engineers
Lieutenant Peter de Chatillon De Kock, MBE, DSC, SANF
Sub-Lieutenant Alfred Harvey Crossley, SANF
PRO DEFE2 1111
Nigel Willmott's exact words –

'Loss of a team appears to me to entail

(a) Possible compromise of a major assault

(b) Major operations may have to be postponed 2-3 weeks before another team, even if available, can produce results and plans be made therefrom

(c) Loss of skilled officers who the Admiralty and War Office describe as unprocurable

(d) Endangering a submarine.'

Nigel Willmott on losses of COPP3 and COPP4

'I have never thought that Reconnaissance could be done on a continuous scale, particularly in winter, the present facilities are most inadequate.'

At the same time excellent information had been obtained in some places; despite the 70% losses of personnel. COPP3 was disbanded and amalgamated with COPP4.

SOURCES

WHITING, Charles, *Slaughter Over Sicily*, Leo Cooper, 1992.

Public Record Office

DEFE2 1116

DEFE2 1111

Imperial War Museum

Lt-Cdr A. I. Hughes, DSC RNR (Retd) archive

Commonwealth War Graves Commission Records Department

CHAPTER THIRTEEN

COPP5 and COPP6 in the Mediterranean

It would be wrong to assume that all attempts to reconnoitre Sicily ceased with COPP3 and COPP4's heavy losses and only partial successes, in late-February and March 1943, but that is to anticipate somewhat.

The incidence of losses in the Mediterranean convinced Nigel Willmott that, even in the face of arguments of operational necessity: he must always insist that all future operational COPP parties follow the full Hayling Island training programme. Also that all parties proceeding overseas must take with them their own, tried and tested equipment – even folbots. The losses in the Sicily reconnaissances were in some measure due to operating with sub-standard, locally-obtained gear.

Before long Willmott had three parties training at the Hayling Island Sailing Club COPP Depot: COPPs 6, 5 and 7. COPP6 was the most advanced in its training; it was commanded by Lieutenant D. W. Amer RNR, who had pilotage experience off Algiers for Operation *Torch*, for which he had won a mention in despatches, as a member of *Party Inhuman*. Don Amer had been a merchant navy officer and was a most experienced navigator. He was also well aware of the heavy losses experienced in reconnoitring Sicily. In principle all recruits to COPP were volunteers for hazardous service. The CO's (S/COPPs) of COPPs7 and 5 were both Royal Navy; 'Pubs' not 'Darts' i.e: Public School entrants not Dartmouth ones. Mind you all that was long behind them; both had considerable navigating experience. They were Lieutenants RN, G. P. D. Hall, and R. N. Stanbury. Geoffrey Hall had been Navigating Officer 15th Minesweeping Flotilla, operating in the Atlantic, Home Waters and around Iceland. This was vital work he enjoyed, but he had wished to become more involved in the war. Ralph Stanbury had served in the Fleet Destroyer *Mashona*; had qualified as a

Navigator and Surveyor in 1941. Thereafter he had navigated the cruiser HMS *Diomede* some 150,000 miles. He had lately brought her back from Montevideo, when he found his way to COPP.

In early days selection procedures for COPP were on an *ad hoc* basis. Geoffrey Hall was interviewed at COHQ, by Lieut L. G. Lyne RN, who had been captured by the Vichy French, in North Africa. Lyne was transferring back into General Service: in a sense taking Hall's place. Geoffrey Hall also saw Willmott and was impressed. He was told to take three weeks leave then report at Sandy Point, COPP Depot, on Hayling Island.

Other appointments seem to have been more arbitrary. Stanbury's Royal Engineer officer, for example, arrived through an error in postings. Another, quite different Captain P. D. Matterson RE, had been intended for COPP. 'Matt' as he became known, nothing loath, stayed and buckled down to his task.

Geoffrey Hall was interested to note that his second-in-command, in COPP7, Lieutenant J. D. R. McLean RNVR, wore a Croix de Guerre. In time McLean explained that this was a result of his service as liaison officer with the Free French Submarine *Rubis*. McLean confided that his friends called him Ruari: spelled in that fashion, because he was Scots: a great advantage with the Free French. Indeed Rousselot, a Lorrainer, Ruari's captain in *Rubis*, was married to a Scots girl. Sadly Vice Admiral Henri Rousselot died in 1994. In fact the Free French had officially become La France Combattante (the Fighting French) on 14 July 1942; though no-one seemed to use that term. The intention was to include Gaullist, patriot resistants in German-occupied France.

As regards the rating members of Stanbury's COPP5. Nick Goodyear, the electrical specialist had not been long in the navy. He had joined as an Ordinary Telegraphist – as had Ruari McLean – Nick had trained at HMS *Vernon*: the famous girls' school. Then very chilly, in the height of winter. When he passed out he had re-mustered as an Electrical Mechanic and had switched bell-bottoms for the less romantic round rig, with jacket and peaked cap. He volunteered after 'Gaffer' Moorhouse, the COPP Depot Main Staff Officer called and appealed for volunteers for hazardous service. When he arrived at Sandy Point his first impression was that he was in a good team, with an excellent inter-rank relationship. Ronnie Williamson, one of the army other ranks, came to COPP5 from a commando. He was a Shetlander and experienced in boat handling and long distance swimming in battledress, including boots and gaiters. Leading Seaman Thomas – a Londoner and prewar ship's steward – joined the team having gained a mention in despatches and a DSM in HMS *Salvia*, during the German occupation of Crete and Greece. So that it may be seen the teams were built up from diversified backgrounds.

John Bowden in Amer's COPP6, was probably the smallest man in the three teams. He was told his size would be a great advantage in submarines. His entry into Combined Operations was perhaps the most dramatic and with scant ceremony. In December 1942, he had been drafted to HMS *Victory*, after having seen his share of action – mostly in escort vessels – having had one bombed and sunk, under him, in 1940. He expected at least three months shore duty. On January 30 1943, however, doubling across the parade ground to a dull job in the mail office, he was accosted by the beckoning finger of the Chief Boatswain's Mate. He was asked: 'Are you excused seagoing duty? Are you married? Have you any relations? Have you ever been in trouble? Do you want to have a go at the Hun?' After answering satisfactorily, he was taken to the First Lieutenant's office, where he saw Geoffrey Galwey, in khaki. His first impression was that though he'd never been in trouble – he was in it *now*: in Combined Operations. And probably for a one-off raid. The same day he was taken to Northney Camp on Hayling Island, kitted out with khaki battledress and interviewed, with a dozen others, by Willmott – who offered them all the chance to opt out: no one did. Probably Willmott was not surprised. Next day John Bowden was transported to the COPP Depot, 'for Commando and COPP training'. He and the other volunteers soon learned that training was considered very urgent and went on day and night.

*

Volunteers for hazardous service were in principle independently minded and critical of dictatorial training routines; in particular nude swimming . . . during the winter months. Willmott had of course already proved to his own satisfaction, the value of 'hardening'. The COPP training routine was deliberately as hard as he could devise it. The ultimate threat of return to General Service for naval personnel; and return to unit for military personnel existed, but they did not have to be invoked for operational parties. Whilst maintenance staff, draughts-men, carpenters, sailmakers, electrical specialists – were in theory non-operational, Willmott foresaw situations where all COPP 'naval party' members might need to be operational as reserves or spare paddlers. So there were no exceptions to the training programme. It saved wrangles. When in time, indepependent medical authorities queried whether such a rigorous training routine was *necessary*: Willmott simply replied that it was *essential*. In any case he did it himself, whenever possible, no-one could argue with that.

All Depot personnel – even permanent, maintenance – staff were constituted on the strength of Combined Operations Command, equipped with khaki Battledress and weapons and equipment. Including, it is said L-pills i.e: instant-death capsules, small arms and fighting knives. They were required to do early-morning physical training and hardening. This applied to Jack Phillis, at that time the sole Writer, in Combined Operations. To whom would be entrusted the compilation of the COPP Training Manual, now preserved for posterity, at the Public Record Office, at Kew.

In principle everyone toed the line. Though there is a canard, that one of the maintenance staff, once refused hardening; remaining in his bunk, and greeting all comers with a levelled, loaded Smith and Wesson revolver. He was censured, but not posted, and on that single day avoided winter swimming. In fact, such training routines paid off: parties posted overseas to the Mediterranean and Far East theatres were agreeably surprised to find themselves operating in warmer waters than they had trained in.

Willmott trained, too, because he was determined that his personal operational tour was by no means over. But his pursuit of excellence: to get the best possible equipment for his COPPists and to replace paddles lost or damaged in training and to obtain a continuous supply of folbots that would stand up to training conditions, no less rigorous than those in operational theatres, sometimes prevented him training with the teams. A folbot team that got into difficulties, navigating off Hayling Island – later in the game – got the rough edge of Willmott's tongue because they accepted aid from a naval vessel. In doing so, he pointed out, they could have compromised the secrecy of COPP's whole training programme. Those concerned became convinced it might have been better had they drowned . . . ! And determined not to get into difficulties again.

Geoffrey Hall's first impressions, at the time, were that Willmott ran a taut ship, with few formalities and just enough discipline for his highly motivated group of trainees. Whilst officers concentrated on navigation, beach surveys and pilotage: ratings' and other ranks' training concentrated on learning to assemble canoes efficiently, making canvas covers and bags for grenades, Tommy guns and the other equipment carried in the canoes. They also waterproofed torches and compasses with oversized condoms. In betweenwhile there was also canoeing, morse code and seamanship, as well as unarmed combat, learning how to use firearms and explosives. Frequent night exercises were of a character-building kind and fostered all ranks' ability to act as a team. Some of the training took place in Scotland. As Geoffrey Hall put it: 'We learnt the virtues of stealth and surprise, we learned self-sufficiency, survival, living off the country, we learnt to kill an enemy in silence – with our hands, with a piece of wire, or with a dagger – and we learnt the techniques of undercover sabotage.' The entire training programme: in Hayling Island and in Scotland, took three to four months. It had to be done quickly, but nothing was skimped. As the teams completed training they went overseas. COPP6 and COPP5 to the Mediterranean; and COPP7 to the Far East. Where we shall hear more of them.

*

COPP5's story in the Mediterranean under Ralph Stanbury has been best described in Ralph Neville (Stanbury)'s Book *Survey by Starlight* – the title alone is most evocative of what COPP did and how they did it. COPP5's first operations were to continue what had been started on Sicilian beaches.

In June 1943 they made successful surveys of the Syracuse south-east Sicilian beaches – undeterred by the COPP3 and COPP4 losses earlier that year – bringing back information on defences that could not have been gleaned from PRU photographs; gun positions embedded in the cliffs, for example. One day before the proposed assault they laid navigation buoys off the landing beaches and their canoes* braved a storm to act as leading lights to guide in the first waves of landing craft – in which other COPPists were embarked in MLs – on 9 July 1943, piloting in the assault force.

They were less fortunate in the Gulf of Gioia, in the Tyrrhenian Sea, Where they surveyed at considerable risk, from HMS/M *Shakespeare* – beaches not used in Operation Husky landings: a pity since COPP5 brought back details of beach gradients above and below waterline, assessments of exits potential and reporting sentry activity on shore and coastal E-boat patrols. By 30 August, almost 150-miles further north, they had begun surveys for the Salerno bridgehead – an obvious case where any slip-up by COPP could have compromised a major offensive – happily they were skilled and proficient and the enemy at no stage

*At Sicily, Ronnie Williamson (COPP5), who was there, has since pointed out; 4 canoes brought in 3,250 ships – by shining torches out to sea.

suspected the presence of the COPP5 teams during several days of intensive reconnaissance. Stanbury, Kent and Matterson acted as COPP5 pilots for the Salerno landing. Frank Berncastle acted as a pilot beacon marker for it too.

*

Don Amer, who had acted as a pilot for the Operation *Torch* landings, returned to the Mediterranean in command of COPP6, with Lieutenant Peter Wild as his second in command. They were sent out to HMS *Talbot*, the Malta submarine base, in Sliema Creek, in May 1943: their brief to survey the south-west coast beaches, between Licata and Cape Passero. The operational party embarked aboard HMS/M *Unison* (Lieutenant A. C. Halliday RN) on 30 May 1943 and did not return until 6 June 1943. Amer took L/Sea F. Phillips as his paddler, and Wild took AB J. Bowden. Both canoes took separate two-day stints and usually worked for 2½ hours to complete each 'run'.

The description of the Salerno reconnaissance has spelled out clearly the responsibilities of an S/COPP in making a swim reconnaissance from a folbot. It is now appropriate to consider the responsibilities of the rating paddler, based on the recollections of Peter Wild's paddler. Peter had chosen 'Shorty' Bowden, because his compactness meant some room for his long legs . . . . As well as being the swimmer's bodyguard, the paddler was jointly responsible for the canoe being maintained in 100% condition and fully operational, with all equipment fitted and stores loaded, ready for immediate use. In the Appendices there is a diagram of a canoe with operational stores. This is taken from the COPP Training Manual and on operations might be varied.

Normally there would always be the P8 aircraft compass, torch, underwater writing tablet, gradient reel and lead-lines, as well as No. 36 grenades for use as SUEs (Signals Underwater Explosive) to contact the submarine in an emergency. These John Bowden primed at the last moment before departure. He would also embark the all-important RG receiver and a Sten gun and ammunition, in case the natives proved hostile.

Inevitably the paddler – frequently a leading hand, or an SBS NCO or other rank – was responsible for the safety of the swimmer; for his successful pick-up and safe return to the submarine. While the swimmer was out of the canoe, the paddler would be on his own, taking soundings and bearings. Keeping calm and mapping coastal defences or other salient features. If there was the slightest gleam of moonlight he would try to keep his eye on his officer swimmer. Even if, to avoid capture, the swimmer should trim down and submerge. On the swimmer and paddler's safe return to the carrier vessel, the rating paddler would share responsibility to ready the canoe for the next operation.

*

COPP6's next operational sortie was in *Unseen* (Lieutenant M. L. C. Crawford RN). The same two teams operated but stepped up the pace, doing two trips each – a total of four altogether, to the beaches. Their third trip was in HMS/M *Unrivalled* (Lieutenant H. B. Turner RN) all their sorties were successful – a vindication both for Donald Amer's leadership and Nigel Willmott's training methods. On D–1 like the COPP5 teams, they were embarked and dropped off at the invasion beach at 2200: the invasion was scheduled to take place at 0600 the following morning. Peter Wild remembers acting as master buoy for the invasion force first waves, using a torch and a given signal. One canoe team Sub-Lieutenant A. G. Sayce and L/Seaman V. F. P. Manning* were not seen again and it is believed they were struck by a glider that fell short, landing in the sea instead of on the mainland. Not long after that the team was recalled to England.

Operating from Malta had posed problems: food was in short supply. Usually it was corned beef, served in one of a dozen ways, with boiled onions since potatoes were in short supply. Beer was rationed to two bottles per week. The 1943 local brew could be purchased but was unappetising. But if COPPists could not often relax with a drink they could relax on a beach and swim, in between exercises.

*

COPP security could pose problems too. When attempting to beg a lift back to the UK, from Naples via Casablanca, on an American aircraft, a puzzled American sergeant, eyeing John Bowden's tropical KD uniform and matelot's cap – no one could accuse COPP, overseas of dressing 'tiddley' fashion! – asked naïvely: 'Are you the King's messenger . . .?'

'The chance would be a fine thing!' replied 'Shorty' Bowden ruefully.

*

* Neither has a known grave, but both are commemorated on the Portsmouth Naval Memorial, as having died on 10 July 1943.

Peter Wild is unstinting in his praise for their submarine carrier-vessel crews:

> Submariners which took us to various destinations were very hospitable, despite the fact that we took up valuable space in conditions which were cramped anyway. Also we must have endangered their lives by having to operate in shallow water – at times five-fathoms depth, most of their time in enemy waters – and lastly we stopped their firing at targets for security reasons.

> Captain M. L. C. Crawford DSC, RN (Retd) – who carried COPPists to Sicily – for two-to-three months, prior to Operatation *Husky*, and in the process didn't get an operational patrol for all that time, had this to say, some fifty years afterwards: 'We did what we could to help the COPPists – creeping close inshore was never popular. Nor were the prohibitions on attacks before and following the special operation.'

The Late Commander Freddie Ponsonby RN (wartime S/COPP8) summed it all up in a short poem in the Visitors' book of HMS *Stoic*, in May 1944:

Submarine Trip

To merely goof at sea and swell
For you one knows is perfect hell,
But we expecting several hits,
Had failed to cater for a blitz,
Which frankly shook us to the tits.

Regret we sat and drank your beer,
And also cost one fish, I fear
But you made comfort every way
To see that we enjoyed our stay.
Our thanks, good luck, Godspeed, good day.

SOURCES

SEYMOUR, William, *British Special Forces*, Sidgwick and Jackson, 1985
LADD, James, *SBS The Invisible Raiders*, Arms and Armour Press, 1983 (David and Charles edition, 1989).
NEVILLE, Ralph, *Survey by Starlight*, Hodder, 1949
Correspondence with former COPP6 member
Commonwealth War Graves Commission records
Correspondence with COPPists

CHAPTER FOURTEEN

Politics

After the Salerno reconnaissances many staff officers made observations on COPP. Some were perfectly reasonable: Captain (S) of the 10th Submarine Flotilla considered that COPP reconnaissances must depend on the weather, the water temperature, the enemy's vigilance and the degree to which COPPists were trained. Willmott could have answered that the almost sadistic 'hardening' routine trainee COPPists went through – was designed to make sure water temperature made damn' all difference to their carrying out their duties. One staff officer, who shall be nameless, suggested that beach reconnaissance was not difficult.

The most perceptive minutes were written by Admiral A. B. Cunningham, then C-in-C Mediterranean to the Chief of Combined Operations. Even he was at times at variance with Willmott's dictums. COPP information he regarded as a valuable source of intelligence, but felt, for that reason, it should be used sparingly – it was extremely arduous and introduced danger of compromise. If it was used more sparingly the COPP teams could be reduced, probably he felt this would reduce casualties. If used other than sparingly, the teams would lose their operational fitness. He felt COPP reconnaissance should only be sea reconnaissance; so that all teams' Sapper officers could be dispensed with. That onshore reconnaissance wasn't essential; nor need each team have its own Sapper draughtsman: Royal Engineers' survey facilities were always bound to be available somewhere handy. Predictably Nigel would never buy that one.

Soundings could be taken by charioteers – as a useful standby – others did not agree. The arguments went backwards and forwards. In particular it emerged that the Admiral was wrong about Charioteers – they grounded long before they reached low water mark. The *Overlord* military planners, fully nine months before the intended D-Day landings, came out strongly in favour of retaining RE officers in COPP teams and vetoed their deletion. Characteristically Nigel Willmott pointed out that sentries posed no dangers to well-trained teams and consequently this disposed of arguments of risk of compromise. The obvious point that beach defences, bearing capacities and beach exits could only be assessed by onshore reconnaissance was eventually re-established.

To his credit A. B. Cunningham never suggested beach reconnaissance was easy. He acknowledged that COPP duties imposed considerable nervous strain. In his memoirs he expressed admiration for those who did them. In 1943, he championed the idea of last-minute reconnaissance; partly because he felt COPP teams would become discouraged if their work was not of immediate operational use. Also because the teams carrying out marking and pilotage for invasion fleets, needed absolutely up-to-the-moment beach information. He perceptively picked up from Ralph Stanbury's Salerno, COPP5 experience that soundings data could be passed by submarine signal. He also noted that COPP5 had been denied Chief of Staff access. One of the mandarins, commenting on COPP5 and COPP6's successes, attributed them to the fact that they had been doing it longer than other teams. That must have been galling for Willmott, engaged as he was in arguing that COPP teams could not be expected to operate indefinitely. He bit back what he thought when the old chestnut: that COPP operations diverted submarines from their primary objective was trotted out.

Willmott was, of course, always trying to improve equipment and procedures. The same policy files contain notes from S/COPPs on the effectiveness of operational equipment. RAF pattern swimmers torches proved unreliable in the Mediterranean and unreliable torches could cost lives: United States Navy pursers' torches were suggested as an alternative. One sounding lead-line and reel might tangle. Why not carry a second? Smith and Wesson revolvers were serviceable, but difficult to strip down and clean – which, of course, was essential after each sortie. There was a French naval pistol (of approximately 8 mm calibre) which could be stripped by the removal of a single screw . . . could it be tested?

None of Nigel Willmott's ideas were first-thought ones: and he was never prepared to allow his teams to suffer, even in noble causes, nor accept second best. It is clear he knew when to fight and when simply to ignore criticism from above . . . and stick to what he'd proved worked best. In fact, experiments involving exploding charges on beaches and even aircraft firing their cannon into them: as means of assessing bearing capacity were tried. Together with examination of aerial photographs

POLITICS

73

to assess beach gradients by the wave-velocity method: neither of these 'scientific' methods proved as reliable as Willmott's swim reconnaissance teams.

SOURCES
PUBLIC RECORD OFFICE
DEFE2 1116
CUNNINGHAM OF HYNDHOPE, Admiral of the Fleet Viscount, *A Sailor's Odyssey*, Hutchinson, 1951.

CHAPTER FIFTEEN

Anzio Saga

It would be wrong to imagine that COPP ME's activities ended with the Sicily reconnaissances, they were also employed prior to the Anzio beachhead.

By November 1943, the Allied advance up the Italian peninsula had been halted at the Gustav Line. An amphibious seaborne operation to outflank the Gustav line was proposed at Anzio. Anzio was a small port sixty miles north of Cassino, where the Allies were also held up. Anzio was conveniently and strategically thirty miles south of Rome. Two recces were carried out: one by a remnant of Z SBS, which had remained behind when unit returned to England. Both operations were made from an Italian motor launch (MAS torpedo boats), operating out of Ischia, with Sub-Lieutenant K. G. Patterson RANVR, of COPP Middle East, in command. Lieutenant Simpson-Jones of SOE (Special Operations Executive) was also carried as conducting officer as the common language with the crew was French. The Z SBS teams were under Captains Alex McClair and W. G. 'Bill' Davies, with Sergeants Ron Sidlow and John Galloway as paddlers. The COPP ME team was Kim Patterson with AB 'Jock' Gordon Lockhead as paddler. Anzio had two sandy, shelving beaches with dunes at the back and false beaches offshore: Nettuno and Anzio. The MAS-boats were similar to German E-boats, with two bow-mounted torpedo tubes and twin Isotta Fraschini engines; they could make 36 knots and were capable of silent running on their underwater exhausts. The boats, were Italian navy crewed.

The MAS boat that launched McClair, put him down off another beach; four miles from his correct one. Undeterred he paddled those four miles and, with dawn fast coming-up, just made it back to the MAS boat: with the vital information that there were definitely two false beaches.

Kim Patterson was luckier on his first sortie, he and Jock were launched off Nettuno, the same night as McClair: 28/29 November 1944. They were able to obtain reasonable soundings, and locate sandbanks that would have grounded LSTs. They too were safely embarked and the MAS boat proceeded back to Ischia.

On the night of 2/3 December the MAS boat was back off Anzio and McClair's, Davies' and Kim Patterson's canoes were launched for a further Anzio beaches' reconnaissance. Again sandbanks: Kim did an extra couple of sounding runs to confirm this. At one point he had to lie low when a beach patrol passed by. Thereafter with the combination of a freshening breeze from the south, a featureless coast – with no landmarks to confirm position – and a northward-flowing current: Patterson's canoe failed to make the rendezvous back with the MAS-boat. His canoe was furthest north and had the furthest to travel back of all three: but even today he is unable to account for why it happened. Patterson and Jock displayed infra-red signals seawards – watched for any return signals – and dropped SUEs; all without finding or being found by the MAS-boat, carrier vessel. Postwar Kim Patterson contacted the late Alex McClair, who could not account for it either. The MAS-boat returned to Ischia and both ME COPPists were reported missing. A sad finish to a successful survey.

Later a further combined sortie (SBS and USNR) was attempted using an American PT Boat as carrier vessel. Davies returned safely but had to be hospitalised because of injuries, from stepping on sea urchins on his second landing. Two US Naval Reserve ensigns – volunteer canoeists – were lost without trace. In the event the reconnaissance evidence of false beaches was discounted – though supported by the British admiral in charge. Instead the Americans relied on the evidence of local fisherman – and several landing craft grounded, at one point 500 American soldiers in full kit stepped out into six feet of water and drowned. Despite this the overall operation – on 22 January 1944 – was a success. It's claimed that the success of the Anglo-American landing at Anzio caused Hitler to divert reinforcements to Italy. Fortunately Kim and Jock, the Middle East COPPists were nothing if not resourceful and their story did not end with being posted missing at Anzio.

*

Kim wrote up his story in an unpublished account entitled *Travels Without a Donkey*. As a first-year medical student, at Sydney University, he had enlisted in the army; but a year later decided to switch to the navy. Commissioned into the RANVR – after sundry courses in the usual places: HMAS *Kybra, Bingera, Rushcutter* – he saw service in HMAS *Gawler*, which eventually took him as far as the Mediterranean. On an escort run from Alexandria to Malta via Tripoli, he answered a signal calling for volunteers for hazardous service . . . believing he'd wind up riding jeeps [Human Torpedoes].

Instead he found himself paddling canoes at Kabrit: HMS *Saunders*. This was a 'stone frigate': a tented camp, midway between the Great and Little Bitter lakes. It was here that Nigel Willmott had set up the Middle East COPP training centre. It even had the dummy side of a ship built at the water's edge, so troops could practise disembarking into landing craft, for practice assaults across the lake. Kim shared a tent, nicknamed 'Wallaby House' with another Australian, Midshipman A. Crookes RNR. Their Commanding Officer was Lieutenant P. R G. Smith DSC, RN, previously mentioned paddling to Malta following a missed rendezvous, after a Sicily recce. Smith's place was taken over by a Lieutenant-Commander Cox RN (ex-*Abdiel*, a fast minelayer).

Training was on the lines of Sandy Point with a few differences: swimming – mostly water polo – PT and folbot handling. They limpet-mined the LCTs anchored in the lake and endured long night, paddling exercises. Patterson and Crookes 'organised' their own motor cycle transport, 'borrowing' army bikes that had been run on to landing craft, they were put over the side with heaving lines attached, whenever MPs appeared. After being beached they were seviceable for trips to far-sited heads and showers at *Saunders*. At a pinch the bikes could even make it as far as Suez or Ishmailia. The pair also bamboozled army motor-transport truck drivers into giving them lifts to shorten the night exercises and, between exercises, learned to drive captured enemy vehicles.

Barely had they heard that their predecessors at *Saunders* had successfully done the Salerno recce, before they were re-mustered as beachmasters, joined a Beach 'Brick' (Beach Reinforcement Independent Unit) tactical landing unit, at Haifa, with units of the 4th Royal Tank Regiment: notionally for a projected invasion of Rhodes. But that was cancelled and they were told their COPP unit was to be disbanded. Some officers were off to the Aegean to man caiques: some were being made ready to go to the Far East. Patterson found himself in charge of a party of two folbots destined for Naples. They took the best two canoes *Scarlett O'Hara* and *Helen of Troy*. They went to Taranto in a four-masted Bibby Line transport *OC Troops*. Thence to Naples where they met up with Alex McClair and Bill Davies. Here they operated from the chateau Mezze Torre that had been requisitioned by SOE for training purposes. Here Kim met Simpson-Jones and it became a joint SBS-ME COPP base for operations with the two MAS boats *No 23* and *No 24*. Here the incident of the perished swim suit occurred and Kim reverted to KD shorts, sandshoes and an Ursula jacket for operations: it seemed safer . . . . The Anzio recces soon followed.

*

When Kim and Jock realised that their MAS boat had left without them they set-off shortly before daylight, paddling south, aiming for the islands of Ventotene or Ponza (some 80 miles away), 20–30 miles off the coast, south of Gaeta. It proved too rough to make any progress, so they lay-to out to sea until the next night, then headed inshore; the canoe broached-to in the breakers, getting ashore, Jock broke his paddle and got the end in his back . . . but they made it in one piece, beached and hid the canoe, and dumped their spare gear. They sheltered in a small brick house, lit a fire and tended Jock's wound. Surprised by a German soldier they hid behind a door, prepared to knock him on the head, having stamped out their fire. Incredibly the soldier left, apparently suspecting nothing.

They set off inland carrying their Sten guns. They checked there was no German transport outside the next house where they sought shelter. It was full of Italians having a party. They held them up with their Sten guns: they were glad they weren't German. They wouldn't have relished shooting that number . . . . Finding the Italians decent farming folk and friendly they joined the party. They spent the night there and were given clothing and boots to replace their sandshoes. As the countryside was reputed teaming with prisoners-of-war, who had released themselves, and discharged Italian servicemen: there seemed little point in carrying the Sten guns. They gave them to a farmer, who promised to pass them on to the *partigiani*.

They took to the mountains where they were to spend all of two months: camping off the roads and tracks at night, in sheephuts and sheds. They had a silk escape map and hoped to get through the allied lines. They met many picturesque characters, including tobacco smugglers from Pontecorvo, lived mainly on Polenta, maize porridge, dried figs, oranges and yellow corn bread, spread with olive oil in lieu of butter; carefully eeking out their Italian escape money. After Christmas, outside Fondi they were put up for the night by the famous writer Alberto Moravia (author of *The Woman of Rome* and *The Fancy Dress*

Party). Moravia was himself hiding in the mountains: he was a violent anti-Fascist. When the area was liberated. Moravia reported to the authorities that he had seen Kim alive and well and heading for the front. This was the first information that reached Kim's family over the six-month period he was missing.

Later, having witnessed the bombardment of Cassino and escaped German patrols and foraging parties, they came to the village of Spignio above Minturno. Here they were only about 1,440 metres from the advancing British 5th Army. They pressed on and came under the fire of the 5th Army 25-pounders. Finally 1km from the allied lines, at Santa Maria Infanti, near Forunia they were captured by a patrol of the *Hermann Göring Division*, having been blown out of haystack by force of artillery fire. By now Kim had a shoulder wound from a shell splinter. They were taken to a prisoner-of-war cage in Forunia, then to Rome and then to hospitalisation in Perugia.

Then following a long train journey over the Alps with two German soldiers going home on leave, Kim wound up at Marlag-Milag Nord, at Wester Timke, the main Naval and Merchant Navy Prison Camp in north-west Germany. The date was 23 February 1944. Kim managed to get from the *Dulag* – interrogation camp – into the Revier (hospital) where his wound was treated. A most unlikely self-styled E-boats' (*Schnellboote*) seaman attempted to question him about Fairmile 'D' Class MTBs' diesel engines: but he knew nothing of them. Sent back to the *Dulag*, he had more interrogations. The Germans expressed surprise that an Australian should be in a European war. He weathered the unenviable situation of having been picked up in a frontline area, in civilain clothing, admittedly with concealed shoulder straps. He couldn't claim to be an escaped POW, as the Germans had lists of these. Although he had identity discs, some elderly German merchant captains, with knowledge of Australian ports questioned him to check that he really was Australian. In time he was released to the main camp and told of his promotion to lieutenant RANVR.

In the main camp he was treated with suspicion until befriended by another Australian, Lieutenant Ivan Black, RANVR, who had been arrested in France. Launched in a dinghy, from an MTB, Black had landed two SOE agents, the boat was swamped, when he attempted to embark Mathilde Lily Carré (the notorious double, agent code-named *La Chatte*) who was being decoyed to England as a double bluff. Arrested in uniform Black had become a POW. Both Kim and his father had known Black prewar, and this established Kim's bonefides among the POWs.

Kim remained in the camp all of fifteen months, the prisoners were guarded by *Kriegsmarine* personnel and coastal artillerymen. There were some notable prisoners, including Lieutenants RN, Don Cameron and Geoffrey Place, both VCs, from the *Tirpitz* X-craft raid. It was at this camp that the 'Albert RN' escape deception was practised, to conceal the absence of escapers on *Appells*, roll calls. Kim had managed to hide and avoid a forced march to Lübeck, by inmates of the rating's compound and most of the officers. The column was inadvertently strafed by the RAF en route. The Milag compound was liberated on 28 April 1945 by armoured cars of the Welsh Guards Armoured Brigade. Kim and other liberated prisoners went sight-seeing in the brigade major's truck. Here and there they accepted surrenders. Patterson annexed one soldier's Schmeisser *machinepistole*, which he took back to Australia and used for kangaroo shooting until he handed it in – with four magazines of ammunition – at Canberra War Memorial, during a clamp-down on automatic weapons. In time repatriation, delousing, kitting-out and debriefing followed. He was still in London for VE-Day and a Buckingham Palace garden party for Commonwealth ex-POWs. Then back to Australia aboard the *Orontes*, disembarkation at Fremantle and flights to Adelaide, Melbourne and Sydney. After leave in Sydney back to HMAS *Rushcutter* for discharge.

SOURCES
PATTERSON, K. G., *Travels Without a Donkey*, unpublished typescript
FOOT, M. R. D. *SOE in France*, HMSO, 1966.

CHAPTER SIXTEEN

Festung Europa

Reconnaissance for the opening of the Second Front, the onslaught on *Festung Europa* was something Nigel Willmott did not care to entrust to others – it wasn't that he didn't trust his teams – I think he would have said simply that there are things that one instinctively feels one should do oneself.

Officialdom didn't agree with Nigel on this point: he was notified officially that he must not land. It was considered he knew too much. Inevitably he was 'Bigoted'. This is not to imply that he was narrow-minded or obstinate in any way. 'Bigot' had been the code word for designating papers that indicated dates and places of offensive landings. It was stamped on such papers, in green, and they might only be seen by the officially 'Bigoted'. This code word had been in use, in precisely this way since at least pre-Operation *Torch*. No-one on the Bigot list might be hazarded on an operation without Winston Churchill's express permission.

Two reconnaissances involving hydrographic landing craft, Bell-Push Able and Bell-Push Baker, were to be carried out on the nights of 25/26 December and 28/29 December 1943. These involved Lieutenant Donald Amer DSC, RNR and Lieutenant Peter Wild DSC, RNVR, from *LCP(L)-190* and *LCP(L)-290*; their taut-wire measuring gear had given problems and although folbots had been embarked with the intention of landing – in what was to become the Sword Beach area – this did not prove possible. None the less, much useful naval research was brought back. The next operation to be undertaken must be to obtain military intelligence; and for that a landing would be essential.

Nigel decided that the next best thing to landing – would be to command the operation. Major General Logan Scott-Bowden – then a major, Royal Engineers – has described it in an article in *The Royal Engineers Journal*, Vol 108 No. 1, April 1944. All quotations in this chapter are from that article.

Willmott was first to be briefed in August 1943 about the choice of landing areas.

The operation would present special problems: the normal COPP methods – tried and tested in the Mediterranean – could not be used. These consisted of a pair of two-man canoes operationg from a S- or T-Class submarine. The Mediterranean had small tidal ranges, but in Northern Europe tidal conditions would not facilitate the use of canoes. And there were other problems.

Normal submarines could not go through the enemy minefields and the Germans had by now acquired sufficient radar skill to detect a surfaced submarine's conning tower. So other means were sought: X-craft provided a possible solution. They would probably pass over the minefields safely and having a neglible profile even with the snorkel raised were virtually undetectable to radar.

As there would be no room for passengers, the operational personnel had to be fully trained as X-craft crews. This meant a two month course at HMS *Varbel*, in Loch Striven, where Nigel Willmott insisted that rigorous physical fitness training be alternated with X-craft training. Once the COPP personnel had been passed as competent X-craft crewman, they returned to the Hayling Island COPP Depot, with the intention that they should await the arrival of their X-craft, by rail before departing on their mission. This was shortly before Christmas 1943. The team were briefed to be ready to be operational in the next dark (moonless) period: 17–22 January 1944.

Circumstances, however, were to decree otherwise – as Scott-Bowden relates:

> Willmott and I were suddenly summoned to Combined Operations Headquarters and told that the scientists had anxieties about the beach bearing-capacity of the Plateau de Calvados beaches for the passage of heavy-wheeled vehicles and guns particularly in the British and Canadian sectors – where in Roman times the coastline and a port had been more than a kilometre further out. Erosion by the sea had covered with sand ancient peat marshes included in an overall review in Latin of the Roman Empire's fuel reserves. I saw this review on Professor J. D. Bernal's desk. He was Chief Scientific Officer to the Chief of Combined Operations.

General Scott-Bowden goes on to explain:

> Where there is peat there is usually clay which if insufficiently covered with sand is dangerous. Similar geological conditions existed on the Brancaster beaches in Norfolk. An RAF bomber had dropped bombs in a selected suspect area on the Plateau de Calvados. The bomber had done this skillfully diving and making smoke to make it appear that it was

damaged and the bombs had to be jettisoned to avoid arousing any suspicion. A similar pattern of bombs was dropped off Brancaster. Over a period the Plateau de Calvados craters were monitored by air photography and checked against those at Brancaster. The results were not sufficiently conclusive for the scientists [to assess comparable bearing capacities].

And there were additional political factors:

Reconnaissance for the invasion was a British responsibility as we had been fighting an increasingly sophsticated air and sea cross-Channel war for four years and knew the form.

The Combined Chiefs of Staff in Washington had been demanding from COSSAC, (Chief of Staff to the Supreme Allied Commander), who had formulated the plans, a firm estimate of the amount of beach trackway required for the invasion, but, because of the scientists' uncertainties, no reply had been forthcoming. An ultimatum came stating that as vital production prorities in the United States had to be changed to meet the worst case optimum estimate, an immediate decision was vital if such requirements were to be met in time for the invasion.

COPP-1 was to prepare for an operation at short notice but as a preliminary test, in 48 hours time, we after some instruction [from the scientists] in collecting samples were to do a night trial at Brancaster sailing out in a tank landing craft from Kings Lynn. If this was successful we might be permitted to do an operation to Normandy on New Year's Eve 1943/1944.

Guards were posted onshore: Professor Bernal among them!

He had the ear of Professor Lindemann, "the Prof", Mr Churchill's scientific adviser.

The LCT quietly closed the shore – the COPPists swam ashore, took samples, eluded the guards, undetected and unsuspected.

The swimmers were Scott-Bowden and Ogden Smith, both heavily laden and in cumbersome rubber swimsuits – grey rubber frogman's suits, without the fin flippers.

Ogden Smith and I being equipped with the additional burden of a large bandolier with a dozen 10-inch tubes with phosporescent numbers on their caps and an 18-inch auger which was efficient pushed fully into the sand and given one half turn, when pulled up it produced a 10-inch core sample from the lower end. It was the dark period and we were in luck as there was some mist.

The two swimmers methodically recorded the positions of their sample bore-holes and, having located all the sentries, crawled back to the water's edge, then walked up the beach, shouting to the frozen

Logan Scott-Bowden.

Peter Wild.

Basil Eckhard, wearing Royal Engineers badges and buttons: 'cover' for a Spanish-speakers' unit.

Richard Fyson.

Nicholas Hastings.

Geoffrey Galwey.

Paul Clark.

Peter Wild.

Prue Wright.

Pam Glencross at Hayling Island.

Jenny Devitt, Robin Harbud, Evelyn 'Kitten' Cross.

Bill' Sykes beside folbot.

'AB Nichol and Ronnie Williamson.

Tubby' Chambers, Stoker Reavel, Bill Tebb

Bill Tebb.

Group including Dennis Mackay, Basil Griffith, Bill Sykes, Ian Mackenzie, with rope.

Basil Griffith, Unknown, Peter Wild, John Hashim, Don Amer.

Smiling group: middle row includes Basil Griffith, John Hashim and 'Shorty' Bowden.

'Tanker' Townson in civvies in front of Temple of Beautiful Thoughts.

Johnny Lamb.

Robin Harbud, Arthur Briggs.

Pam Glencross with a group that includes Mackay, Griffith, Gambrill and Mackenzie.

Peter Wild, Rollo Mangnall.

sentries. Later they displayed their samples, in the dimmed headlights of a 15-cwt truck. The trial had been completely successful.

Two days later COPP were told that a reconniassance had been approved. They were to examine a suspect area of beach west of Ver sur Mer, on New Years's Eve, when the Germans might be less than normally vigilant.

*

Quite apart from that no sane person would think of making a swim reconnaissance in the bleak mid-winter, but then COPPists needed to be a little mad. And many had swum stark naked in Chichester Harbour and Loch Striven, in December. Willmott's COPP1 team comprised himself, as naval commander, and for the military reconnaissance Major Logan Scott-Bowden and Sergeant Bruce Ogden Smith, East Surreys and formerly HAC. The party would travel from Gosport in two MGBs, which would tow two shallow-draft landing craft specially designed for hydrographic survey.

It was planned that the MGBs would stop short of the minefield and transfer the COPPists to the landing craft. Lieutenant N. C. Glen RN, was navigation officer; Lieutenant Peter Wild RNVR (COPP6) was signals officer and Lieutenant Richards RANVR, was craft officer. *LCP(L) 290.* Back-up would be provided by Lieutenant Geoffrey Galwey RNVR (COPP1) as senior officer in *LCP(L) 291*, with Sub-Lieutenant W. D. A. Waters RNVR, as craft officer.

On the night in question the sea was officially deemed 'slight', with the qualification that this would be moderate to rough as applied to very small craft. The party embarked in *MGB-312* (Lieutenant-Commander Nye) and made the crossing without incident beyond the fact that the QH navigation system was playing up and the wind had freshened to Force 3, rising to Force 5. With QH unreliable the party were glad to be able to check the Ouistreham, Ver sur Mer and Port en Bessin lighthouses. The COPPists, however, were less happy: never having expected to have to land under the glare of a lighthouse beam, rotating every 65 seconds. There had been no mention of this during any of their briefings.

The operational party transferred to the landing craft, closed the shore, checked their position and the two military swimmers went over the side with four-hundred yards to swim. They had a strenuous swim and were swept three-quarters of a mile east of the area to be examined, by the strong cross-current of the rising tide. The official report says that they heard enemy activity but were undetected. Scott-Bowden questioned by the author was more explicit: 'The Germans were having a carousal in the village, we could hear them singing and shouting, when we reached the shelter of the seawall, which screened us from the lighthouse beam at Ver sur Mer.' They were careful to keep below high water-mark, so that the rising tide would wash away their tracks. When they came into the sweep of the lighthouse's rotating beam they had to flatten themselves on the beach, each time it passed, until they were sufficiently far west in the area to be examined. There was no question of the beach being mined, at that time, Scott-Bowden, knew from his briefing that with tides and moving sand, no mines would stay there for long. But behind the thick barbed wire a minefield in the dunes, extended far to the west.

When he and Ogden Smith had filled their bandoliers with heavy samples of wet sand, taken according to the required pattern and after examining a potentially dangerous area of exposed peat, which had stood out clearly on the aerial photographs. Scott-Bowden recalls:

> We went out into the surf festooned as we were with our personal gear, plus loaded bandoliers and started swimming; we were smartly flung back. The wind was still strenghtening. We quickly tried again rather harder with the same result. The prospects did not look too good. Nothing could be abandoned for fear of compromising secrecy. We sat as far out in the surf as possible to work out the wave pattern, hoping to be able to time the best moment to go: the lighthouse beam helped in this. At the third attempt, timing it right we made it through the surf and swam hard to be sure of not being swept back again.

On the swim out, Ogden Smith fell back several yards and was shouting. Scott-Bowden swam back, thinking he was in serious trouble – a leak in his swimsuit, or he'd got cramp – in fact he was yelling: 'Happy New Year.' Scott-Bowden shouted at him: 'Swim, you b***** or we'll be back on the beach . . . !' Then he wished him one back. As he told the author: 'there was no question of his just being my bodyguard: we shared the tasks between us, Bruce had been rejected for officer training, in 1939, when he was very young – and he refused to apply again.' Later, after being driver for General Sir Bernard Paget, C-in-C Home Forces, Ogden Smith joined SBS and took part in their raids on the Channel Islands.

Having swam well clear of the breakers, which could have endangered the recovery craft, they signalled with their personally-waterproofed torches: taking care in the rough sea to point them away from the shore. Signalling only when on the top of a wave. So they could be seen. It seemed a long wait before they were helped aboard, soon after 2359, feeling very wet and cold.

Eventually picked up on RG, the MGB was contacted. Tow to Spithead proved impossible, an attempt was made against the wind to reach Portsmouth. On Lieutenant-Commander Nye's suggestion, C-in-C Portsmouth approved their running before the wind to Newhaven.

During their struggle to get out through the breakers, the swimmers had lost their augers and a fighting knife, below the water's edge but it was felt that they would become buried in the sand. A perceptive Frenchman did, however, find an auger, recognised it for what it was and realising its probable significance, hid it till after the war.

*

The subsequent operational report acknowledged that impressive results had been obtained but conceded that there had been seamanship problems. In fact, there had been no time for a rehearsal with the specialised landing craft and their skilled and operationally experienced crews: a calculated risk had been taken at the highest level, in authorising this operation to obtain crucial information. Had the X-craft been available: the risk would have been greatly minimised.

Although the geologists knew the bearing capacities of the United States beaches were almost all good, doubts were raised about a few areas which showed up differently from the rest on the aerial photographs. The Americans, therefore, requested a reconnaissance of their beaches, too, to check this and obtain other general intelligence; pointing out that the British had already done theirs.

A reconnaissance of the American beach – Omaha Beach – was approved: to be carried out by COPP1 and the X-craft and crew with whom they had been specially trained and with whom they were well integrated. Willmott was in overall charge of the operation; Ken Hudspeth from Hobart Tasmania, as X-craft captain, together with Lieutenant (E) Bruce Enzer from Northern Ireland; Scott-Bowden and Ogden Smith, who also had crew duties, were to carry out the military reconnaissance. The operation which took place 17–21 January 1944 was code-named *Postage Able*. Before it Willmott and Scott-Bowden were briefed with a final update on the operational situation, by Rear Admiral Sir Philip Vian, VC, at The Royal Yacht Squadron, Cowes. Vian – the hero of the *Altmark* affair – had recently been appointed to command the British Invasion Fleet.

X-20, to conserve fuel and make good speed, was towed out into the

Channel, by the trawler HMS *Darthema*. Shortly before the tow was slipped the telephone cable in the towing cable broke and had to be repaired.

After release the X-craft went on alone, on the surface overnight, submerging at dawn to close the coast.

There were fishing boats ahead, with armed German soldiers aboard them no doubt to prevent French fishermen escaping to England. Scott-Bowden, at very close range, observed one German soldier – through the periscope – greatcoat collar turned-up, contently smoking a curved cherry-wood pipe. The X-craft downed periscope and passed slowly about twelve-feet below him, avoiding the craft's nets.

She later bottomed at periscope depth and took bearings through the periscope – it was no thicker than a man's thumb – taking periscope observations was, in fact, extremely tricky as one person changing position to take periscope watch could be enough to upset the boat's trim and cause its bow or stern to break surface . . . unless water was adjusted between the fore and aft trim tanks. Close in-shore the periscope could only be raised a foot above the water's surface. With care however, all the observations could be made, and then the craft eased off down the coast to a different position and the process of observing begun again. Scott-Bowden and Bruce Ogden Smith's COPP equipment was stored in the area above the battery compartment: a mere 2 foot 5 inches high (0.736m). Badges of rank were sewn on to the sweaters they wore beneath their swim-suits and, on Scott-Bowden's insistence to the outside of their rubber swimsuits. A Combined Operations directive had established the point that an officer, or other rank in uniform, wearing special clothing, was still in uniform. It was no different from aircrew wearing flying suits. Scott-Bowden and Ogden Smith didn't carry lethal pills; probably because neither of them planned to get caught. They knew the risks and had been briefed on the probable consequences of capture: interrogation in Paris, initially by the armed forces, then by the Gestapo.

In the daylight hours the perisope reconnaissance techniques developed off Kyntyre were used. It was known that Field Marshal Rommel had recently taken command. It was plain that he had stirred things up: hundreds of soldiers could be seen working vigorously on defensive positions. From water level one could see under the camouflage netting and get a clearer view of construction than from an oblique photograph. With accurate cross bearings it was possible to check some of the blockhouses for the photographic interpreters:

whether they had anti-tank or machine-gun embrasures. It still was winter, of course, and the early onset of twilight stopped their interested observations. Scott-Bowden remembers:

> We withdrew offshore and then that first moment after surfacing when a hatch could safely be opened brought intense relief from the build up of air pressure and the shortage of oxygen. We moved out, still on the electric motor, far enough offshore to start the diesel where it could not be heard for charging the batteries which took about 3 to 4 hours. During this time we had to listen to the BBC news; if it contained a certain phrase, that was the order to return to base immediately.

Scott-Bowden and Ogden Smith in turn, struggled into their bulky swimsuits and equipped themselves, in the X-craft's battery compartment. It wasn't easy getting kitted-up in less than the X-craft's internal diameter: 5 ft 11 inches (1.803m).

They swam in from about four hundred yards, leaving the vessel through the wet-and-dry compartment. It didn't have to be flooded up for this purpose. They landed on what was to become the left-hand sector of the United States Ist Division beach. Three-hundred yards of beach were available for inspection above the rising tide. There were no obstacles below high-water mark. They tested the firmness of the beach with their augers. When examining a large shingle bank at the back of the beach they heard voices and two sentries passed by on the track inside the wire.

The recovery went extremely smoothly. Nigel Willmott records that Scott-Bowden seemed very cheerful – allowing for the fact that they had to go out again the next night. The second night – the swimmers proceeded in-shore, some 200-yards east of the Vierville reentrant and were lying and watching in shallow water when an alert sentry shone a powerful torch directly on them. They just stayed where they were, slowly and gradually easing their way back into the waves out of range of the beam and swam eastwards to a more deserted sector. Perhaps the sentry took his sighting for seals. As he stood guard *behind* the wire, he couldn't readily come and investigate. Aboard the X-craft Willmott spotted the light at the water's edge and was worried.

Ogden Smith and Scott-Bowden probed the beach with their augers and examined the shingle bank – which was a potential obstacle for tanks – as requested in their briefing, bringing back a 5-inch diameter sample. Scott-Bowden remembers:

> Whilst we were ashore a Bomber Command raid had been laid on in the River Orne area to distract sentries' attention. Surprisingly the flashes

from successive bombs' explosions many miles away lit up the X-craft well out to sea. It was very visible to us onshore and that was disturbing. We crawled back knowing our tracks would be erased by the tide, swam in the calm sea for about half a mile before signalling for recovery.

On the following day the X-craft observed fishing boats at very close quarters and even had her periscope fired at from the shore, the shells exploding unpleasantlly close. Probably the narrow sticklike rod had been mistaken for a marker cane, on nets or drifting crab pots. Had their periscope been hit the X-craft would have been blind from then on. Whilst a third night's reconnaissance had been scheduled; Willmott decided it should not be attempted. There seemed little point, it was better to return with the wealth of information they had accumulated, than to compromise the operation striving to obtain more: they had tangible evidence the enemy were vigilant. They moved submerged until dark, then on the surface to their base at HMS *Dolphin*, Gosport, arriving the following afternoon.

Summoned to Supreme Headquarters, at Norfolk House, St James's Square, the next Sunday, Scott-Bowden thought he was in for a short debriefing by Rear Admiral Creasy. In fact, without any warning, he found himself facing five more British and five American admirals. Not only that but also United States Lieutenant General Omar Bradley – just appointed to command the US invasion armies – and Major Generals Bedell-Smith and Bull, and the British Major Generals Brownjohn and Inglis from Supreme Headquarters. He was told to give an account of the reconnaissance, then had to answer questions. After the meeting dispersed General Bradley took Scott-Bowden back to the large-scale map and pressed him for answers to many questions, mostly related to getting tanks from the beach onto the ridge above: he was concerned that the four main re-entrants providing exits, could be made impassible by demolition for a long time. The one diagonal track, traversing up the ridge on the left hand sector was a possible route. Scott-Bowden was able to say, that he'd had seen two Percheron horses, in tandem, pulling a small cart up the slope from a construction site; so the track should be suitable for light tanks; but that he could not assess its width for the wider Sherman tanks, from his low angle of view. After his interrogation he told General Bradley that COPP's other duty was assisting in assault pilotage and that he hoped they would be allowed to do that on D-Day. Bradley said he would see what he could do to fix that.

Bradley's last words were: 'Be sure to give my personal thanks to Sergeant Ogden Smith.'

SOURCES

COPP to Normandy 1943/44 – a Personal Account of Part of the story article by Major General L. Scott-Bowden CBE, DSO, MC*, in *The Royal Engineers Journal*, Vol 108 No. 1, April 1994.

STRUTTON, Bill and PEARSON, Michael *The Secret Invaders*, Hodder and Stoughton, 1958

MILLER, Russell *Nothing Less than Victory*, Michael Joseph, 1993

LADD, James *Commandos and Rangers in World War II*

LADD, James *SBS The Invisible Raiders*

MITCHELL, Pamela *The Tip of the Spear*, Richard Netherwood, 1993.

Public Record Office

DEFE2 971

CHAPTER SEVENTEEN

COPP2 First and Second Commissions

COPP2 First Commission

In 1942 Lieutenant F. M. Berncastle RN had been appointed by the Hydrographer of the Navy, Rear Admiral Edgell (later Sir John) to the staff of the Chief of Combined Operations, Lord Louis Mountbatten. Berncastle was briefed that his immediate requirement was to ascertain gradient, suitability and nature of enemy-held beaches for raiding and landing operations. This was to be done from specially-built ships and craft then being brought into service.

Admiral Edgell suggested that gradient could be measured using echo-sounding gear and a taut piano-wire measuring machine could give horizontal distance. Rocks, sandbars and other obstructions likely to cause a vessel to ground short of the shore, could also be picked up by echo-sounder.

Lord Louis emphasised his point soon after Berncastle had joined COHQ, by telling a story – perhaps apocryphal – at Richmond Terrace, to a high-ranking US Army officer – how Lord Lovat, leading the Lovat Scouts, had leapt from a landing craft as it grounded, only to disappear beneath the surface of the water. Apocryphal or not the story made its point.

Berncastle was soon joined by Sub-Lieutenant L. K. Scott RNVR – whose services were to prove invaluable, and with whom he is still in touch – who helped procure craft and equipment, and commanded a craft on operations.

They were allocated two LCP (Landing Craft Personnel): 32 ft long, camouflaged, with a low profile and a radar signature not readily detectable by the enemy. Single-engined, the craft performed quite well at 3 knots, the required speed for taking soundings, but the engine, fitted with an under-water silencer, gave less than 10 knots on passage. The engines also proved unreliable as did the echo-sounding machine. The newly-designed taut-wire machine also gave trouble it had a 9-mile rotating drum of piano wire, and compared poorly with the 140-mile static drum, then fitted in survey ships. At the start of the soundings the wire was anchored to the seabed by a cast-iron sinker, and at the end of the soundings the wire would be cut: so it sprang clear of the craft and her screw. Berncastle and Scott were sent to Dover to work-up and practice on local beaches. They were involved in one cross-channel raiding operation, when the echo-sounder did not perform well. They were joined by Sir Malcolm Campbell, holder of the land-speed record, complete with his 'Pogo-stick' for measuring beach bearing capacity. He joined them on operations though his night vision was poor. They also took Captain Day, Chief of Staff, Dover, an hydrographic specialist. They took care not to have to return from France and admit that they'd left Sir Malcolm stranded on a French beach. In time, because Sir Malcolm was recognised, they found themselves stared at in pubs.

At long last moon and tide were right: and on the night of 9/10 November 1942, they obtained a line of soundings off the Normandy coast north of Le Hardelot. One craft only was used, towed into position by an MGB (Motor Gun Boat), with a second in support. In an attempt to establish the exact position a time bomb had been left behind on the beach to make a conspicuous mark as the tide receded. Next day its crater failed to show up on a PRU photo.

On 27 February 1943, both craft were towed from the Solent by MGBs to a position 20 miles off the Iles St Marcouf in the Baie de la Seine. From there they attempted to close the shore under their own power, but met up with an enemy convoy and came under fire, though they were not hit. They turned away and carried on with their operation. They were now fitted with QH navigational, electronic positioning-apparatus and carried a specialist operator to use it. QH had been developed for use with the RAF and this was a trial to establish its reliability with a low aerial. Visual taut-wire fixes were compared with QH ones and valuable data resulted. Berncastle had no means of knowing that the operating area was that selected for the Second Front Landings.

Close inshore accurate bearings were taken on distinctive French villas, identifiable on PRU photos, building up very accurate surveys. Berncastle had trained as an hydrographic surveyor, under Captain A. G. N. Wyatt RN (later Rear Admiral and Hydrographer of the Navy), using principles traceable back to Captain James Cook. Captain Wyatt was happy to pass on the great man's requirements for accuracy to eight young Reserve officers posted to him, who provided surveys for use in the Normandy landings and elsewhere.

LCN-154 and *LCN-201*, as they were now designated, were shipped aboard two LSTs (Landing Ships Tanks) and after midnight on 10 July 1943, lowered into the water off Sicily. During that day and after the initial assault, they surveyed beaches and advised beachmasters and individual ships where best to land their forces.

For the Salerno assault they put out from Bizerta and suffered an unpleasant five-day tow in heavy weather. On arrival they found the marker vessel: an American PY-boat, larger than an LCN, being shelled from onshore and unable to hold her position. However the LCNs were able to take bearings of their position and run a taut-wire distance to the required position off the coast – despite a featureless coast. They held their position, flashing a pre-arranged signal seaward, until the convoy arrived at at 0100 on 9 September 1943, and continued to mark throughout the night. A daylight survey revealed generally good beaches. The survey teams remained on the Salerno beaches assisting, until sent to Capri, by then defects had developed with their engines and the craft were shipped back to Malta. Berncastle was ordered back to London. He flew, being delayed in Marrakesh where he discovered Gracie Fields had priority for her London flight. He arrived back in time to attend a meeting, in Norfolk House, on 21 October 1943.

Rear Admiral G. E. Creasy, Head of British Naval Branch of planning for Operation *Overlord* was in the chair. It was decided that first priority should be given to the two Mulberry Harbours – then known as Projects A and B. Two more LCPs were being converted for survey work, with a promise of four other craft soon. Berncastle suggested he could train the crews for the first two craft, to operate during the no-moon period beginning on 25 November. He naturally pressed for the return of his trained crews from the Mediterranean, though he was unlucky in this. He was to work under Commodore J. Hughes Hallet, commanding Force J, at Cowes. He joined Hughes Hallett's staff in Cowes, while the craft and crews were based at HMS *Tormentor* at Warsash.

Lieutenant N. C. Glen RN (H) was appointed to assist Berncastle and Lieutenant D.W. Hay RNVR, an experienced flotilla officer with LCPs, was appointed in charge of craft and personnel, destined to become the 712th LCP (Survey) Flotilla. Extensive training exercises had had them ready for the first – and most successful – survey operation of the Normandy Landings.

712th Landing Craft Personnel (Survey) Flotilla

The first recorded operation was on 26/27 November 1943 and it undoubtedly contributed to the success of the Arromanches Mulberry Harbour – and consequently to the whole Allied D-Day landings. Three LCP(Sy) were towed to within 20 miles of the French coast and proceeded under their own power to the Roches du Calvados – the site of the Arromanches Mulberry harbour and established their positions by sounding for the three-fathom line, following it and crossing it with one of the QH lattice lines. A bearing on St Come-de-Fresne Church confirmed it. One of the boats was anchored as a mark boat, and from it they 'starred' four lines of soundings, using taut wire to the shore, from the ends of which, in a depth of 5 feet or less they took bearings on distinctive villas. Once plotted, these results enabled them to cover the area for the 'Phoenix' units which were to form the Mulberry's northern breakwater. Seabed samples were obtained with a hand lead armed with tallow. Tidal stream rate was measured at the mark boat, by means of a weighted wooden pole let-out on a marked line.

The same craft and personnel carried out a similar operation on the night of 1/2 December 1943, for an area 12 miles westward – the site designated for the second Mulberry – though this was not known at the time. Berncastle was relying on QH to bring him in sight of the Pointe de la Percée, to establish a point from which a line of bearings could be established. After searching for 40 minutes, what was thought to be the tower was sighted, a bearing was taken, the taut-wire distance run and the mark boat anchored. A QH fix, however, put them on dry land: although they were in 7-fathoms depth. Bercastle's own diagnosis was that the bearings had not been taken on the tower, but on the spire of Vierville Church, thus placing them 2250 yards to the eastward. Perhaps, he considers, this is why the American Mulberry never got built. But the soundings obtained must have been useful for the landings on Omaha Beach. In fact it produced nothing not already available from the existing charts although it did add detail. It was a scientific adviser who produced something different (probably Dr Bernal). On the return passage the wind increased to Force 6 and both boats made Newhaven under their own power after what seemed a very long 24 hours. Rear Admiral Vian – of destroyer *Cossack* fame – who had taken over from Hughes Hallett, came down to meet them when they came alongside at Cowes. He was readily persuaded that they should carry self-heating tins of soup in future.

The next operations did not take place until the dark period of 25–29 December it involved Donald Amer and Peter Wild and has already been described in the *Festung Europa* account. Similarly two of the survey craft and their personnel, including Lieutenant Glen took part in the operation led by Nigel Willmott: Operation *KJH*.

The last of these survey operations prior to 6 June 1944 D-day, took place on the night of 30/31 January 1944; to provide further soundings of the Arromanches Mulberry site. Thick fog and visibility down to 50-yards were encountered. It may well have been the first electronic positioning survey carried out in darkness – nowadays quite a common practice. Two USN ensigns were present.

Star shells were fired from the shore – the craft must have been heard – it couldn't have been seen. Commodore G. N Oliver, the naval commander, commented that he hoped this would be carefully weighed before further operations in this vicinity were undertaken.

Some idea of the complicated processes involved in taut-wire surveys may be gained from Frank Berncastle's own account:

> We were allocated two Landing Craft Personnel (Large) (or LCPs), 32-ft long, camouflaged and with a low profile not easily detected by enemy radar, but having only one engine (fitted with a silencer) which gave a speed of rather less than 10 knots on passage and did not perform well at the speed of not more than than three knots required for sounding. The engines did, however, prove reliable. Of the hardware, the recording echo-sounding machine was a continual source of of unreliability and frustration, having an electrically energised pen rotating over special damp sensitive paper. There were also problems at certain speeds caused by aeration under the boat, masking the oscillators fitted in the bottom. The newly designed taut-wire machine containing a 9-mile drum of piano wire which rotated also proved troublesome. This compared with the standard 140-mile static drum with a rotating peel-off arm fitted in Surveying ships at the time. At the start of a line of soundings, the wire was anchored to the seabed by attaching a cast-iron sinker. It then ran through a recording dial and after every 100-ft of wire paid out the operator pressed a button which recorded on the echo-sounding machine's paper. At the end of the line of soundings, the wire was cut which then sprang clear of the boat and its propeller.

Admiral Sir Bertram Ramsay passed a letter congratulating all officers and crews, saying: 'On these operations depends to a very great extent the final success of Operation *Overlord*.' Mindful of the need for security Berncastle did not pass it on till after D-day.

On D-day 712th LCP(Sy) Flotilla acted as pathfinders for Duplex-drive tanks, and when their launching was cancelled went inshore to buoy and mark best approach channels and landing beaches liaising with beachmasters. Later larger markers were anchored, using lifeboats from sunken merchantships forming the Gooseberry Harbours. Lieutenant Glen assisted in the navigation of an Headquarters craft off Arromanches and Berncastle did likewise off Courseulles. By now they had QM, which had superseded QH. QM is now marketed as 'Decca' navigator. When the Gooseberry Blockships arrived LCP(Sy)s played a vital role marking and guiding them into position before they were scuttled.

*

Lieutenant D. W. Hay established his headquarters in the superstructure of one of the sunken ships, and it was from her that Sub-Lieutenant (E) F. V. Brown RNVR operated his staff maintaining the ship for a whole month, including repair of damage from the 19-22 June gale. During the gale the ship took a list, frozen meat aboard turned putrid and the ship became uninhabitable.

Berncastle carried out a survey of the Courseulles area, discovering that 'rocks' diagnosed by an expert was 6-foot lengths of Kelp or seaweed on the seabed, that floated, sundried on the rising tide and looked just like rocks. He couldn't help feeling that however well you know your job – you can always learn.

SOURCES
Sounding in the Dark, The Hydrographic Surveying of Beaches for use by Assault Craft and Prior to the landings on the Coast of Normandy, 1944 – a privately printed account by Lieutenant-Commander F. M. Berncastle DSC*, RN (Retd) FRICS.

*

The recommissioned COPP2, under Lieutenant R. H Fyson RN, trained at Sandy Point during the winter of 1943–44. In February COPP2 moved up to the Clyde for training with a submarine, practising loading and disembarking a canoe, leaving on a night exercise sortie and then homing back to the submarine by RG. It wasn't easy they found. The whole RG receiver was scarcely larger than a pre-war box camera. One had to peer closely at its screen – constantly speckled with pin-points of gree, infra-red starlight – and try to pick up the more distinct, green spots which were the submarine's morse dit-dit signals.

Then back to Hayling Island, playing hide-and-seek with the Chichester police and Arundel Home Guard. And they were made to march 20 miles with a 40 lb pack and sleep rough in a wood in a snow storm. Inevitably they spent hours immersed in a freezing cold sea. It was scant consolation but COPP4 under Lieutenant D. H. Mackay RN was undergoing training at the same time. On 29 March 1944 it was almost a relief to sail in the troopship *Highland Princess* to Oran. On 24 April 1944 the main party sailed from Algiers aboard *Royal Scotsman*. Two days later they had set up a base camp at Porto Vecchio. Night exercises with the canoes were organised. Their operational boss was Lieutenant-Commander Whatley at Naval HQ Ajaccio, Corsica, where the allied liberation had been completed some seven months earlier. Fyson, plus Mike Dawson and Derrick Freeman attended a briefing session in HMS *Royal Scotsman*, on 14 May 1944. They learned they would be required to provide markers for an assault on Elba by French commandos. The same night a signal was received that Fyson's wife, Ella, had given birth to a son on 9 May 1944. A riotous celebration party was held in the Transit Officers' Mess.

Six days later Operation *Sniff*, a recce of Elba was mounted using two American patrol boats: *PT 210* (Lieutenant Nugent USN) and *PT 209* (Lieutenant Macarthur USN). Lieutenant Devol USNR was in overall command. The return passage, against short head seas induced seasickness. Back at Porto Vecchio the party trained with plywood Mark III canoes. Their bow and stern sections had so-called watertight hatches for stowing emergency rations and water. The canoes' hatches leaked badly, they were extremely heavy – requiring four men to carry them, when loaded – much heavier than the canvas Mark 1s.

16 June 1944, Operation *Brassard*: the only operation that COPP2 took part in while based at Porto Vecchio. Two canoes were dropped off Elba by the PT Boats. Fyson and L/Sea Irvine marked a small beach to the west of Campo Bay. Mike Dawson, mounted on the rock Scolio Triglia, provided a beacon to the entrance to Campo Bay. Derrick Freeman marked the eastern promontory to the bay. French Commandos in Landing Craft Assault passed well away from the markers, ran into a beach with rocks instead of the intended shingle one and had to be extricated. Shells began to fall all round the markers. They later found a German flak lighter was engaging the invasion fleet and the COPPists were 'copping the overs'. Fyson's canoe upped its tangled anchor line, moved out of the line of fire and paddled into open water to rendezvous with Derrick Freeman on Scolio Triglia rock. Here they had a grandstand view of the assault. LCRs, landing craft fitted with banks of rocket-firing tubes, laid down a creeping barrage – just ahead of the troops landed from the LCAs.

Whilst the fireworks were impressive they later found they had not been very effective against well-prepared German positions. The troops had to fight hard to hold their bridgehead. After breakfast and a sleep on their rock the COPP2 party hitched a lift home in an LCT.

From Porto Vecchio Fyson travelled to Basti. Here Senior Officer Inshore squadron, Captain Black RN, advised they could set up camp in Chateau Fornali, St Florent, now vacated by French Commandos. They'd be sharing with Captain Ronnie Renton, of ISLD, but there was room. In fact, it proved ideal: about the size of a house, it had garages for storage and the front of the house was shaded by a vine-covered pergola. In addition there was a boathouse, a jetty and a bathing raft. The chateau belonged to an Englishman and his Czech wife. She agreed to cook for the party, assisted where necessary by AB Gillingham. By now Fyson had grown a beard and was; accordingly known as Fuzz. Other team members acquired nicknames.

Fuzz made many visits to staff in Bastia and Naples: he met an American Colonel Burhams, who wanted to do a reconnaissance of the seaward side of Ile de Port Cros off Toulon, preparatory to an assault by the US 7th Army on the coast of Southern France. On 27 July 1944, Fuzz and Mike Dawson embarked with Burhams in HMS/M *Untiring*. Exercises were tried, launching Burhams from the submarine, whilst willing he was not proficient in canoe-handling and it was a relief that he contented himself with periscope observations. On 30 July *Untiring* returned to port without having once launched the canoe.

August passed agreeably with little for the personnel to do but enjoy themselves and experiment with different sailing rigs on the Mark III canoes. Alan Wallwork had considerable success with his craft rigged as a yawl: perfect for pleasure sailing, but too unwieldly for operations. There were frequent visits to Bastia, Naples, Ajaccio and Corte. They also explored the north-west coast as far as Calvi. From one trip to Naples Fyson brought back Donald Amer and Ian Mackenzie of COPP6. They were based at Ischia in the Bay of Naples.

12 September 1944 COPP2 left the Chateau Fornali with all gear packed. Light stores and some personnel were loaded aboard the trawler *Unst*; the remainder with heavy stores were embarked in an Italian LCT. The next day, once *Unst* and the LCT had sailed, bound for Piombino, on the Italian mainland, Fuzz Fyson set off for Rome leading a convoy of two trucks, christened *Jabberwok* and *Bandersnatch*. The next day, despite misrouting and motorcycle break-downs they were in Rome. Pressing on from there, by Friday 15 September 1944 they were in Naples, billeted at Nisida Barracks. With local leave they took the

opportunity to visit Pompei, with ratings from *Unst*. Fuzz went to see Sulfatara, the active volcano near to Pozzuoli: small pools of boiling water and cracks in the lava crust were an alarming sight. It was said if Sulfatara erupted Vesuvius would do so a few days later.

By 29 September 1944 orders had come for COPP2 to move across Italy to Bari in four three-ton lorries. Next day they had arrived at the Villa Nitti in San Giorgio. The villa stood at the end of a short lane, leading down to a small bay with a low, rocky shoreline. Jose a local olive-grower became the COPP2 volunteer butler, asking for a fortnight's leave to harvest his crop. At the same time racketeers commandeered an RAF petrol bowser, filled it with olive oil and sold it at a profit in Naples. They were caught on their second trip.

Mid-October 1944 Mike Dawson and Jim Younger left COPP2 to join up with SBS and RM Commandos for an assault on the Gulf of Corinth. They were later in Corinth and in Athens where they drove through the streets with the Commandos, being pelted with flowers by the local population. They returned to base, to a less rapturous reception, on Sunday 22 October. In their absence Fyson, Derrick Freeman, L/Sea Irvine and AB Gillingham had joined a joint-services party, commanded by a brigadier, that was required to reconnoitre the port of Dubrovnik, to assess its suitability as a supply base for Tito's Yugoslav partisans. The Germans had left the area only two days before. The party was ferried across the Adriatic by ML and quartered in an hotel; they drank a local wine called Tiger Milk with enjoyment. Early next morning, after a tour round the picturesque fortified town, they learned that the local commissar had vetoed any reconnaissance. It took a personal signal from the Brigadier to Tito before they were released from house arrest. Whilst Derrick looked at port facilities, Fuzz went off to a local quarry in search of a reported store of sea mines. L/Sea Irvine broke the padlock on a door in the quarry face and Fuzz opened the door – and was knocked unconscious by the resulting deafening explosion of a concealed booby trap. Irvine, uninjured, was blown high into the air. Their guide took the full force of the explosion; he died later of his wounds. Fuzz had been hit by part of the door, he was taken to a nunnery converted into a field hospital and treated for a four-inch scalp wound. The party were shipped back to Bari in an LCT. Fuzz was taken to hospital there and later to VIII Army orthopaedic hospital at Barletta. X-ray examination revealed a depressed fracture of the skull. It would be ten weeks before Fuzz was back on duties.

On 5 November 1944 Lieutenant John H. Hashim joined COPP2 as a temporary relief for Fuzz. Fuzz meanwhile had returned from hospital and spent a fortnight making a walnut dining table: good therapy he considered it.

24 November 1944 Alan Wallwork and AB Cox left in LCI for an unrecorded operation. Five days later they were reported under guard in Yugoslavia, having done quite a good job and had a good time. In early December various members of COPP2 did a parachute course at RAF Gioia. 18 December Fuzz and Mike Dawson went over to Naples to see the C-in-C's Staff. All they learned was that COPP10 was returning to Britain. With no operations scheduled a Christmas party was thrown at the Villa Nitti on Saturday 23 December. This was followed by another party to the small hours at the flat, in Torre-a-Mare of Joan Thompson of SOE, where there were several other FANY present. On Christmas day after Fuzz, Hashim and three ratings had been to church, the officers gave a party for the ratings and other ranks. It was a great success: a large cockerel had been specially fattened by Jose, and even fed port, which may have improved his flavour. The meal was better than the one at the Allied Officers' Club in Bari, that night. New Year they hardly celebrated at all: Jim Younger was still in hospital with jaundice, Derrick Freeman was down with suspected malaria, and it was bitterly cold. It didn't prevent exercises with Mark 1** canoe, in choppy seas. They practised surf landings, not daring to attempt them in their operational Mark III plywood canoes, so rough and shingly were the beaches. On 9 January 1945 Fyson visited one of the Trulle houses around Martina Franca: houses, barns and cowsheds, circular in plan, with thick stone walls and conical stone roofs. He felt them a bit like stone igloos.

COPP2 was instructed to do the necessary reconnaissance work for a crossing of Lake Commachio, just north of Ravenna. Fuzz took a party to witness trials of amphibious tanks – called Fantails – on Lake Trasimene near Perugia; he, Mike Dawson, Alan Wallwork and L/Sea Irvine. They took two canoes, on a three-tonner to the beautiful old fortified town of Perugia. The Fantails resembled high-sided landing craft with a propeller sticking out at the back. Here, with a hard lake bottom, they performed well; in the thick mud of Lake Commachio their tracks dug channels till they bellied immobilised.

From Perugia they drove to Ravenna to reconnoitre a forward base. It was the direct route, but all the bridges were blown; they should have gone via Florence. At length, having found a suitable base, they drove back to Bari, along the coast road through Rimini and Ancona. Ancona

was the base of the Inshore squadron MTBs and MLs, under Captain
Black RN.

23 February 1945, arriving back at the Villa Nitti, Fyson arranged a
priority flight to England to pick up new Mark VI's canoes; these were
Mark III hulls fitted with a Robin Hood outboard engine; it could be
lowered through a trunk and out through the boat bottom, between the
paddlers' legs. It was proposed to use the Mark IV's engine for long
distance approaches, then retract it and paddle silently for the last half-
mile or-so. It seemed a good idea, but in practice the engines did not
always run well. Even when retracted, engines and propellers imposed
tremendous drag.

Next day, Fuzz flew to England from Naples – a bitterly cold journey
in a converted Wellington bomber – he spent a week with Nick
Hastings' help collecting the canoes and arranging for the construction
of a special light buoy, with up to 24-hour delay mechanism, that would
be necessary for the Lake Comacchio marking. He even managed to
spend a little time with his wife and ten-month old son Jonathan, whom
he was seeing for the first time.

On Sunday 4 March 1945 he flew back as the sole passenger in a cargo
plane, with four crated canoes. Without oxygen he fell asleep when the
plane reached 14,000 feet. After refuelling at Marseilles, he and the
crates were transferred to a Dakota and flown to Ravenna on a fighter
airstrip near to the front line – had they overshot they'd have probably
been in enemy territory!

Then followed a period of intense activity, when COPP2 were
operating by night and left their canoes, close to the water, in the safe
care of partisans. Between 8 and 18 March six sorties were carried out,
mostly successfully. On one, American personnel – probably OSS, were
involved – sentries were observed more than once, but adroitly avoided.

During the next two months Alan Wallwork made frequent visits to
Zara. Once Fuzz obtained a lobster and it was cooked in a steel
ammunition box on top of an improvised brazier (60-gallon oil drum).
It proved delicious and there was plenty for all.

COPP6's S/COPP, Lieutenant David Kay, and his E/COPP Captain
Johnstone RE appeared on the scene and set up a branch in Ancona.
COPP2 never carried out any joint operations with them.

Early in April Derrick Freeman took part in a raid with 'Popski's
Private Army' – 'Popski', the Polish Colonel Vladimir Peniakoff – had
gathered round him a a small force of highly trained commando style
troops: they became famous for their raids behind enemy lines. Derrick
assisted in coastal navigation on the coast near the mouth of the River

Po. COPP2 met another picturesque character Anders Lassen, 'The Mad Dane', later to win a posthumous VC in Operation *Roast*.

Operation *Roast* was a 2 Commando Brigade assault from Lake Comacchio on the Spit, a narrow stretch of low-lying land, 600-yards wide between the Adriatic shore and the shallow waters of Lake Comacchio. German defenders were well dug-in at the southern end of the spit and could not be dislodged by frontal assaults.

The assault took place on the night of 1/2 April 1945, a clear flat-calm night when sound travelled. Two COPP2 two-man teams, each with an army signalman and portable wireless, in flat-bottomed punts provided markers 200-yards offshore. Fuzz and Mike Dawson, in one boat and Alan Wallwork and Jim Younger, in the other remained in position watching the Allied artillery barrage till the Assault craft passed them.

The special time-delay marker buoys appeared from England in time for their use to be considered for a waterborne attack on the north-west, German-held corner of Lake Comacchio. On the ominous date of Friday 13 April 1945 COPP2 undertook a recce operation to find a suitable landing point for commandos. They were some twenty-miles distant from their launching point. Fuzz took Mike Dawson in a Mark VI canoe. Sub-Lieutenant Jim Younger and L/Sea Irvine also started off in a Mark 1 canoe, but could not keep up with the headwind they encountered.

Launched in daylight Fyson's canoe made it to islands held by partisans, rested till dark and set off again under power for their next 12-mile leg to the distant shore. Half-a mile from shore they found a mass of small islets only a foot out of the water and covered by coarse grass. Plainly they had to find a way through them for the assault craft. Eventually they made it to the shore and found themselves only a mile to the south of their intended beach. Fuzz made a foray on shore and on being confronted by a notice '*Achtung Minen*' carefully retraced his steps to the canoe. Shortly afterwards Mike and he found themselves illuminated by a cluster of flares dropped by the RAF. Scanning the shore through binoculars, Fuzz spotted two heads turned in their direction. 'Mike, we're being watched!' he exclaimed. Almost immediately came a burst of machine-gun fire. They turned end-on and paddled for the islands. Guessing the Germans would be firing on fixed lines – zeroed on open channels – they made for the nearest inlet and safety. With coastal defences alerted, any further reconnaissance was out of the question.

When they tried to start the outboard it proved impossible. They paddled for the partisan-held islands; it took six hours. The partisans fed them a cooked breakfast. After that, astonishingly, the outboard started at the first pull and they motored back in fine style.

*

It was the last reconnaissance by COPP2. The Eighth Army's advance bypassed the Lake. COPP2 did take part in its own liberation parade in Comacchio – a miniature Venice. On 12 May 1945, COPP2 sailed for England on the troopship *Georgic*. On 23 May they were met at Havant by Nick Hastings and WRNS driver Jenny Devitt. Official demobilisation and one-week's leave followed.

SOURCES

NIGEL CLOGSTOUN-WILLMOTT: aide memoire prepared for Earl Mountbatten of
    Burma, dated 18 March 1977
SEYMOUR, William *British Special Forces*, Sidgwick and Jackson, 1985
Log of COPP2, Compiled by R. H. Fyson from 1944 and 1945 diaries
COURTNEY, G. B. *The SBS in World War Two*, Robert Hale, 1983.

CHAPTER EIGHTEEN

How did one get into COPP?

How did one reach COPP? – For some it was simplicity itself. Arthur Ruberry after mustering as an AB was posted to Combined Operations, trained as a coxswain on landing craft and on qualifying was promoted leading hand. Thereafter he was drafted to COPP and found himself at the Hayling Island Training Depot. Of course, had he known what he was in for, Arthur would have volunteered: he was that sort of person.

Whilst some case histories have already been sketched, the process gradually increased in sophistication.

Alec Colson, was a sapper lieutenant instructing at 140 OCTU Royal Engineers' (Field), Newark-upon-Trent. In the Military Duties Wing he was required to take each class of cadets through its first six weeks: drill, mathematics, fieldcraft, tactics. The last of the seven weeks he'd spend with the course at the Battle Camp, at Penmaenmawr. Each class then went on with its Sapper training programme: demolitions, mine-warfare, bridging etc. Once the Battle Camp was over Alec went back to start a new class on its seven weeks. Alec had been commissioned on 15 February 1942. He began instructing at Newark in September 1942. When the Dieppe raid occurred, on 19 August 1942, it was subsequently written-up in Army training Memoranda. Alec, as an instructor, saw these secret documents. He decided that he had had enough of a safe instructing job and that he should volunteer for service with the Commandos. When his posting to OCTU had come through he'd asked if it was likely to be a short posting. No, it wouldn't, his commanding officer told him, adding reasonably: 'If you wanted to stay with the unit you shouldn't have done so well in the "blood and guts" course!' It had been a tough course, with little spared but drenching with ox blood, during bayonet practice, that had featured months before*.

* Saturday May 23, 1942, C-in-C orders an end to 'bloodlust inculcation' in British battle training. It had involved bayonetting Ox blood-filled bladders.

Alec decided his best course of action would be to contact his previous officer commanding, Major Edward T. Collins, at 75 Chemical Warfare Company. Collins, he found had moved to Combined Operations Headquarters as a lieutenant-colonel. It made sense, Collins had believed in training all the men under his command to commando standard. He had marched his Company 75-miles, in 46-hours . . . and on another occasion, at the end of an ordinary working day, 36-miles to the ranges at Colchester. Edward Collins led from the front and was top-scorer with the Lee Enfield rifle. His reply to Alec's letter was an invitation to dine at the Junior Carlton Club. They ate in silence for some time, no mention being made of Alec's application. Alec began to get impatient. Collins said quietly:

'I've put your name down for something better than a commando, but I can't tell you more than that.'

'Can you tell me what sort of work it is, sir?'

'I'm afraid not you'll have to wait until they send for you.'

*

Alec hadn't had to wait long: the next stage was a trip up to London, to Combined Operations Headquarters, at Richmond Terrace, W1, for an interview with a Lieutenant-Commander Moorhouse. The entrance to the building bustled with activity. The women's services were well in evidence; it must be true, what people said, that the best looking girls were sent to work with Mountbatten. Alec waited with three other sapper officers; two were captains, the other a subaltern like himself. It was May 1943 – around the time the Allies captured Tunis and Bizerta. Moorhouse appeared and ushered them out onto a flag-paved terrace. He wore no cap and his wavy grey hair was brushed straight back. With his arms folded on his chest, it could be seen that his sleeves bore the intertwined lace of the Royal Naval Reserve. He looked intently into each of their faces in turn. Apparently satisfied he began to speak.

'You've volunteered for hazardous service – service that will take you an anchor's throw from the enemy's nose. You may find the weather takes the enemy's side. Submarine trips will become as commonplace as bus-rides. Casualties are high and the enemy shows no mercy to those he captures . . . hope none of you are married. But if you are, or if you've got any doubts . . . just take one pace back and the whole thing will be forgotten. No one will think the worse of you.'

Alec looked down the leafy drive opening onto Whitehall, feeling like a murderer gazing out of his barred window, the morning of his execution. The others stood silently: not one moved, or thought of asking questions. 'Gaffer' Moorhouse was Personnel Officer for COPP, a former actor he probably relished the spine-chilling dialogue he had delivered. He was convincing, effective, frightening.

'Well, that's about as much as I'm permitted to tell you. You can collect railway warrants for the next stage of your selection procedure. Report to Hayling Island.'

Moorhouse's reference to submarines could mean he was thinking of the Mediterranean theatre, what the work would be – was anybody's guess.

*

The party, perhaps a shade chastened, travelled to Hayling Island, not far from Chichester harbour. From a small railway station they were driven by a WRNS driver – in a 15-cwt truck, on a four-mile bumpy journey, over island roads, past barbed wire – to what had been the pre-war Hayling Island Sailing Club. It was a modern two-storey building with flat roof and large plate glass windows.

Inside, at first-floor level, in the wardroom, on a baize-covered table were laid out bundles of papers giving more information, in précis form of the duties they had volunteered for: they were requested to read through it. The candidates were then interviewed separately by Lieutenant-Commander Nigel Clogstoun-Willmott DSO, DSC. Many people have written of Nigel's arresting manner, piercing light-blue eyes and the intensity with which he spoke.

He explained beach reconnaissance in simple terms: the use of submarines, canvas canoes and swimming suits; and the all-important fact that one landed alone, by night. Alec swallowed, he'd always hated the dark and found difficulty swimming one-hundred yards.

He confided to Willmott that he wanted to take the job but was a poor swimmer.

'You needn't worry about that,' Willmott assured him. 'When you've got a heavy swim-suit on, the air-belt keeps you afloat and there's little difference between a swimming champion and a lame duck.'

Back in the wardroom, the party had been reduced by half: now just Captain Logan Scott-Bowden and Alec Colson remained. Scott-Bowden had a brushed up moustache and a relaxed, confident manner. Ordered to see Major Roger Courtney, the officer-commanding Commando Special Boat Section, for a final interview in London, Alec travelled back to Whitehall. Courtney's office proved empty. It wasn't long, however, before he appeared. Roger Courtney MC, King's Royal Rifle Corps and Special Boat Section, was short and thickset. He had a jagged scar from his forehead to his mouth, strongly suggesting a German sentry's bayonet. He told Alec he would be under his nominal command, though he would see little of him from now on. He would, however, wear Commando SBS, shoulder titles and big circular Combined Operations patches on upper arms of his battledress and Courtney did not want the SBS name disgraced.

'Never let them capture you, fight to the end.'

Those were his last words. He never mentioned the precise nature of COPP duties. By now Alec was aware that their designated unit was partly naval, partly military and that swimming and folbots would be involved. He was also told that on posting down to the Hayling Island Depot he could put up his third pip. That evening Scott-Bowden and he ate at Lyons Corner House. It seemed appropriate: Alec felt he'd had quite enough excitement for one day. One thing was certain: he could forget about instructing for the duration. Weeks later he learned that Courtney's scar dated from a pre-war party, when he'd fallen down some basement steps.

Alec was unaware, at that time, but Scott-Bowden was no ordinary recruit to COPP. He was already Commando trained – he had first joined Special Forces in 1940, when he saw action, in Norway, in 2nd Independent Company – it had been agreed that he should be joining COPP Depot as Senior Military Officer, with the rank of major, on the strength of Willmott's COPP1.

Sadly Lieutenant-Colonel Collins – Alec Colson's sponsor into COPP – was to be killed after D-Day.

SOURCES

Hazardous Beginnings unpublished article by Alec Colson
Conversations with Arthur Ruberry, John Bowden DSM and Nick Goodyear and other former COPPists.

CHAPTER NINETEEN

COPP Training and Conditioning

Nigel Willmott has been quoted as saying that it took three months to train an S/COPP who was already a Navigator, and five months to train one who wasn't.

What were COPPists training needs? In principle all COPP members had to be able to fight their way out of any situation they might find themselves in – but only as a last resort, if say their boats were in danger – avoiding trouble and avoiding compromising the mission was the top priority; so they needed scouting and stalking skills; an agent's ability to brazen out a cover story; extreme physical endurance and, in an emergency, evasion and survival skills.

Whilst naval and military components of reconnaissance intelligence were quite different, in the event of casualties, S/COPP's and E/COPP's duties had to be interchangeable. Thus all operational officers practised all duties. Nigel Willmott was in any case adamant that all personnel should have done a Commando course. So that naval personnel went over assault courses, practised unarmed combat and sharpshooting. Above all, all COPP operational officers needed to know all Combined Operations Staff needs – from strategic planning, downwards to quite small matters of detail: landing craft, types and navigation; beachmasters and naval commandos; and all military, naval and even RAF aspects of amphibious landings.

The E/COPP – army officer – in any COPP inevitably did less seamanship and navigation than his naval counterparts; but he was expected to do a mine-clearance course and impart that expertise to the rest of the COPP. Apart from technical expertise a COPP, in 'the field' had to be self-supporting, pay its personnel, insist that proper facilities were accorded them, and avoid being browbeaten by staff officers claiming higher priorities.

*

The COPP8 Log Book account is probably the most detailed available and may be regarded as fairly typical record of training: for a total period of almost four months. COPP naval and army officers did most of their training together; COPP naval ratings had different training needs and so trained separately until allocated to a particular COPP. They were quartered in nissen huts at Sandy Point and a brief account of their training and conditions will be given after the COPP8 Log Book material. The ratings and other ranks for each COPP were allocated once officer training was complete.

*

The log book account begins with most of COPP8's and COPP10's officers proceeding from COHQ to COPP Depot, Hayling Island. From Havant station on the mainland they would be driven to Sandy Point by a WRNS driver. Here they attempted to get settled in and draw stores. All was frankly uncongenial: training was reputed to be very tough and, they learned, living conditions were terrible. Training might last twenty-hours out of the twenty-four. All this was on Tuesday 1 June 1943, the day Allied Naval forces commenced a round-the-clock bombardment of Pantellaria.

In the morning they planned to proceed to Marine Barracks, Eastney, to draw more stores. A surprise awaited them, however, they would be permitted to do nothing – until they had done their compulsory PT and 'hardening' at 0700. No one had been shooting a line last night, they discovered: after PT they were, indeed, required to swim nude in the cold sea of Chichester Harbour – before breakfast – this 'hardening' was all part of a plan to make them very tough indeed. They were lucky it wasn't winter, they were told: the routine would be just the same . . . ! In the afternoon they unpacked, thoughtfully, and indulged in a little friendly unarmed combat with Corporal Ogden Smith, East Surrey Regt, Honourable Artillery Company and Commando SBS.

Bruce Ogden Smith was held in some awe – it was popularly believed he'd already had hand-to-hand experience of commando fighting: and had despatched a German SS man with his Sykes-Fairbairn fighting knife. Anyway he knew his stuff. Inevitably there was more skinny-dipping at the end of the day.

Next morning PT and before-breakfast swimming, were taken by the CO, Lieutenant-Commander Nigel Willmott DSO, DSC. The routine was noticeably harder. Willmott led them in their swim – without his decorations. Questioned by the author in 1989 he said: 'I always insisted they swim quite naked – and I did it myself – got a seven-inch cut on the thigh in the process . . . from a gash bully-beef tin! I still don't like swimming; even now when I live in Cyprus.' At the time trainees would have sworn he revelled in it – they did not: but got used to it. Willmott always led by example – he knew COPPists' future performance and survival could depend on how physically tough they were as well as on how finely trained.

That Thursday was to prove a hectic day: after breakfast a short talk by Lieutenant Nick Hastings DSC, RNVR, on canoes followed by two hours practical experience handling them. At 1200 they embussed for Portsmouth (HMS *Dolphin*), for DSEA (Davis Submarine Escape Apparatus) instruction. They ate lunch during a good lecture on how to use the apparatus. After that they tried it out in the training tank, known as 'the pot': not as deep as the present 100-foot one, but quite frightening. All the party passed with flying colours, except for 'Gussie' Talbot of COPP10, who had a blocked ear. Their WRNS driver turned up early with a basket of strawberries which she passed round. They persuaded her to drive them to the strawberry shop, where they bought and ate the entire stock. In the evening Nigel Willmott delivered pep-talks to pairs of Trainee COPPists. He began disarmingly by stating:

'A lot of people would rather die than think. A lot of them do!' A quotation attributed to George Bernard Shaw.

After that they were quite glad of a few drinks at the Nab Club.

Next day Alec Colson left the party for a War Office Selection Course. This was to determine whether he became a regular officer or not. It was at that time a matter of sublime indifference to him, but asked to deliver a short lecture, he gave the lunchtime HMS *Dolphin* DSEA one, and heard months later that he had passed. He followed the rest of the course up to HMS *Armadillo*, The Royal Naval Commando Training School, at Ardentinney, on the Forth of Clyde, just at the entrance to Loch Long. They were in Scotland to learn all aspects of beach organization. They spent eight days here, learning the essentials on Beach Commandos, Beach Signals Organization and the RAF Regiment detail requirements, interspersed with practice in 'Shanghai shooting' – pistol and Tommy-gun instinctive, snap-shooting without time to take proper aim – and a quick run over an assault course: that almost killed one of the lecturers. They visited all the ships in the Rothesay anchorage, enjoyed their hospitality, and bivouacked on a midge-infested hillside after an operation they had been intended to see had been cancelled. Later, after more Shanghai shooting, they did see a night operation on the Isle of Bute. This was on the day the Allies landed in Sicily.

Next day found them Cutter sailing and by Sunday 13 June 1943 the party had organised their own sleeping quarters in a barn.

Early next morning, at 0200 to be precise, the embryo COPPists felt a wish, to let-off steam and to show what they'd learned. So they raided the nearby 'stone frigate' HMS *James Cook*, the Landing Craft Navigation School.

It was totally unofficial, of course: that way it would be more realistic and testing. The guards naturally would be armed; no one seemed certain whether they'd have live ammunition. One thing was certain: they wouldn't have blanks. . . . *James Cook* was situated at Tighna-bruich, at the north-west end of the Isle of Bute. The COPPists had the advantage of knowing its geography: Freddie Ponsonby, the CO, had been its chief instructor and Mike Peacock one of his instructors. Whilst it may sound rather silly and dangerous: the raid in conception and execution was typical of many unofficial exercises of the period.

Ponsonby led the attack. Mike Peacock rang the fire bell to create a diversion. Keen not to let the side down, Alec Colson tackled a petty officer they found inside the main building. The Log Book says he was the Quarter Master and that he 'squealed' long and loud. The drill for a sentry armed with a rifle was one they'd all frequently practised. This one was unarmed. In the event, however, it didn't go as planned. The 'defender' plainly had also been taught close combat and knew how to parry the attack. He was also bigger than Alec. So he wasn't slung over Alec's shoulders as planned: instead Alec went over his. Even so with concerted efforts the 'opposition' was overcome. 'Negotiated' as the SAS say nowadays. The party left notes showing where they had notionally placed explosives, then departed having let off smoke floats inside the building.

Honour satisfied, COPP8 embarked in a cutter and rowed off into the night. It had some of the atmosphere of a college spree, but someone could have got killed. In commando training, with live ammunition, some trainees were indeed killed. In fact, all COPP8 survived to eat a good breakfast and lunched at *James Cook*, with no one unduly annoyed at their nocturnal disturbance.

They made good time sailing back to *Armadillo* and were given a picture of life 'at the sharp end', by two beachmasters who'd been at Dieppe. Alec Colson left on compassionate leave and, in his absence Mike Peacock's 21st birthday was celebrated at Rogano's at Glasgow. Now based at the Marine Hotel Troon, the party were instructed on '*The*

Task of the Beach Group and its Composition'. Other lectures – chiefly aimed at army officers followed – RASC in Combined Operations; the same for RE, RAC and even naval aspects. They had an opportunity to see Alligators and amphibious DUKWs and were given a short (and wet) sea trip in a DUKW. Four days were devoted to landing tables and dumps.

Then three days viewing types of landing craft and gaining beaching and handling experience proved far more popular. By now quite a few of COPP8 had unaccountably become painfully sunburnt, basking on assault beaches. The last day of June 1943 finished with COPP8 quartered in Dundonald RE Block, with the knowledge that their next two days were to be spent with the RAF.

The first day at Dundonald aerodrome was a lecture chiefly devoted to photographic reconnaissance. Then a lot of pointless chat on gremlins; no doubt intended to put them off flying on the morrow.

Next day they flew: Freddie Ponsonby and Mike Peacock in a Bristol Blenheim and Alec and 'Gussie' Talbot in an Avro Anson. After that they went to Newton Bay, just south of Strachur and watched an unopposed landing from behind smoke cover. They had just time to catch the train for Glasgow and a last slap-up meal at Rogano's before boarding a sleeper for London.

3 July 1943 found them back in London. Week-end leave was awarded. The E/COPPs to report to Ripon afterwards. On arrival there they found they were unexpected. The Brigade Major ordered them to do the course as offered or leave. Finding it was infantry mines course, delivered by infantry officers, Alec phoned COHQ. The E/COPPs spent the next day visiting the American SME (School of Military Engineering) and collecting data with the help of Major Livingstone-Learmonth. They went drinking with him that night at the Spa. The E/COPPs were glad to leave Ripon next day. Then back to Hayling Island, where it is sufficient to pick out the high-spots of their training.

Soon COPP8 had drawn all their suits and had practice assembling and dismantling canoes. Freddie 'Poonby' delivered a lecture to E/COPPs and ratings on Beach Pilotage. 16 July was memorable for canoe speed-trials. None of COPP8's turned turtle. Ten-days leave followed, then straight into the routine of early morning PT and skinny-dipping. All their Siebe Gorman swimsuits were found to require alteration to make them fit. Some strenuous swimming in good weather and practice taking soundings floating in a Gieves suit. After a demonstration of fieldcraft, COPP8 took on COPP10 in a simulated night exercise, wearing dark glasses. Geoff Richards (M/COPP) distinguished himself.

Day stalking was less practical. So E/COPP and M/COPP gave S/COPP and A/COPP some motorcycle instruction. At the week-end Neville McHarg DSO, RNR and Captain Rice RE, appeared from abroad.

Monday 2 August marked the start of training in earnest. Willmott lectured on stores. There was swimming practice in the Siebe Gorman suits. In the evening stripping and assembling pistols. Next day Willmott on recce sketching, and the course in the wardroom attempting to draw the silhouette across the water. Some pistol and Sten shooting, then back to the wardroom to finish the drawings. Then in the evening a canoe exercise. Willmott lectured next day, on homing methods with a great many tips. Some grenade throwing followed and a depressing night exercise in which many things went wrong. Next day was spent in plotting soundings previously taken.

6 August 1943 Alec gave a lecture on mines, detonators, booby traps etc. Followed by an exercise in mine detection, using a 'coin minefield'; although 5/6d (27.5p) had been laid the recovery rate was disappointing. Alec later almost cut a finger off trying to open a door by pushing in a glass panel. As a result he missed that evening's exercise of RG transmission and reception, and eventually homing. More well-filled days and a memorable lecture by Surgeon-Commander Murray Levick on Polar exploration. Next day was spent making torches watertight prior to a night exercise, which wind and weather washed out. Next day Alec had recovered enough to fire 200 rounds through eight of the Sten guns. The week ended with the allocation of ratings and other ranks to COPP8. Sunday's Divisions, Church parade, bathing and sunbathing were followed by an air raid, with a proportion of delayed-action bombs dropped.

So on Monday 16 August: the billet had to be evacuated so the bomb disposal squad could attend to a UXB. The forenoon was spent packing operational canoes. After lunch all sailed for an 18-hour exercise on Copnor Point. Whilst lying up on Pilsey an Me 109 was shot down from 36,000 feet, with a direct hit from an AA shell. A truly remarkable feat.

A full moon spoiled the exercise making it too easy for the defender sentries. The party took up their beds and walked . . . back to the billet. Bomb disposal subsequently reported the bomb as probably a 1,000 pounder. Then that it was an unexploded UP (unrotated projectile) anti-aircraft rocket. All COPP8 and 10 personnel took part in RG exercises – using infra-red signals, only visible as green traces, through a special receiver lens. Naval personnel received instruction in QH, otherwise known as Gee: an early form of what is now the Decca Navigation System.

Sunday 22 August was declared an ordinary working day and all gear was packed and mackerel fished for, without success.

Monday included a lecture from Willmott on canoe launching and recovery from submarines. It all sounded terrifying, in the evening surf trials at Eastoke Point. Alec and Geoff overturned their canoe and the Wrens took off their skirts to bear a hand. Inevitably they were swamped too. Days followed preparing for the submarine course up at Greenock.

This was to take a week, and begun with practice using the periscope and launching and recovery from a stationary submarine, with night drills and RG practice. Their allotted submarine was HMS/M *Stonehenge* (Lieutenant D. S. Verschoyle-Campbell DSC,* RN). There followed a couple of nights of exercises, one using 'handie-talkies'; another when the submarine missed the RG signals; and next night a booze-up in the Depot Ship HMS *Wolfe*. on 3 September 1943, the day the Allies established a beach-head in Italy. Next day back to London by stages.

One of the first night exercises on return to Hayling Island was one involving creeks, with canoes bottoming in the mud and failing to reach the beaches.

The last three weeks were occupied with a visit to COXE (Combined Operations Experimental Establishment at Torridge House, Westward Ho, Plymouth); and to Oxford to ISTD (Inter Services Topographical Department). More exercises, unarmed combat, firing practice and an interesting lecture on the Japanese and their ways by an intelligence expert. By then 19 September various farewell parties began – WRNS, base officers and the Captain, Nab Club – were all included. With a return to the Depot on Sunday 26 September to do final personal packing. By now it was certain they would be going to India.

*

Peter Wild has contributed the following piece on Night Scouting training, at Hayling Island:

This was the most instructive and subsequently, the most useful training we ever had there. A "sentry" was placed on the shingle, with a storm lantern beside him, after dark. We would take turns, crawling up to him – nine times out of ten, the crawler would give himself up, long before "the sentry" had seen him. The moral was to realise that if a sentry glanced or even stared in your direction, and you'd be convinced he'd seen you – almost every time – you'd be wrong: he'd not seen you at all. Had you fired at him – and the temptation was very strong – you would compromised the area being reconnoitred. And with that particular beach "blown" – any planned operation would have to be aborted.

*

Whilst the foregoing account concentrates on officer training the needs of ratings and military other ranks were carefully assessed. Training courses had to depend on previous experience.

Soldiers fresh from the Commando Depot should do three weeks SBS training. Seamen were required to do Naval Beach Commando Training four weeks at HMS *Armadillo*. Maintenance mates should be trained in canoe repairs, with possibly a week at the builders. Maintenance artificers should be trained on radio navigational aids, including repairs: three days at Northney. They should also be able to maintain and repair canoe hulls and skins: 1–2 weeks at the builders. They should also spend a week at Seibe Gorman's on swim-suit repairs.

All ranks of both services, of course, did boat training, and commando training: basically physical training, fieldcraft, weapons' training and unarmed combat.

SOURCES

STRUTTON, Bill and PEARSON, Michael *The Secret Invaders*, Hodder and Stoughton, 1958.

COPP8 Log Book: kept in various hands, at the time (by Freddie Ponsonby, Geoff Richards, Alec Colson, Mike Peacock and Peter Crafer) subsequently transcribed as a typescript by Alec Colson.

Conversations with COPPists.

CHAPTER TWENTY

The WRNS at Sandy Point

Throughout the span of COPP Depot's tenure of occupancy of the Hayling Island Sailing Club clubhouse, COPP was allotted three trucks and these were driven by four WRNS drivers. The Wrens' team was in the charge of Leading Wren Prue Wright, a tall good looking blonde girl, later to become the first Mrs Nigel Willmott. The team for the greater part of the Depot's operation was Prue, Pam Glencross, Jenny Devitt and Evelyn Cross. Prue was 5' 11" tall, but Evelyn – always known as 'Kitten' – was only about 4' 11".

The Wrens always took pains always to look smart. For duty they wore uniform with bell-bottoms: it was practical for driving. Though Nigel Willmott insisted that Number Ones with skirts be worn for Sunday Divisions (Church Parade). A frequent VIP visitor at COPP depot was Sir Malcolm Campbell. He had devised his 'pogo-stick' a device for testing the bearing capacity of sand, originally for his speed record run in *Bluebird*, at Daytona Beach, Florida, when he achieved a record of 276.8 mph, on 3 September 1935. He felt it could be useful for COPP and was always ready to render them assistance. Sir Malcolm would be collected from Havant railway station and rushed back in time to catch his train back to London.

The COPP Depot vehicles consisted of two fifteen-hundredweight trucks – named 'Tweedledum' and 'Tweedledee' – and a three-ton lorry named 'The Grand Lama of Tibet'. In the course of duty, the Wren drivers took things in their stride: the rutted, cratered, largely unmade road that was the only access to the Depot, for example; and driving a three-tonner, long before the days of powered steering. In time the Depot also acquired an amphibious jeep; technically designated Ford Amphibian Jeep GPA, which became named 'Jemima Puddledukw'. All the vehicles had neat name boards with their names and the Combined Operations emblem, sign painted by 'Tubby' Chambers.

Initially WRNS quarters were in one of the Depot ground-floor,

workshop-cum-storage areas and the four Wrens ate in the Petty
Officers' mess. They were billeted in civilian homes on the island. They
cheerfully worked long hours: mustered for duty early in the morning
and drove their vehicles back to their billets late at night. They were
expected to have their vehicles ready and in working order whenever
required for duty and immobilised by removal of the rotor arm,
whenever parked. They thought nothing of driving to lonely places on
late nights in the line of duty.

They were at all times on good terms with Depot staff; including the
three-badge killicks who looked after the central heating and all cordage
and tackle. They took their meals with the Petty Officers until a
'Wrenery' was built: a small brick, ground-floor structure, under the
first-floor gallery on the south side of the clubhouse building. Nigel
Willmott wittily christened it 'The Temple of Beautiful Thoughts'. Its
outside appearance, however, was more like that of a blockhouse, with
windows, and it was just as substantial. Indeed it is still standing and
its present use is for as a dry-goods store for present-day catering at the
clubhouse. Roughly 10' × 10' on plan: its living space was L-shaped, the
remainder being taken up by the loo. It was the place where the WRNS
waited to be notified of their duties. In fact they messed there as well.
There was an electric fire for heating.

The Wrens had a tight camaraderie: they didn't want promotion or
commissions, which would have taken them away from Hayling Island.

They enjoyed working as equal members of the small team and in the
1940's there were no sexist objections to being ordered about by men.
No one wanted to alter the set-up. Their most frequent journeys were
backwards and forwards to Havant railway station; to other bases on
Hayling Island for victuals, mail and stores and to Portsmouth
Dockyard; as well as to and from the Combined Operations Headquarters in Richmond Terrace, W1. Their vehicles parked in the carpark at
COHQ sometimes invited comment from senior officers. 'Why is your
vehicle called Tweedledee?' received the Wren driver's disarming reply:
'Well, I suppose because the other is called Tweedledum, sir.' An
occasional late night trips to Thorney Island airstrip, or one of the other
bases would be all part of the job. As was the occasional puncture. One
Wren, on her own couldn't change a tyre on a three-ton lorry, but two
could and did.

In time all COPP teams spent up-to three months training at Hayling
Island; apart that is from the early teams rushed to the Mediterranean
in great haste. Consequently the Wrens got to know the trainee
COPPists quite well. Their last duty would be to load them up, with all

their equipment, including canoes, on completion of their training and take them, sometimes to RAF Lyneham, to be flown overseas. After the Sicily recces the COPP operational teams never again relied on being able to find servicable folbots in their operational, overseas station.

Happily for posterity group photos were sometimes taken before their departures and some of these wartime snapshots survive. In them the naval parties members' facial expressions reflect diffidence, resignation and bravado, in about equal quantities. Whilst the Wrens may have been glad to send the operational teams, on their way with a smile, their ultimate responsiblity was to get their vehicle back to the Depot for the arrival of the next teams to be trained.

Then the whole process of getting to know the teams and finally driving them off with their equipment would begin again.

*

At Hayling Island the ratings names on the nominal rolls may have raised the occasional chuckle, for example, there was a Fish and a Pond. There were also some excitements of a romantic nature. *The Secret Invaders* relates how Midshipman Robin Harbud RNVR, courted 'Kitten' Cross, who initially rebuffed him. In time his qualities triumphed, they married and had over forty happy years together.

Nigel Willmott's and Prue Wright's wedding was a moment of great excitement. It was a typical wartime one: with everyone in uniform. All the Wrens went. The service was on 27 March 1944. Roger Courtney was among the wedding guests and his gift of a silver plated, inscribed commando dagger was to remind Nigel of their joint recce of Rhodes – the Island of Roses – as if he could forget that. The bridal car left the church, drawn by ropes pulled by COPP HQ ABs and SBS other ranks, quite possibly because petrol was rationed, like almost everything else that made life bearable. The ceremony was memorable and a good pretext for a spree; though characteristically Nigel made sure the training schedules wouldn't suffer. Nigel was treated with great respect, not quite affection: the girls knew he had high standards – none higher than those he imposed on himself. After Prue and 'Kitten' were married, other Wren drivers took their places; one an American who was known as 'California'.

Later that year came D-Day, when the sky over Hayling Island was almost completely covered by gliders crossing the Channel. All the nearby anchorages were full of landing craft. It seemed amazing the enemy was prepared to believe in Pas de Calais landing beaches.

A week later the V1 offensive began. When the noise of the pilotless flying bombs' pulse jets was seldom absent. In the early days, sirens sounded almost continuously. Jenny Devitt was driving Nicholas Hastings, who had won a DSC on the Vaagso commando raid, who – though RNVR – was in every sense of behaviour real RN type. Jenny remembers, during the 'doodlebug', V1 period that Hastings had not long put up his commander's third stripe and brass hat. On a trip to London, at a duty stop, when the engine was switched off, a doodlebug was heard overhead. When the V1's noisy engine cut out, it was too late for Jenny to get out of her cab and take cover; so she remained at the wheel till the explosion came. As the echoes died away, she climbed down, to find Nicholas Hastings, unruffled, wearing his braided cap, standing by the rear of the vehicle, holding a tray full of coffee cups.

'The age of chivalry is not yet dead,' he told her. 'The good lady carrying these wanted to take cover. I said I'd hold them for her. . . .'

During their stays at the Depot, the teams' work and details of their training was something they kept quiet about and would never discuss. Wrens and COPPists talked, instead, about other happier things – like Hugh Maynard's piano playing. In the final days, at Sandy Point, just after the end of hostilities, before demobilisation started, the South African, Gerry Kuyper, painted a set of amusing murals: of which sadly no trace – or even photograph remains today. By then all the COPPists – the personalities, whose secrets and companionship the WRNS were privileged to share, had gone or were packing.

In fact the Wrens were told very little about COPP and they asked no questions. They knew of course that they were part of Combined Operations and that their work was secret. In particular the word reconnaissance was never mentioned to them. How many people did know about them? Evelyn Waugh, for example, in his wartime diaries referred to Roger Courtenay (sic) setting up a folbot section, but seems to have been unaware of the COPPists. So that it would seem COPP's secret existence was kept even from people at Combined Operations Headquarters.

The Wrens, one cannot help feeling, by not gossiping or asking questions, but quietly getting on with their duties – contributed to the tight security maintained at Sandy Point.

SOURCES
Conversations with former COPP personnel

CHAPTER TWENTY-ONE

COPP7 and COPP8 in the Far East

In many ways the fortunes of these two COPPs are interconnected. They were destined to see action in the Far Eastern theatre although probably their team members had assumed when interviewed that they were destined to serve in the Mediterranean. The background to the start of their training periods, however, unquestionably was clouded by events in the Far East in 1942–43. The Japanese capture of Malaya, Singapore, the Dutch East Indies and Hong Kong had been alarming and sobering as had been the Japanese pre-emptive strike on the American Pearl Harbor Naval Base – inspired it is said by the Fleet Air Arm strike on the Italian Fleet at Taranto.

Around Easter 1942, Winston Churchill had worries about the safety of Ceylon – with reason as it was to turn out – he confided his worries to Roosevelt, who replied that this was an area in which he should be able to look after himself. Fortunately a Japanese task force was spotted en route for Ceylon by a Consolidated Catalina flying boat. The Catalina radioed a sighting report and – the 'most dangerous moment' – was avoided: and a surprise attack prevented.

The Allied 'Summit' conferences at Quebec, in August 1943; and Teheran and Cairo, in November and December 1943, helped to co-ordinate global strategy and culminated in the appointment of a Supreme Allied Commander South East Asia – in the person of Lord Louis Mountbatten, appointed on 15 November 1943. Before very long in Burma, where in 1942, the Japanese had consolidated their conquest, allied offensives and seaborne operations would be mounted, with consequent need for beach reconnaissance.

COPP7 was the first COPP to reach India and, indeed, the first to reach and to operate in the Far East. They cannot have expected this: Geoffrey Hall had taken his E/COPP, Bill Lucas, and A/COPP Ruari McLean to ISTD (Inter-Services Topographical Department) at Oxford

– Ruari knew the place: he considered he had only escaped from there through Geoffrey Galwey's good offices – here they had studied aerial photographs of Sicilian beaches.

So it was probably no surprise for them when Naval Party 735 – their cover name – was ordered to the Mediterranean by troopship. They were to have a frustrating time, arriving too late for the Sicily landings, they found no-one, at Allied HQ Algiers, who knew anything about them. So it was with relief they received a brief signal 'Proceed to India'. Their first step, to Alexandria in HMS *Barham*: produced problems when a COPP7 rating accidently fired his pistol and wounded a PO of the ship's company. S/COPP7 has spoken of a certain coolness of relations with the commander by the time they disembarked.

Geoffrey Hall decided to fly to Delhi, with E/COPP Bill Lucas. Naval HQ New Delhi had never heard of COPP. They eventually reached Admiral Miles, Senior Officer Force C: the novel idea of reconnoitring beaches in advance of invasions appealed to him. He gave them every encouragement, and a whole folio of charts and invited them to pick a site for a training centre. They chose Cocanada, 100 miles south-west of Vizagapatam. Cocanada was at the mouth of a small river, there was an artificial harbour, with port facilities and much wild and desolate coast. Hall and Lucas visited it after a 1,000 mile railway journey to reach it. HQ was established at Inverlair, a bungalow standing in 1½ acres of shady grounds. Other people were interested in the bungalow but Geoffrey Hall had been given carte blanche. In time it would be designated as the establishment RN Cocanada. At that time it had to be set-up without disclosing its true function. Geoffrey Hall produced a cover story that the unit was really ISSP (Inter-Service Security Patrol) told the local police superintendent and told him to keep it under his hat.

By the end of August 1943, the place was ready to receive the main body of COPP7, under Ruari McLean; they arrived by sea from Alexandria. They were first in the field and A/COPP7 has recorded his impressions of a first night exercise:

> This evening we did our first swimming from canoes, and for me it was the very first time I'd tried to take beach gradients in the water (in India). Lucas was sick so Geoffrey Hall went with L/Sea Nicol and I took AB Witham (L/Sea Kennedy, my paddler was in hospital). Jennings was in charge of the LCP and we went out with the two canoes on her decks, to the buoy, then ran inshore. I dressed in the LCP – in denim battledress, with a webbing belt to which was fastened revolver (loaded) fighting knife, beach gradient reel, and lead line (the lead in my trouser pocket).

I had on a Mae West (ordinary naval issue inflatable lifebelt) and a torch with a lanyard round my neck was tucked down the inside of my battledress, I had a bag of copper acetate crystals (to keep off sharks!) in one pocket, pencil in another: and when I swam I had my underwater writing tablets strapped on my left wrist and luminous water-tight watch on my right wrist and gym shoes on my feet.

The canoe launch was successful and we paddled inshore in company and the LCP (with underwater silent exhaust) made off quickly. When about one mile offshore and on the correct bearing of the landmark we were using, we turned north and paddled for half an hour. It was a darkish night though the moon was about a quarter full: there was a windy sky and a slight wind astern of us which helped.

We were quite close to the breakers which were roaring continuously and showing, when they broke, a long rather ominous line of white. Sometimes we were close enough to see the spray tossed in the air at the moment the wave pounded down: beyond the breakers – how far it was impossible to see – was a line of palm trees.

I left Hall (he was going to investigate there) and paddled on for another half hour to my beach. Witham now told me he had no watch. Oh no, he hadn't forgotten it, he said in an aggrieved tone, but in the rush of leaving the house he'd left it on his bed.

After paddling parallel to the shore for 30 minutes we stopped, I shipped my paddle and gave my binoculars to Witham: took off my bushwhackers hat, gave that to Witham and gave him his final instructions (I was to be inshore for an hour – he was to keep a look out for my torch. If he didn't pick me up – but the whole schedule depended on accurate timing and I had the only watch – so I had to be picked up!) Hall was to rendezvous with us at 0130.

At 2335 I went over the side of the canoe, repeating to myself 'Sharks will keep off from the copper acetate, barracudas don't strike at night or at black men'. (I was in dark-coloured clothes and wearing black gloves, but I hadn't blackened my face).

I swam on my tummy towards the breakers: there was a colossal undertow and I thought I'd never make it. However I got into the breakers and more or less rolled up the beach in one, and found I could then stand, and waded in the rest. It wasn't realistic, but there was now a bright moon, and if it had been a Jap beach I would not have been able to walk brazenly up it. However, I did that, found a very fast stream, about twenty feet wide; crossed it (nearly getting carried away), found the far side was not suitable for a landing as the stream curved round behind it; recrossed and plugged in the BG spike and walked into the sea, taking soundings. There were three runnels about a foot deep; then I got gradually into deeper water. It was about up to my hips, and I had my back to the sea and was preparing to sound with the lead when I was hit by an express train and knocked A over T up the beach. It took ages to coil up the reel. Then I saw two men coming towards me. I tried to give myself up to them but they were coastal watchers and seemed keener on identifying themselves to me. They had been warned about us. One luckily spoke English. When they departed I swam out again and got one sounding and found I'd lost my pencil in the previous wave. And quite frankly, I funked floating about in the deep water and it was bloody difficult to sound whilst keeping the BG line taut and then write down the depths on the tablet whilst imagining that every other splash was a shark coming up.

About 0400 I swam out through the breakers and started flashing for the canoe. It seemed ages and this was the worst time, floating absolutely alone in the night sea and wondering how the devil the canoe could find me. I could flash only when on the crest of a wave. But Witham arrived, and I was back in the canoe by the scheduled time, 0100.

Geoff was very late: he'd had difficulty with his torch and had been an hour late in being picked up.

Rendezvous with the LCP was effected after some anxious delay: ended our first swim in Indian Waters.

Wednesday September 15, 1943.

Hall and Nicol in one canoe, and myself and Sapper Morrison in another, set out at about 2130 from the Tiffin shed to provide gradients from two beaches some miles from the end of the groynes. We paddled in company to the first beach (on which Gimson was established, and as we learned later occasionally firing his revolver at jackals).

There were many night exercises using their own three LCPs as carrier vessels for canoes and swimmers. In October, Hall and Lucas were summoned to Delhi and later, Force 136 HQ, Calcutta, for briefing on their first operation: a reconnaissance of Akyab Island, code-named Operation *Provident*. The operation was mounted from Chittagong British Forces' Advanced Base. Three canoes landed the operational personnel for what might be termed the *hors d'oeuvre*: a reconnaissance of Oyster Island.

Geoffrey Hall's plan called for a party of six, in line abreast, armed with Stens, should move across the islet as a 'reconnaissance in force' firing on anyone encountered during their advance. In the event four landed and the islet proved empty, but a valuable lesson was learned – if the line wasn't kept properly there was a danger of the party firing on the man out of line . . . this almost happened.

The following night, Friday 10 September 1943, the ML moved in silently – with ship completely darkened, to within two miles of the Akyab beaches. Geoffrey Hall and Ruari McLean were launched, in a single canoe. The canoe paddled to within a cable of the shore and Hall set off, paddling breast stroke, trailing clouds of blue-green shark-repellent. Hall's task was to measure four gradient lines, spaced about thirty yards apart. Relentlessly battered by surf, to say nothing of the danger from sharks, Hall found when taking his final line of soundings, that his lead-line had wound itself around his legs and that he could no longer swim properly. He was sinking inexorably. In desperation he turned on his blue-shaded waterproof torch, held it above his head and swept it seawards in the direction of the anchored canoe . . . and passed out.

Fortunately Ruari had seen his signal, weighed anchor and come to his rescue. He came to being hauled across the fore-part of Ruari's canoe, coughing and retching. Ruari lost no time in cutting away the lead-line. It didn't stop Geoffrey Hall making a second sortie with Lucas* the following night. They were hampered by an RAF raid on Akyab: plainly a liaison slip up . . . with the sky lit-up with flares and searchlights, those on the beach felt naked. The plan was for the canoe to return to the LCP, which would embark the canoe and rendezvous with the ML. In the event the ML failed to make its rendezvous. The LCP, however, had plenty of fuel and the party successfully made it back to Chittagong.

*

COPP8, following fast on COPP7's heels was quartered in the Depot Ship HMS *Adamant*, at Trincomalee, by December 1943: all set to proceed on a recce for Operation *Buccaneer* – the proposed occupation of the Andaman Islands by Indian troops – for which two months of planning had been undertaken, when this was cancelled on 12 December 1943. Following a move from Cocanada, India, to the SOG (Small Operations Group) Hammenheil Fort, Jaffna, Ceylon, COPP8 executed Operation *Bunkum*. on the Mayu Pensinsular.

Reconnaissance of Northern Sumatra by COPP7 and COPP8 – for proposed Operation Culverin

There were at various times plans for the invasion of Sumatra in an Operation that might well be termed the Operation *Torch* of the Far East. The first one had been undertaken by COPP8: the second one had

*COPP8's log is at variance with COPP7's: COPP8's log has Lucas in hospital at this time.

been undertaken by COPP7 with Alec Colson of COPP8 as an additional officer.

In mid-April 1944 a team that included Lieutenant Freddie Ponsonby and Sub-Lieutenant Mike Peacock, travelled in HMS/M *Stoic* (Lieutenant P. B. Marriott RN). S-class submarines were smaller, more cramped and crowded than the T-boats. It had been a disappointing experience. After observing surf conditions through the periscope, the COPP8 team were prevented from carrying out a full-scale reconnaissance of the beaches observed – by the terms of their operation order.

Later in the patrol reconnaissance of Lho Somawe (21 nautical miles north along the coast from Diamond Point) was intended but Marriott and Ponsonby attempted to visit Biroen, 26 miles to the north, first – so as to have tried out all equipment at a quiet spot beforehand. On 23 April 1944 in fitful visibility, only able to pin-point their position by mountains ashore, they attempted to launch a canoe from a position two-miles offshore. The canoe capsized on launching, its slings fouling *Stoic*'s casing; it floated upside down in the water. She was righted partially pumped dry and hoisted inboard again. The gear was all checked and Ponsonby managed to get away at a second attempt and made an in-shore reconnaissance. The RG, having been immersed, no longer worked. Without RG a dimmed Oldhams light was displayed on the periscope standards as an alternative. The canoe was recovered as dawn was breaking, with all personnel drenched: though no personnel or equipment were lost. PO Gascoigne was the paddler.

The following day Sam Marriott was presented with a target, off Lho Samawe, but prevented by the attack prohibition following a special operation, from mounting an attack on a merchant vessel of 1,500 tons. The merchantman was escorted by a submarine chaser and other vessels, these and many outrigger canoes hampered observations of the shore: they did demonstrate a marked tidal effect close inshore. Most of the day – 'a thoroughly bad-temper making day,' Marriott termed it – was spent making sketches through the periscope. After sunset a flash of gunfire was observed near the harbour. As this could have meant her periscope had been spotted, *Stoic* went down to 60-feet depth. About ten rounds were fired; either by the submarine chaser or shore batteries. *Stoic* was in a vulnerable position three-quarters of a mile offshore. Silent routine was observed when Asdic picked up hydrophone effect indicative of a vessel apparently bent on stalking her.

Next day Ponsonby did his best to persuade Marriott that the gunfire had been an exercise and the hydrophone effect from vessels putting out to sea from the harbour. Marriott agreed to close Lho Somawe's beach. Its inshore waters were littered with driftwood and wreckage: so a periscope shouldn't be too conspicuous. After observing the shore *Stoic* bottomed in 160-feet of water and waited for dark. After nightfall she surfaced in a good position – one mile from shore, and 1½ miles south of the town – the hatches were cracked and a canoe made ready but rain squalls and bad visibility ruled out any sortie that night. *Stoic* withdrew and spent the silent hours battery-charging well out to sea.

On 26 April the procedure was repeated and a canoe with Mike Peacock and L/Sea Neil in it was launched eight cables from shore. He completed a satisfactory observation of the shallows and was re-embarked. This provided the information needed and Ponsonby ruled against making a landing. With the COPP8 operation complete Marriott was free to apply himself to his patrol's primary purpose: sinking enemy shipping. Off Lho Somawe, once the attack ban was over Marriott fired two torpedoes at a ship, with no observed results. Her escort responded with fifteen retaliatory depth charges.

*

Operation *Frippery* brought COPP7 back to the same shores in August. The operational team was led by Geoffrey Hall S/COPP7 with Ruari McLean for the naval survey; and Bill Lucas E/COPP7 and Alec Colson for the military recce. Other ranks would be Corporal A. A. Morrison and L/Sea. Kennedy, and ABs Witham and Seagust.

Both COPPs had recently taken delivery of Welrod pistols. These had the advantage of being completely silent; but the disadvantage of having no trigger guard. The Welrod resembled a bicycle pump with a pistol grip. Its small calibre (.32-inch) and short barrel meant that it had poor stopping power and could only be used at very short range. It had been designed as an assassination weapon for use by European resistants. Even so as they'd been issued it was felt they should be used.

The operation orders gave signs that lessons learned on the earlier COPP8 Sumatra operation were being implemented. The Commanding Officer of COPP7 had freedom to select the beaches to be reconnoitred, but at no stage would the submarine approach closer than the ten-fathom line. Up till now some submarine commanders had been known to go in to the five fathom line .... It was also spelled out that *Frippery* did not take precedence over operational requirements. That enemy shipping, if met would be attacked and *Frippery* resumed afterwards. The COPP party must wear uniform, it was stated. Alec Colson interpreted this as meaning – wear a shirt with pips on its shoulder straps under your tropical swimsuit. The next stipulation was that no prearranged contact was to be made with any person ashore. Well, that one certainly had his vote.

Lho Somawe and Biroen were again the primary targets, with Koetaradja, Lhonga and Idi as secondary ones. Bongle was to be used instead of RG for homing. It had been proved that the metal trip hammer strikes of a bongle might readily be picked-up by asdic and tracked on. It was reliable, simple and mechanical, without batteries to be waterproofed. Special escape equipment and local currency was issued before sailing.

It was a relief to find that the party had drawn a T-boat HMS/M *Tudor* (Lieutenant S. A. Porter RN). They would be sailing from Trincomalee and it could be quite a long patrol. The party were at Trinco by 1 August 1944 and harbour and sea drills were completed before sailing.

Tudor sailed on 6 August and was off Biroen at dawn on the 11 August. As with the April Operation it had been decided that Biroen was the easier landing proposition. No fishing vessels were sighted, but smoke hung over the shore and the area appeared reassuringly quiet. Periscope sketching was carried out. After nightfall, while surfaced seven-miles offshore, various shore lights some fires and what looked like a powerful signalling lamp were observed. Having sighted similar signals in the Mediterranean, Sam Porter was not totally surprised when, some five minutes later, *Tudor* was chased by fast anti-submarine vessels. She dived to 90-feet depth and went into silent routine. It worked: no depth charges were dropped and the vessels' engines were heard receding. As no aircraft had been spotted, and *Tudor*'s periscope could not have been spotted from the shore, it seemed most likely she'd been spotted by radar watch. The landing operation was temporarily suspended to give the area a chance to 'cool'.

Next day off Lho Somawe minefields were observed by Asdic, seven tonkangs fishing gave a good idea where the mines ran out. Even so Porter decided to cancel both the proposed landings in the Lho Somawe area. Plans to return to Biroen had to be abandoned when SSO Eastern Fleet signalled a new patrol area, south of Butang, to be reached by dawn on 15 August.

By first light on 17 August *Tudor* was back in the Biroen area. Indications were picked up of radar transmissions, but they were not strong or very frequent. *Tudor* submerged, later closed the coast at Biroen and made a periscope reconnaissance of beaches from 1½ miles distant. The area seemed quiet. There was no offshore fishing. By nightfall, *Tudor* had manoeuvred end-on to land, to present as inconspicuous a silhouette as possible and two canoes were ready for launching:

Sorties were made using a pair of two-man canoes each time:

	First canoe	Second canoe
17 Aug	Geoffrey Hall*	Bill Lucas* (*lone recce)
	Ruari McLean	Morrison

With their canoes launched and cleared, the crews exercised their Bongle. Then, in accordance with plans, *Tudor* submerged and bottomed. Three-and-a-half hours later *Tudor* picked up Bongle transmissions, she surfaced used RG and found the folboats only one cable (600 feet) away. Both folbots were recovered, one capsized in the swell.

The following night back off Biroen a pair of folbots was again launched:

	First canoe	Second canoe
18 Aug	Ruari McLean*	Alec Colson* (*lone recce)
	Kennedy	Witham

The folbots were gone well over three hours. There was a false alarm when two small charges were heard exploding and taken to be SUEs (Signals Underwater Explosive): *Tudor* had surfaced in case the folbots were in trouble but had seen nothing. *Tudor* again surfaced when Bongle transmissions were heard. She was some 500 yards from the folboats. They reported she was invisible at 150 yards distance. The night was dark, hazy and cloudy. By 2304 the folbots had been recovered. Alec Colson came aboard still toting his Welrod: he'd penetrated a fair distance inland and come back with useful information. *Tudor* proceeded seawards on the surface to charge batteries.

*

Thereafter the patrol took *Tudor* east of Diamond Point and next day near to Idi. The coast was hard to identify: the navigational pilot data inaccurate, mines were searched for and *Tudor* found herself in a minefield, and it took an hour's careful manoeuvring to work clear. Signals were passed to base about the new minefields and a progress report on Operation *Frippery*.

On 22 August *Tudor* closed Biroen for periscope reconnaissance. Then things started to happen. First a twin-engined bomber was spotted; then a three-masted junk. Sam Porter decided the aircraft was probably the junk's escort, but thought he'd sink it anyway. He surfaced

at a range of just under a mile and commenced gun action. In six minutes
the junk had sunk: hit by ten out of twenty-nine rounds fired by the 4-
inch gun. As Porter put it: 'Excellent for morale!' *Tudor* dived and cleared
the area. There was some wreckage but no survivors. Forty minutes later
a twin-engined aircraft was searching the attack area.

Tudor returned to Lho Somawe and Biroen. It had been noted that
coastal defences were being built in the area and it was decided to
investigate.

On the night of 23/24 August two canoes were launched:

First canoe	*Second canoe*
Geoffrey Hall	Bill Lucas (swam)
Alec Colson (swam)	Seagust

Bill Lucas and Alec Colson both swam ashore – Alec armed with a
Sten – and were recovered four hours later having gained details of the
defences being constructed.

At the end of this chapter is an extract from Sam Porter's
observations on launching and recovering folbots. There are also three
pages of drawings showing information obtained – and quite how
accurately tidal sets can be plotted, even when navigating in a folbot,
by a navigator of Geoffrey Hall's calibre. Geoffrey Hall and Ruari
McLean received DSCs for their part in reconnaissances in Burmese
waters. Alec Colson and Bill Lucas received MBEs for their part in
Operation *Frippery*.

Tudor's patrol lasted from 6-30 August; a long patrol by anyone's
standards. The COPPists on board were glad to get ashore and amazed
to find Trinco harbour flooded with oil as a result of an accidental
discharge of a torpedo by HMS/M *Severn* – which sunk a tanker.

*

If one is tempted to pose the question: was it worth it, if we never
invaded Sumatra? There can be no doubt of the answer. Operation
Culverin, the proposed assault on Sumatra, was planned in fine detail.
It was to take place not earlier than 1 March 1945. It was no token
diversionary exercise as indicated by the scale of forces considered
necessary:
– Four Commandos
– Four and two-thirds Divisions
– Three and a half Beach Groups
– One Tank Brigade, plus one Armoured Regiment

– Force HQ
– Corps HQ
– Engineers for three Forward Airfields.

Note: the Divisional slice was estimated as 35,000 strong. Operation *Culverin* was no flight of fancy.

Annexe to HMS/M Tudor*'s Report of Operation* Frippery
METHOD OF LAUNCHING FOLBOTS
The submarine was trimmed right down and folbots were launched and recovered at a position alongside the casing between the fore hatch and 4-inch gun. The gun being trained athwartships to help control the tail line. Provided there is little or no swell, this method works quite well, as there is enough water to float a loaded folbot over the ballast tanks of a T-Class submarine at low buoyancy. However, in any swell, with movement on the submarine, the folbots were liable to capsize alongside, as once happened on recovery. Listing the ship on No. 4 main ballast tank is a considerable help, but on a dark night, the ship is liable to be in a dangerously low state of buoyancy with many hands on the casing and bridge.

It is considered that, for folbots, this position of launching is much better than from the fore planes and in practice, proved much quicker.

From surfacing to diving again which included launching two double folbots and getting enough buoyancy to open fore hatch, average time was twenty minutes.

RENDEZVOUS PROCEDURE
The system used was for the folbots to come out to the 10 fathom line on the return journey and anchor in the estimated position of the submarine. When anchored "Bongle" was commenced and submarine then steered for the "Bongle" bearing, showing RG on the bearing to show that contact had been made. The folbots were closed till sighted visually, by which time they had weighed and were ready for recovery.

In practice this method worked perfectly. The "Bongle" was very clearly heard while the submarine was bottomed and the "Bongle" bearings accurate enough for surface homing. The minimum homing range was 100 yards, maximum 500 yards, during the operation, so the "Bongle" did not have a long range test, but I have no doubt it would work up to some miles. In the area of operation there was considerable noise from surf, but this did not affect Bongle reception.

The submarine end-on was invisible at over 150 yards and beam-on at a slightly greater range. Without such homing devices on a dark night, the problem of recovery is considerable.

ACCOMMODATION AND PRIORITY
The accommodation of 4 extra officers in the wardroom and four extra ratings for a whole patrol period of 24 days was crowded.

It is suggested that for such an operation, the patrol be shortened and have only the operation as the objective, it being stated before the ship sails exactly what reconnaissance is required, since landings can take place nightly to investigate each tree or coconut which looks suspicious through the periscope and the length of the patrol extended until supplies of stores and the patience of the Commanding Officer are exhausted.

*

COPP8 and the Jungle Warfare School, Shimoga, Mysore
Briefly COPP7 and COPP8 military personnel moved from Cocanda, via Madras and Bangalore to Shimoga – a distance of 750 miles, in the period 1–4 April 1944. In the same period the sieges of Imphal and Kohima were taking place; as was Orde Wingate's second long range penetration expedition; and the decisive Admin Box battle in Arakan. So that Jungle warfare was a particularly important matter of the moment – and instructing in it was far from being a sinecure. Quite a lot of Wingate's Chindits were instructing and COPPists were on their toes to defend the reputation of COPP. Lessons learned as instructors were passed on by Bill Lucas and Alec Colson in Jungle Training in Ceylon – no doubt to the benefit of all – at all events, four naval members of COPP3 survived months in the Malayan jungle after having failed to make a submarine rendezvous. Quite possibly the survival training they had received helped them to survive.

SOURCES
RN Submarine Museum
Operation Frippery operation order
Public Record Office
ADM199 1862
WO203 3006

TRENOWDEN, Ian *Operations Most Secret*, William Kimber, 1978 (reprinted Crécy Books, 1994).

CHAPTER TWENTY-TWO

COPP8: Operations David and Deputy (Snatch)

Towards the end of September 1944, COPP8 was still at Hammenheil Fort, with no prospect of an operation. None the less they kept up training and PT. On Tuesday 26 September 1944 all that changed. Colonel H. T. Tollemache RM called and warned them to be ready to embark on a warship with a view to establishing an advanced base for operations. Consequently morale soared. On 3 October 1944, with all stores embarked in two LCPs with eight canoes. The party – most wore bush-hats, though the military retained their green berets – rendezvoused with HMAS *Nizam* and sailed for Chittagong. Days were spent here and the conversion of a Mark 1** canoe to a three-seater completed.

By Wednesday 11 October 1944, Freddie Ponsonby had spent time with the Senior Officer Arakan Coastal Forces, Commander Ashby DSC, RNVR, and their target was known. Alec attended Chittagong airfield and, with a minimum of formalities was taken up in a Beaufighter to overfly the area. It seemed a far cry from the Dundonald training flight. There was no seat for him and he stood behind the pilot. In order to provide any Jap observers with a pretext for their flight, the pilot fired a burst of cannon, into a creek alongside a native fishing craft. Next day, once operational packing was complete, the party were all set to go, but days of waiting – with annoying air raid panic alarms were spent – before the operational party sailed on 12 October 1944 in *ML-829* (Lieutenant R. J. Williams SANF(V), supported by *ML-382* (Lieutenant V. Bartholomew SANF(V). It had been decided to use the three-man canoe conversion. The line of battle would be as follows:

Onchaung		*Ondaw*	
Canoe No.1:	Ponsonby/Gascoigne	Peacock/ Neil	
Canoe No.2:	Peacock/Neil	Richards/ Duffy	

Canoe No.3:   Colson/Cumberland/   Colson/Cumberland/
               Duffy   Gascoigne

On the first first night, 16–17 October 1944, the ML was not in place
1½ miles offshore, from Onchaung Beach, till 40 minutes later than
hoped. That meant only 1½ hours on shore. Ponsonby decided to restrict
the survey to the western beach; he himself fixed the position of offshore
dangers and took soundings between them. Alec Colson and Crawford
Cumberland found their progress impeded by a suspected look-out post.
They returned to sea but had difficulty trying to swim round it. In their
buoyant suits they were thrown back on to the shore: a nude swimmer
might have succeeded, but clothed and weighed down by valuable
equipment, it could not be done. They regained their canoe with difficulty
and all three canoes made it to the rendezvous despite a 2½ knot cross
tide. The journey back to Teknaf was made without incident.

On the second night, 18–19 October 1944, all three canoes were off
Ondaw Bay, Elizabeth Island, Lieutenant Geoff Richards RNVR swum
ashore, as did Colson and Gascoigne. Mike Peacock anchored their
boats in the waiting position and then himself swam for the shore,
leaving the canoe 200 yards from the shore intending to take a line of
soundings west of the spit and, if time permitted, determine the limit
of shoal water in the bay's western corner. Peacock wore a tropical
swimsuit, with buoyant kapok waistcoat and inflatable lifebelt. He was
armed with a .38 pistol and fighting knife and heavily weighted down
with sounding gear and the usual equipment. He was not seen again.
For the rest of the party, the beach's rocky spit made identification
straightforward, but it did create dangerous surf conditions. Despite the
problems, they completed their tasks. On discovering Mike Peacock had
not made the rendezvous Richards and Neil, and Colson and Duffy took
their canoes back inshore and made a careful search for Mike, Alec
searching the surf along the beach where he was known to have been
operating. It was not then known that Mike had suffered from dysentery
during the previous day. The search had to be abandoned eventually;
the party stayed till the last possible moment and left, hoping D-Day
would not be far distant and that Mike would prove to be in good hands.
In fact, with the full force of the out-going tide behind them, all three
canoes were carried beyond the ML and were spotted only after she'd
begun to weigh anchor and they'd made frantic torch signals.

In the circumstances it was decided to abandon plans for reconnaissances of Pyanbaung and Kyanthaya, on the next two nights. Colonel
Young evidently considered COPP8's findings so vital, that he again

came aboard for a verbal report. Alec Colson was subsequently awarded a mention in despatches for his work that night as was Geoff Richards.

*

Operation Deputy, *November 1944*
On 22 October 1944, COPP8 had moved to Chittagong. Some days were spent here and tasks included packing-up and listing Mike Peacock's kit. On Friday 27 October, after a good meal the previous night at the New China Restaurant, COPP8 officers arrived at the office to find a note requesting two officers to be sent to the forward base to search for Mike Peacock and obtain information. Freddie Ponsonby and Alec got the necessary gear together and prepared to leave. They enjoyed the Irving Berlin film *This is the Army* that night. On the morrow they sailed in an ML flotilla to Teknaf. Some preliminary planning was done and aerial photographs studied. Colonel Young, the deputy commander of 3 Commando Brigade – a veteran of early Commando raids, in the Channel Islands, Vaagso, Dieppe, and other small-scale raids, to say nothing of the Sicilian, Italian and North-western European campaigns – asked pertinent questions about the look-out post at Onchaung.

'Why did you think it other than an ordinary fisherman's hut?' he asked.

Feeling as though he was on trial Alec explained: the hut hadn't been seen from the Beaufighter – so it was camouflaged; it was well placed for concealment and to cover both beaches; a light had been seen there long after all lights were out in Onchang village; and it had mosquito nets.

Colonel Young seemed satisfied. Operation orders were drawn up, roneoed and Duffy, the COPP8 draughtsman prepared the maps.

On Sunday 29 October they met Major Jock Cunningham, in command of the proposed operation, expected to be done with a force about 30 strong. Freddie Ponsonby, who had seen his share of naval fighting, and had served in HMS *Cossack* and *Cairo* seemed excited at the thought of taking part in a fighting raid. At Teknaf the plan was explained – the party would land at Ondaw, to avoid Onchaung's heavy surf, then march 2½-miles across the island to Onchaung. They would, it was hoped, be able to creep up to the look-out post, lob in the explosive and take a prisoner. They would have interpreters in the party, who could interrogate the natives for news of Mike Peacock.

Major Cunningham discussed details with Alec. A Mills bomb thrown in through the door would be likely to kill all the occupants; so there would be no-one to take prisoner. As an alternative Alec suggested a quarter-pound charge of gelignite, whose explosion would have much the effect of a modern stun-grenade: a dazzling flash and no flying fragments to injure the post's occupants. Experiments were made with various methods of igniter fuse. A fuse capped by match composition and struck on a matchbox – like a thunderflash – proved unreliable.

An experienced corporal, skilled in handling explosives, produced a version in which the removal of a pin fired a cap to light a short fuse. He demonstrated it successfully.

'Let's throw one or two for luck,' said Cunningham.

Alec threw one that performed perfectly. Cunningham pulled the pin out of his and it went off instantly, blowing his hand clean off. The Commando's medical officer* fortunately was on hand and applied a tourniquet to the stump. Alec went with Lieutenant-Colonel Fellowes to explain the accident to Colonel Young. Subsequently it emerged that the length of fuse employed was so short, that pressure developed and the normal calculations of fuse-length and burning-time no longer applied. Alec had had a lucky escape.

Next morning NAFCA (Naval Assault Force Commander Arakan) Commander Nichol arrived, and tried to prevent the operation taking place by refusing the use of a landing craft. Colonel Young was utterly determined the operation should go ahead – even if he had to go in the COPP canoes. That wasn't required. The Corps Commander, Lieutenant-General Christison visited the Brigade in the morning and offered to lend Colonel Young his private landing craft personnel. Major Michael Davies – a prep school friend of Alec's – was to lead the operation in place of Cunningham. General Christison left after a morale-raising inspection in which he shook all officers hands.

Next morning, 3 November, they boarded the MLs at 0700; the Senior Officer of 49th Flotilla led in *ML-380*, with COPP8's old friend, Vic Bartholomew, following in *ML-382* towing the LCP.

The landing was made as planned, guides were recruited, but had a tendency to stop and have discussions. Covering 2½ miles took some time. As the Commando force neared the huts, they had to advance in single file, without advanced scouts and hampered by their nattering guides. A corporal in a leading assault group inadvertently fired two rounds from his Tommy gun – and the element of surprise was lost.

The Japs opened fire but their shooting was inaccurate and was returned. A Jap broke cover and was promptly fired at and hit by two American Garand self-loading rifles and a Tommy gun. The Jap fell, got

*Capt. F. Rodger RAMC.

up and ran screaming, down the beach towards the sea. He was cut down at the water's edge, by a Bren gunner firing from the hip. The assault party retired in short order, covering 2½ miles in forty-five minutes. Villagers streaming out of Onchaung, for an instant gave a scare that the Japs might be about to ambush the party.

The landing craft came in, embarked half the force, then broached to, and without steering way, got a kedge line round her screw. Marines attempted to paddle the boat out. The boat officer Lieutenant Lang RNVR, went over the side and made several dives to cut four turns of 4-inch rope with a hack saw. It took him some twenty dives, before the screw would turn . . . . The rest of the force were embarked, some having to swim to the landing craft. The LCP returned to the MLs and unloaded. It was discovered that Corporal Chappell, a Bren gunner, was missing. The LCP returned to look for Corporal Chappell, but returned without him. The party had taken no prisoner, there was no definite news of Mike Peacock.

The MLs returned to Teknaf where George Barnes of SBS was briefed on picking up Chappell. Plans to seize Elizabeth Island and use it as an offensive base were abandoned. There was no definite news of Mike Peacock until his release after the fighting in the Sittang bend, April to May 1945. He had made use of a cover story concocted by Alec Colson: that as a naval officer he'd been scouting for a suitable place to establish a dump of gasolene and oil, for use by MLs as an advanced operational Base.

Operation *Deputy* – the raid on Elizabeth Island, was the last of COPP8's operations, before they handed their equipment over to the newly arrived COPP3 under Alex Hughes and left Hammenheil on 17 December 1944. Their stores and equipment of course included the folbots. It must have been an emotional moment for Freddie Ponsonby to part with *Dusky Maiden*; and for Alec Colson to be parted from *Jenny Wren*.

SOURCES
RN Submarine Museum
Operation *Frippery* – operation order
Public Record Office
ADM199 1862
WO203 3006
COPP8 Logbook, transcribed by Alec Colson
COLSON, Alec *Double Handle*, unpublished manuscript on Operation *David*
TRENOWDEN, Ian *Operations Most Secret*, William Kimber, 1978 (reprinted Crécy Books, 1994)

CHAPTER TWENTY-THREE

D-Day Marking and Assistance from COPP

Ken Hudspeth was back in command of *X-20*, off the Normandy coast, in early June: his crew were Sub-Lieutenant Bruce Enzer RNVR and ERA L. Tilley. Also in *X-20* were two COPPists: Lieutenant-Commander Paul W. Clark RN and Sub-Lieutenant Robin Harbud RNVR. Clark had not long taken over as CO COPP HQ: Nigel Willmott's health having finally packed up and he was in hospital; and thereby prevented from doing duty as one of the navigational beacons for the D-Day invasion fleet. Something he had been determined to do personally.

X-23 was commanded by Lieutenant George Honour RNVR, who had as his crew Lieutenant J. H. Hodges RNVR and ERA George Vause; His two COPPists were S/COPP9, Geoffrey Lyne and James Booth. George Honour had come to X-craft through volunteering for hazardous service, whilst serving as an RNVR officer in the Western Desert. Eventually this brought him back to Britain and to a concentrated course at HMS *Varbel* at Rothesay: electrics, diesel engines, navigation and diving as a frogman. X-craft crews were all frogmen – they had to be prepared to leave the craft to cut through nets and attach limpet mines. After commanding *X-4*: mainly used for training purposes he was given command of *X-23*, early in 1944, when *X-23* and *X-20* had both been detached from the 12th Submarine Flotilla to act as navigational beacons off the D-Day beaches. For this purpose they were based at Gosport and their ultra-secret craft – 52-feet in length and 6-feet in diameter had to be transported by rail. Conferences at Hayling Island meant that George Honour was pretty well informed on COPP requirements.

Both X-craft had been modified by the addition of welded buoyancy cylinders, in place of their explosive side-cargoes: the added buoyancy was necessary to compensate for increased all-up weight. Their complement had been increased to five: three crew members and two COPPists. *X-20* came from the workshops of Thomas Broadbent & Son, Huddersfield. She had an echo-sounder fitted, a gyro repeater compass mounted on deck and a long sounding-pole, secured to the casing. *X-23* had been constructed by Markham of Chesterfield.

The crews had all had their photos taken in civilian clothing – along with other COPPists selected for D-Day tasks – that way they'd have photos available for false identity cards: if they had to ditch and go ashore. It had been rather a jolly occasion, Wren 'Kitten' Cross had her photo taken with the others. Bruce Ogden Smith appeared in khaki battledress – probably because he had a certain contempt for the enemy and didn't plan to get caught by them. Bill Tebb was photographed in a British steel helmet; probably for the same reasons.

The detailed plan was that the X-craft should cross the channel submerged and undetected to their marking positions. Honour's craft one mile off Ouistreham, Sword Beach; Hudspeth's further west off Courseulles, Juno Beach. Both vessels passed through the Channel minefield. *X-20* found herself in a shoal of jellyfish and, at one stage, had a dan buoy cable fouling her screw. Even so both boats reached the French coast on Sunday, 4 June 1944, just as dawn was breaking. On passage George Honour had periodically raised *X-23*'s induction and run the engine for a few minutes, to 'guff through' the boat, changing her air supply and thereby husbanding her oxygen. A fixed red light, at the mouth of the Orne river, was burning: it gave them a good navigational fix. Both craft bottomed. Inevitably all on board knew the full details of the forthcoming operation. Having sailed from HMS *Dolphin* they had no means of communicating with headquarters, though they could pick up their signals. As soon as they began their listening watch they picked up the signal that D-Day had been postponed. It was something of a body blow, but it made sense: the weather was pretty rough thought *X-23*'s crew. Further down the coast *X-20*'s crew wouldn't have agreed: to them things seemed pretty moderate. Either way both boats charged batteries and ventilated their interiors, then down to the bottom for eighteen hours.

*

Others suffered similar frustration. Ralph Stanbury had laid special sonic navigation buoys in mid-Channel from a HDML (Harbour Defence Motor Launch). He was a special navigation pilot for Juno Beach: Staff officer (Navigation). QH was used to positon the buoys, with a reputed accuracy of three yards in fifteen miles. The buoys had special timing devices. They would pop-up to just below the surface in the small hours of June 5 1944. Once laid they could not be recovered or their timing devices altered. Had the Germans appropriate receivers they could, in theory, have picked up their signals.

*

Before putting to sea *X-20* and *X-23* had embarked oxygen to breath during their prolonged submergence. This was contained in a dozen aluminium cylinders salvaged from shot-down Luftwaffe aircraft: they were simply the best article available, frogmen used them too. During their long wait the X-craft captains and COPPists were able to verify their positions very carefully, plotting bearings from onshore landmarks on specially detailed charts with a Douglas protractor.

George Honour has described evocatively how, near the estuary of the River Orne, that Sunday morning, before submerging, he could see clearly the lights of aircraft landing on Caen's Carpiquet airfield – fully seven miles inland. Once securely anchored in their 'billets' the crews had little to divert them beyond listening to the BBC Home and Forces programmes. It seems likely that they heard the popular *Monday Night at Eight* programme. They had plenty to do, of course, condensation had to be mopped-up continually. Lying one-mile off the beaches they could make periscope observations of the shore. George Honour saw lorry loads of German soldiers swimming: a good sign. It meant one beach that wasn't mined. His periscope gave him a clear view but he couldn't tell if the Germans wore costumes. Speculation on this subject made a change from wondering how long the oxygen would last. Briefly surfaced during the hours of darkness, they could pick up wireless messages from the Isle of Wight's powerful Niton transmitter. Many coded messages for the French resistance were received: their volume hopefully indicative that the postponement would be not over long.

On Monday night they surfaced after dark and received the message that the invasion would begin at first light on Tuesday, 6 June 1944 – in spite of rising wind and sea. Both boats remained submerged until just before dawn. At 0400 they broke surface and set up their 18-foot mast and commenced flashing their navigation beacon seawards, at 0530. The water was still rough enough to make entry and exit through the hatch difficult. Whilst Willmott could not be with the markers he was certainly there in spirit. He would have approved Robin Harbud's approach to the identification problem – he had acquired a cruiser's ensign to fly on *X-*

20. She began signalling with a shaded light after sighting an aircraft attacking shore targets and the naval bombardment began. They also made use of a Bongle trip-hammer and a tiny radar beacon. Would the invasion fleet never come? Suddenly through the murk, lines of landing craft appeared, surging past them in the rising sea. LCRs (Landing Craft Rockets) poured seemingly endless salvoes overhead. It is said that the crew's report was so understated it read like that of a ship in peacetime. *X-20* had planned to put a rubber dinghy over the side with an officer and other signalling gear, but it was judged too rough for this.

George Honour is on record that he found the invasion fleet's battleship shore bombardment reassuring. With the X-craft trimmed low in the water, one landing craft soldier has spoken of his surprise at seeing a naval officer apparently 'walking on the water'. At sunrise *X-23* substituted a naval code D-Flag – yellow-red-yellow, equally divided vertically – for the signal lamp. It was soon clear that the landings were succeeding and that the midget markers had played their part. The Duplex-drive, swimming Sherman tanks: one of the most important vehicles they had marked for were playing their part. Once the Commandos and tanks had gone ashore the X-craft had done their work and Operation *Gambit* was complete. The crew of *X-23* cut her anchor rope – they were too exhausted to pull it up. A trawler waited just outside Gosport, to shackle on the towline and tow them into harbour, through the swept channels. On arrival the two boats were greeted by ships sirens . . . for a successful operation. Operation *Gambit* had taken 72-hours; and 64 of them had been submerged. Happily, unlike the pawn in a chess-game gambit, neither had been thrown away. Their crews were back in *Dolphin* in time for a bath and a snifter before dinner.

*

Other COPPists marked for DD tanks on D-Day COPP6 among them. In the early dawn of D-Day, Lieutenant Peter Wild RNVR, in a landing craft, guided in a squadron of 13th/18th Royal of Hussars Duplex-drive Sherman tanks, to Juno Beach.

Away to port Don Slater, also COPP6 was similarly occupied, at Sword Beach. Lieutenant D. G. W. Slater RNVR had joined COPP6 after the loss of Sub-Lieutenant Sayce. He came to COPP via HMS *Tormentor*, Warsash and Force J. To encourage his landing craft's load of soldiery, he fired off four magazines from a Bren. As the magazine takes thirty, but no more than 28 rounds are recommended, that would be over 100-rounds. As the barrel was by then frying hot, he decided not to change to the spare barrel, but pitched the weapon over the side; knowing it was 'scrounged' and on no one's charge. He himself, had been encouraged, during the run-in to see a bit of coast he recognised. He'd been briefed at the Bodleian Library, in Oxford, where he'd been shown maps and a panoramic photo of Sword Beach, but not permitted to take notes. As he could see no further than about two-miles – low down in a landing craft, not far above water-line – he was certainly on the ball. He knew troops hated getting their feet wet: so he ran his American-constructed, LCP timber-hull craft right up on to the beach, in any case it didn't have a ramp . . . .

*

It has been suggested that the Americans refused COPP markers for Omaha beach. In fact, from a COPP point of view they were not necessary – unlike in the case of the British and Canadian beaches. Rightly, the American Force Commander at Omaha, welcomed pilotage assistance for the final assault run-in.

So Logan Scott-Bowden was present on D-Day to assist in piloting in the American troops to Omaha beach, as was Bruce Ogden Smith.

Scott-Bowden has told the story vividly in an article in *The Royal Engineers Journal*:

> Ogden Smith and I were mainly with US V Corps for briefings for Omaha Beach. We answered various questions, and the fact that we had been and seen the beach seemed to give them some encouragement.
>
> For D-Day we were assigned to Naval Force 'O', commanded by Rear Admiral J. L. Hall, Jr, USN to assist with pilotage and had attended the major rehearsal exercises. We sailed in the Admiral's flagship from Weymouth and stopped briefly before dawn. The very small pilot boats were launched and we went down the scrambling nets to board.

Scott-Bowden had opted for the right hand US 29th Division; Ogden Smith went in with the US 1st Division on the left. Scott-Bowden's account continues –

> The pilot boat which I was in, was commanded by a very experienced US naval lieutenant doing his fourth assault landing. He had a crew of two: a coxswain and a gunner of Mexican extraction, manning a four-barrelled 'pom-pom' for anti-aircraft fire, but which could be directed horizontally.
>
> We sped rapidly to the head of the fleet, taking station in front of the eight Landing Craft Tanks (LCT) carrying the 32 amphibious Sherman tanks which would be the first to land; the LCTs deployed in line abreast.

We took position on their left as we approached the 1,500 yd position, the decision then had to be made as to whether to stop and launch the tanks so they could swim ashore under their own propulsion – or go straight in to put them on the beach. The US navy lieutenant was responsible for this decision. The major commanding the tanks was in the turret of his tank in the left-hand craft and he by signs made very clear he wished to be taken on in. I think out of courtesy, the lieutenant asked my opinion. I said 'It is far too rough; we should go right in.'

We looked east to see what was happening on the left. Their eight LCTs were stopped and were discharging their tanks into the sea. We later learned that out of their 32 tanks, 26 were drowned with their crews. Then things happened fast.

Our gunner opened up and I gave him some targets mainly embrasures. He was enjoying it. The LCTs grounded on time and in exactly the right place just short of the beach obstacles full of mines, downed their ramps and the amphibious tanks emerged, still with their canvas flotation gear up which they then had to blow free. Some had difficulty as they were being hit by intense machine-gun fire. Soon they were being knocked out by anti-tank gunfire. Not many tanks survived. From among the obstacles we heaved inboard some tank crew survivors.

Smaller Landing Craft Assault (LCA) were now beaching closer in to off-load infantry and engineers.

Not far from where Scott-Bowden had gone ashore five-months earlier – and a sentry had shone a powerful torch beam on him – the advance was halted.

Destroyers closed in and naval support gunfire started being effective. Even the battleship USS *Texas* had closed and was visible broadside-on firing its main armament.

Gradually with immense courage the infantry and engineers, some using man-pack flame-throwers worked along the ridge destroying the rabbit-warren of bunkers as the naval gunfire moved just in front of them. It was a magnificent display of navy and army co-operation.

When they went back to the flagship to report, they found that Admiral Hall was already aware that the battle was being won.

*

On D + 2 Scott-Bowden, back from the front, was on the ridge overlooking Omaha beach and saw that a few of the US Mulberry harbour blockships appeared to be sunk in too deep water. Snipers were also active, having remained hidden in the rabbit-warren of defences, and had just killed a USAF major, close by, at the back of the beach.

Around D + 5 Scott-Bowden ceased to be a free agent:

After the British and American link up at Port en Bessin, I was standing at the then small crossroads, at the head of the harbour when Brigadier Basil Davy saw me and demanded to know what I was doing. I was looking somewhat disreputable, having had to discard my battledress which was saturated by oil from knocked-out tanks on D-Day, and I could only acquire a pair of US waterproof trousers and a sort of golf jacket. I said: 'Absolutely nothing, Sir, my job is finished.' I did not add that I was supposed to go back to the UK after D-Day.

Scott-Bowden was sent to 3rd Infantry Division; their engineers had suffered severe casualties. That evening he reverted to being an orthodox engineer, taking command of 17th Field Company after dark, laying 5,000 mines, in front of 185 Infantry Brigade positions, across the expected line of attack by *21st Panzer Division.*

*

So ended Scott-Bowden's service with COPP:

Apart from a threatened Court Martial, for failing to return to the UK, from the new Chief of Combined Operations, Major General Robert Laycock, via Commander-in-Chief 21st Army Group to CRE 3rd Infantry Division Lieutenant Colonel R. W. 'Tiger' Urquhart. Fortunately Tiger knew Bob very well and thus I escaped indictment to soldier on happily ever after.

He went right through the campaign, was twice wounded and was awarded a bar to his MC.

*

Ralph Stanbury was on the beaches too – for six weeks – as Staff Officer (Movements), sustained by Camembert cheese and Whisky. It was better than the bully beef and cocoa he seemed to remember doing his COPP training on.

Other COPPists were there too: among them Geoffrey Lyne, who landed with AB Bill Tebb as bodyguard. Bill Tebb had been on the very first Human-torpedo attack mission: against the *Tirpitz.* The 'Jeeps' (human torpedoes) had been lost from their carrier vehicle (the trawler *Arthur,* under the command of Lief Larsen of 'Shetland Bus' fame) in bad weather. The attack had to be aborted and the operational party had had to evade and had escaped only through Bill Tebb's shooting a

German. One of the party, wounded in an exchange of shots, had to be left behind and was subsequently executed. Understandably Bill Tebb had no love for Germans and Geoffrey Galwey says he seemed pleased that orders were that no German prisoners were to be taken. The full story of the Human Torpedo attack on *Tirpitz* is told in *Above Us the Waves* by C. E. T. Warren and James Benson, published by George Harrap, 1953, and it is worth reading.

Geoff Galwey was off the beaches – detailed to make contact with marker midget *X-20*. Once this had been done, PO Briggs and Cecil 'Billy' Fish, who were with him, were both determined to go ashore, where they joined in and enthusiastically assisted RAMC stretcher bearers. Even so Geoff knew he had better get them back to the Depot pretty quick – both were highly trained ratings, likely to be wanted for duty elsewhere. He also knew that unwounded personnel, on landing craft carrying wounded were likely to be declared deserters. So he arranged for the three of them to return to Britain by MGB.

*

Others suffered the frustration of being trained and ready for operations, but still at the Depot when D-Day dawned. Sergeant Jack Powell RE was one of them. He had trained with COPP5, but was to join COPP9 under Lieutenant John Morison RN, before going overseas. The Navy List gives S/COPP9's names with exactly that spelling. In fact, many wartime papers have Morrison (with double-r) and many of Morison's friends knew him as Ian.

*

Ronnie Williamson was at OTU on D-Day. He felt a bitter sense of frustration – to be concerned with Brasso and blanco, when all the action was across the Channel in France. He had returned from his Mediterranean service with COPP5 – for which, though he didn't know it, he had been recommended for a military medal – hoping to be employed on D-Day landings reconnaissance. As he had not been employed on this duty he had taken a commission. Whilst D-Day may have seemed a disappointment, he did go from corporal to captain in fourteen months, and susequently served with No 1 Commando and the SRS (Special Raiding Squadron).

*

Decorations for Operation Gambit were a DSC for George Honour, a second bar to the DSC for Ken Hudspeth and a Croix de Guerre for Jim Booth and mentions in despatches for other crew members.

SOURCES

Major General L. Scott-Bowden CBE, DSO, MC*, 'COPP to Normandy 1943/1944 – a Personal Account of part of the Story', article in *The Royal Engineers Journal*.

Correspondence with George Honour.

Discussions with former COPPists

Lieutenant-Commander K. R. Hudspeth DSC**, RANR (Retd) '*X-20* in the English Channel', article in Naval Historical Review.

WARREN, C. E. T. and BENSON, James *Above Us the Waves*, George G. Harrap 1953.

Correspondence with COPPists and Gus Britton.

CHAPTER TWENTY-FOUR

Final COPP Operations in Europe

As Geoffrey Galwey put it:

After D-Day General Montgomery became very keen on COPP reconnaissance. Of the first three teams I trained, two were used for the advance through the Lowlands and Germany, one under Lieutenant Harvey Winship SANF(V), for the Rhine crossing for which he was awarded the DSC. The other under Lieutenant John Hashim RN, now a trawler owner in Lowestoft, surveyed the Elbe crossing.

As General Eisenhower had put it:

TOP SECRET TELEGRAM

1. It is anticipated that our operation in the spring will be on a very large scale and may require a quantity of equipment particularly for crossing the Rhine which with its strong currents, flooded areas and difficult embankments will be a specialised undertaking, calling for the utilisation of of all our resourses and ingenuity. It will entail the use of appropriate craft and special devices. The advice of authorities who have specialised in the study of river crossings will be needed. Would appreciate assistance of COHQ and Assault Training Centre in this respect and would be grateful if you could arrange this with CCO [Chief of Combined Operations] and War Office.

2. A meeting of the three army groups is being called at this HQ commencing 1400 hours on Friday 12 January to discuss the experiments, plans already made to disseminate all available information. The presence of representatives of Combined Operations Headquarters and of Assault Training Centre at this meeting would be much appreciated. The names of officers designated at this meeting would be much appreciated and ETA assist in providing appropriate billets arrangements which will be made here.

Circulation:
1st Sea Lord
CIGS
CAS
CCO
Defence Officer

PRO DEFE2 1276. *Crown copyright: reproduced with permission Controller HM Stationery Office.*

*

Rhine Reconnaissance

Interestingly one notes the First Sea Lord at the top of the distribution list. No one seems to have been in any doubt that this must be a combined operation, with Royal Navy participation, right from the start.

No archives survive on the Rhine reconnaissance. The testimony of a surviving participant confirms that it was entrusted to COPP5(1) under the command of Lieutenant A. H. Winship SANF(V) – known to his friends as Harvey.

Harvey Winship's number two was A. G. 'Peter' or 'Hamish' Hamilton; who has been kind enough to supply facts. The army officer in the team was Captain R. F. Preedy RE. The team probably also included Petty Officer Young, AB Armstrong and Lance Corporal Hinkley RE.

The most detailed secondary-source accounts state that the reconnaissance was made at Wesel, at twenty-four hours notice, on the night of 22/23 March 1945, in bright moonlight conditions – operating with 15th Scottish Division – without benefit of artillery cover. The batteries were in transit, being moved forward after several nights of bombardment. Even so, swimmers completed their reconnaissance, breasting a 4-knot current, without suffering casualties and checked the enemy bank for mines. They had to be right the first time as the assault was planned for the following day.

Operation *Plunder/Varsity* was executed as planned, on the night of 23/24 March, with a typical Montgomery prelude: a crushing artillery bombardment of over 3,000 guns, along a front of twenty-five miles. The 1st Commando Brigade made an attack with tracked amphibians and assault boats, in the area of Wesel at an H-hour of 0200. They made their landing almost undetected, infiltrated the town while the defenders were still dazed, and occupied almost all of it during the hours of darkness. At 1000 hours the airborne assault began, by British 6th Airborne Division and 17th US Division.

Mark 1** Folbot being handled by her crew, prior to launching from a beach.

Preparing to embark the swimmer – a training exercise in daylight.

Hammenheil, Jaffna, Ceylon, panoramic view by Basil Griffith.

Operation David – Captain F. Rodger RAMC, on right, Alec Colson squatting in front of him, aboard ML.

Jack Phillis in rickshaw.

Above: Alex Hughes, below: members of his COPP – both photographs at Jaffna.

Ruari McLean.

Geoff Lyne.

Alex Hughes.

Alex Hughes and Joan marry in Saint Andrew's Kirk, Kullupoijya, Ceylon.

COPP8, Inverlair, Christmas 1943.
Back Row: Rourke, Pond, Spence, Duffy. Middle Row: Peacock,
Richards, Ponsonby, Colson, Crafter. Front Row: Gascoigne,
Neil, Cumberland.

COPP7: Mike, Alec and Geoff
Richards holding Chota, the
monkey.

COPP7 and 8, Inverlair, Christmas 1943.

COPP7's LCP
which took them
to Rangoon.

COPP reunion 1977, at Hayling Island Sailing Club.

Earl Mountbatten of Burma KG, and plaque unveiled by him.

IN THIS BUILDING AND THE SURROUNDING WATERS THE
COMBINED OPERATIONS PILOTAGE PARTIES (COPP)
TRAINED FOR THEIR SECRET ROLE OF BEACH RECONNAISSANCE
AND ASSAULT PILOTAGE DURING THE YEARS 1942-45.
TO MARK THEIR REUNION AND IN MEMORY OF COMRADES
LOST IN ACTION THIS PLAQUE WAS UNVEILED ON 18th MARCH 1977
BY THE FORMER CHIEF OF COMBINED OPERATIONS,
ADMIRAL OF THE FLEET THE EARL MOUNTBATTEN OF BURMA K.G.

Nick Goodyear Secretary COPP Association, Willmott, Earl Mountbatten.

General Logan Scott-Bowden, Nigel Willmott and Earl Mountbatten, in background the Commodore's wife and Sheila Goodyear.

COPP reunion 1977, at Hayling Island Sailing Club: Earl Mountbatten of Burma KG, Nigel Willmott, Alec Colson, Petto Colson.

Geoffrey Galwey, Evelyn 'Kitten' Harbud, on left.

Earl Mountbatten, Nigel Willmott and Bruce and Sylvia Ogden Smith.

1977 COPP Reunion – Earl Mountbatten, Alex Hughes and Joan Hughes.

Nigel Willmott and Ronnie Williamson photographed alongside X-20, in Portsmouth, in 1989.

The run-up to COPP Operation Overlord operations.
COPPists and X-Craft personnel, photographed in civilian clothing, prior to D-Day. Individual portraits from this group were to be enlarged, to be attached to identity cards the French Underground would provide. Each man had to invent his own cover story. Back row: Bill Tebb, 'Billy' Fish, Jim Booth, Paul Clark, Ainsworth Davis, Bruce Ogden Smith and Granger. Front row: Arthur Briggs, Bruce Enzer, George Honour, Wren 'Kitten' Cross, Robin Harbud, Geoff Galwey and George Starn.

Elements of four other divisions were also involved. The COPP reconnaissance made a vital contribution to a major offensive. Montgomery later said he considered the attack across the Rhine an outstanding success.

Elbe Reconnaissance

The record of this operation is based on correspondence with surviving participants. The reconnaissance was entrusted to Lieutenant John Randolph Hashim RN. Hashim had begun the war as a midshipman. After commissioning he had seen service in HMS *Ajax*, collecting a mention in despatches, at the time of the Greek withdrawal. Following five months of COPP training, under Geoffrey Galwey – as has been seen – he had been sent out to Italy to relieve 'Fuzz' Fison in COPP2 – after S/COPP2 had been injured by a booby trap. During his period overseas a number of weeks were spent living with the Yugoslavs in Zara. A number of the teams completed a seven-drop parachute course in case this mode of delivery of a COPP team might be an advantage in the future. Returning to the United Kingdom he had reconstituted COPP7 – referred to as COPP7(1) in the tables. Hashim had as his second-in-command Lieutenant Alastair Ernest Henderson RN.

Around 16 April 1945 a signal was received at Hayling Island stating that COPP were required to survey the far side of the River Elbe. The team was augmented: Major J. B. Griffith brought along Company Sergent-Major Francis McNally. John Bowden, who was on leave, was recalled by telephone: he was not over pleased, as he'd been sunbathing on a beach with his fiancée when the news was received. Warned to report back to Hayling Island, he was told on arrival that he was joining Hashim's COPP7 because he was the only rating available with operational experience. The team weighed and packed their equipment and were taken to Thorney Island. They had been told that two C-47 Dakotas awaited them. In the event one only was used – somewhat overladen – the other one that had been ear-marked was dropping food to the Dutch population. They were flown to Celle, in Germany, complete with canoes. Celle is twenty-six miles north-east of Hanover. At Celle they transferred to an army 4-ton lorry and were driven for about four hours to a Brigade Headquarters. From here an advanced party went forward by jeep – and a two-mile walk, down a farm track – and reached the river bank, somewhere near to Luneburg. They observed the far bank through binoculars. Débris floating down the river gave an idea of the speed of its flow: it was *fast*. Given the choice of that night or the following, the team prayed for rain, wind or fog. The following night proved dead still – with crystal-clear moonlight. Plainly this would not be a classic reconnaissance-with-canoes and recovery by RG infra-red reception. It could only be a swim recce.

Hashim, Henderson and Griffith were all allocated separate objectives on the far bank to be investigated. Hashim today says he remembers little beyond the fact that the swimmers detonated no booby traps, proved none can have been floating in the water. Griffith and Hashim, Henderson believes, were both shot at. Griffith remembers being passed by evaders coming in the opposite direction.

Henderson remembers that he walked upstream about 1½ miles through grassland, then entered the water, an hour before midnight and swam silently, without moving his legs. He arrived at his intended destination; a small bay with a beached, flat-bottomed lighter. He wormed his way up the beach, taking samples and withdrew when he heard sentries voices. Halfway across, with his suit flooding badly he was obliged to jettison dagger, revolver and compass. He retained a whisky flask. He landed at about 0400: it was uncomfortably light. He had a good pull of whisky and walked up a steep bank to be challenged by a Glaswegian corporal with a small patrol. They were very suspicious, Griffith had drifted far downstream; he was in a different army command and did not know the password, taken to the corporal's CO at gunpoint he managed to establish his identity.

There must have been a fourth officer swimmer, as John Bowden went to the rescue of a Canadian RN officer, whose name he can no longer remember. After a low cry for help, he found him tangled in barbed wire, on the allied bank, with his ripped suit flooding . Walking back to forward base, in single file, both were almost shot: not having heard two challenges . . . . The officer gave the password: 'Kill the Hun!' on the third. John Bowden, bringing up the rear, was uncomfortably aware that he – a seaman – was in advance of British army forward positions.

On their return to Celle the party saw numerous pyjama-clad skeletons: newly released prisoners from nearby Belsen. The party were flown back to Thorney Island, cleared customs refusing to open boxes marked Secret Equipment, and were driven back to the Depot by Jenny Devitt. The requisite reports were made. This was the final COPP operation carried out in Europe; only a few weeks before the cease fire.

Whilst the United States 9th Army did establish a bridgehead at Magdeburg placing them only 50 miles from Berlin, for political reasons, no immediate major attack was made in the area reconnoitred by

Hashim's COPP. On 25 April 1945, however, Russian and American troops linked up at Torgau on the River Elbe.

SOURCES

Correspondence with former COPPists
Strutton and Pearson op cit
PRO DEFE2 1276 Combined Operations for crossing the Rhine
Geoffrey Galwey *Op cit*
JEWELL, Brian, *Over The Rhine, The Last Days of War in Europe*, Spellmount Ltd, Tunbridge Wells, 1985.
LADD, James *SBS The Invisible Raiders*, David and Charles, 1983.
WILLMOTT, Chester *The Struggle for Europe*, Collins, 1952.

CHAPTER TWENTY-FIVE

COPP10's Odyssey

C OPP10 was numerically the last team to be trained and sent overseas. By this stage in COPP's development, in order to recruit the right personnel for COPP teams, notices were being posted in naval barracks throughout the Fleet asking volunteers to put forward their names if they were prepared to undertake 'duties of a hazardous nature'. No indication was given of what those duties might be.

There is of course a long established view in the navy that one should never volunteer for anything; despite this an assorted bunch of volunteers came forward. Most of them were seen by Nigel Willmott at the Hayling Island COPP Depot – he easily spotted those who were volunteering simply to get away from what they were already in and discarded them. Inevitably they may have included the unlucky in love and those with death wishes. Many were rejected because they did not have the required experience or swimming ability. It's said that one candidate was accepted who had killed a Royal Marine after a run ashore and that the COPP CO's decision was proved right.

Army volunteers were inevitably keen types and frequently were prepared to accept a reduction in rank in order to be accepted. Naval volunteers were glad this did not apply to them. Whilst S/COPPs were required to be straight-lace Navigators or Hydrographers – extremely unusual for special service – other officers frequently came from Landing Craft flotillas and were, therefore, well aware just how difficult it was to find the right spot to put troops ashore – approaching a strange coast, on a dark night. Also how exasperated the soldiery might be, having trained for a particular operation, to be put ashore at some completely unrecognisable place.

Once Lieutenant (N) J. S. Townson had assembled his team, it was not long before his nickname 'Tanker' Townson became known. The team soon made contact with the Mark1** canoe, which was said to have been made by Harriss-Lebus and with the Mark III, marking canoe, said to have been designed by Uffa Fox and Chris Rattrey.

COPP10's training followed the usual pattern and began on Tuesday 1 June 1943. It was complete by Friday 24 September 1943. Whereupon all members proceeded on embarkation leave, prior to being sent overseas. They proceeded overseas on Tuesday 2 October 1943.

Before embarking on reconnaissance in the field, Tanker, Captain J. C. Lamb RE Commando SBS and Lieutenant A. E. Stanley tried out their swimsuits – they experimented with tying the bulky trouser legs so that they didn't flap about – it worked. The best rig seemed to be skin-tight trousers and the blouse buttoned on to the trousers. Wearing a thin vest underneath served to keep the swimmer warm. The kapok lining had sufficient flotation to keep the swimmer afloat. This, no doubt, was the tropical suit, an early 'wet suit'; which was not watertight. Townson reassured the party that all was working well by taking a line of soundings 110-yards long.

*

Some of COPP10 had a remarkable trip out to India. Hugh Maynard, A/M COPP10 has provided a remarkable record in an account written c1948. He and Alf Stanley and five ratings were taken to Poole by Pam Glencross. After a night in a Bournemouth hotel and a false start, the party – in civilian clothes – took off in a BOAC Boeing flying boat. They refuelled at Foynes, where they sampled Irish coffee, wandered round the town before flying on to Lisbon, at that time popularly believed to be the espionage capital of Europe. Here they enjoyed bright lights and an absence of blackout, but encountered no blonde spies.

The next flight with pineapple, bacon-and-egg and bananas in-flight refreshments took them to Bathurst. It was now very warm in the plane and they changed into tropical uniform. On landing they had much needed showers and decided to go for a swim in the local siesta time. They soon found a sandy beach with Atlantic rollers. Used to hardening they went in skinny-dipping, only to be warned by one of their aircraft's crew of the local Barracuda and its propensities. Happily all survived unbitten and repaired back to their hotel for a two-hour meal of unfamiliar food that included Paw Paw. Their next flight was to Lagos – where they saw the local fire brigade attending a 'shout' on a modern appliance, in loin cloths and brass helmets. In an open-air cinema they saw the film *Casablanca*. After a short night's rest they took off for Leopoldville. This time in a Sunderland flying boat, in which many passengers seemed to be VIPs. Stanleyville and the marvellous Stanley Falls and Khartoum followed in quick succession. Then came the final lap to Cairo. After the pyramids, Groppi's and Shepheards Hotel, Bahrein, on the Persian Gulf, was their next stop. Then on to Karachi; and a 3-day train journey to Cocanada, where they found COPP7 and 8 already in residence.

*

At Cocanada they experimented, strapping their canoes under the wings of flying boats and the personnel did parachute-jumping courses. They were disappointed to find their canoes broke up trying to get in to land over big surf; so they trained in the use of surf boards. They had every expectation of moving up to Burma.

This was not to be, before long Hugh Maynard was back in Karachi awaiting the arrival of the rest of the party. Then followed an uncomfortable Dakota flight to Beirut, where they celebrated the New Year. From there to Alexandria in a 3-ton lorry. Then another Dakota flight to Naples, with a refuelling stop at Benghazi then to Ischia and the chateau Mezza Torre.

There was an initial hiccough, when the building containing all their stores (laboriously collected from Naples) went up in flames: assumed to be the work of a German raiding party. Thereafter operating out of Ischia during most of 1944: they carried out thirty-one operations, reconnoitring and marking the Anzio beaches, using the Mark III canoe with outriggers. They added to the canoe's stability when one was climbing out or in, but its mainly balsa construction was a disadvantage if rammed by a Landing Craft (Assault). 'Gus' Talbot found the Landing Craft (Rockets) impressive: 900 rocket projectiles, each equivalent to a 4-inch shell, not only did they neutralise the opposition, but they also set-off some of the beach mines. Eventually, with the task over, the markers transferred to a small ship which took them back to Mezze Torre. During their stay in Ischia they saw nearby Vesuvius erupt and Hugh Maynard and Gus Talbot enlivened the evenings with the chateau's grand piano and a homemade double bass.

Thence to Maddelena, a small island between Sicily and Sardinia. It had a convenient small harbour and they were able to use their Combined Operations Police Patrol cover. Before long they were ordered to pack up and depart by lorries to Bari. From Bari they crossed the Adriatic to Vis, from where they made surveys of Adriatic Islands for Tito's partisans, preparatory to retaking the individual islands with a combined force of RN landing craft and partisans. Meanwhile MTBs patrolled the inshore shipping lanes, keeping them free of enemy ships. Many running battles ensued.

On Mljet a COPP10 party watched two Germans making a COPP-type survey from a canoe. On one of the raids Hugh Maynard discovered that the CO of the LCI was none other than (Sir) Alec Guinness. They had been to school together.

Alfie Stanley and George Talbot left with their rating teams and went on separate missions into Albania. They had a lively time and it was some time before the whole party met up again in Athens.

Surveys and raids continued at a rate of about one per week until all the islands up to Split were re-taken.

*

A most memorable raid was the recapture of the harbour on the island of Korkula. An LCI with a false funnel rigged, looking like a frigate, patrolled backwards and forwards within range of German batteries on the Peljesac Peninsula, firing blank ammunition with lots of smoke. Meanwhile other landing craft landed field guns onto a beach, from where they could fire over a hill into the harbour. For a while firing from the beach synchronised with the 'frigate's' fire. When they realised the deception the Germans promptly got the range and bracketed the LCI, which withdrew unhit. They then opened fire, with shrapnel shells on the beach field-gun party – and that party were withdrawn inevitably with serious casualties. The harbour installation was badly damaged, however, and the German E-boats fled and did not return. The story demonstrates the variety of tactics that were necessary in the islands' *guerre de course.*

Hugh Maynard and his wife visited Korkula in recent years and found a touching memorial tablet in the town square.

*

Months later the remainder of the party was ordered back to Greece and billeted in naval barracks at Piraeus. In the course of the Greek civil war that erupted Leading Seaman Harding was shot dead in an outbreak of crossfire. He was buried at sea, with full naval honours, in the Gulf of Corinth. After that, detailed to go to Salonika, through heavily-mined waters, they sailed there by caique, with all their stores. They arrived after the Germans had left and acted as beachmasters for a large fleet of troop carriers. In Salonika Hugh Maynard celebrated his twenty-first birthday. With the landings successfully completed, 'Tanker' Townson, S/COPP10, was ordered to hand over his command to Lieutenant Harvey Winship SANFV. By 22 December 1944 Townson's party was back in England, for leave, return to the Depot and paying off. In all their tour of operations had covered Italy, Yugoslavia, Dalmatia and Greece.

SOURCES

Imperial War Museum

COPP10's Boxes – George R. Talbot DSC, RNVR.

Unofficial Semi-Official *Log-Journal of COPP10*, Naval Party 745 (First Commission) in training and in India and mainly in the Mediterranean Sea especially Adriatic and Ionian, from 1943 onwards. Property of Commander J. S. Townson DSC, RN, loaned by his wife, Mrs Nation.

MAYNARD, Hugh manuscripts: *My Trip to India – November 1943* (written c1948), and *COPP10* (written 1994).

CHAPTER TWENTY-SIX

COPP3(1) under Alex Hughes

A recommissioned COPP3(1) sailed for the Far East, aboard a troopship which before the war had been called SS *Strathaird*, on Sunday 16 July 1944 – six weeks after the Normandy D-Day landings – under the command of Lieutenant Alex Hughes RNR. The London Gazette gives his name as Alexander Hughes – though some of his postwar friends knew him as Ian Hughes – and his home town as Pittenweem, Fife. Fife is a peninsular Scots county, bounded by the Firths of Tay and Forth, and by the North Sea. Certainly Alex was Scots and spoke with a slight Scots accent.

When the new COPP3(1) sailed, Alex was just turned thirty-years of age, and therefore almost ten-years older than some of the ratings in his party. All in all, his attitude was a pretty mature one. He believed in, and in his personal diary championed the reserve officer's viewpoint, as opposed to that of RN, permanent officers, as he saw it. Briefly, Alex felt, the reservist view amounted to doing one's duties, but avoiding any pointless worrying or brooding. He had met some permanent officers who seemed to him unable, or unwilling to relax, between sorties. Alex knew – none better – that his party were well trained and would be needed for action at short notice – therefore, whilst awaiting orders, his credo was: relax, keep fit and carry out training exercises and equipment maintenance . . . and development of improved operating techniques . . . . Above all, on no account, brood on what the next assignment *might* be.

*

Alex was popular with his officers and non-commissioned team members. He got results in his own way and had the gift of handling people of all ranks. Before the war he had been in the Merchant Navy, had sailed with the Clan Line all over the world and had plenty of experience of navigation. That, of course, had appealed to Nigel Willmott. When Alex came to COPP he had given up the plum job of navigator in the escort aircraft carrier HMS *Slinger* to do so. So that Nigel had no doubts on that score. Alex readily accepted the aphorism that 'Some people would rather die than think'. He was used to doing his own thinking and had survived almost five years of war. If he found, 'in the field' that he could improve on what the team had been trained to do, he'd do just that. Interestingly he has contributed a very detailed picture of what life was like in COPP3, as he left behind a diary kept – strictly against regulations – at the time. Before drawing upon that source, however, it will be necessary to sketch briefly Alex's war, up to the time he came to COPP.

One of the so-called 'Hungry Hundred', Alex had entered the Royal Naval Reserve before the outbreak of war. He had been appointed (probationary) sub-lieutenant on 29 March 1939: probably he avoided being a midshipman because he was already twenty-four years of age and held a master's ticket. As RNR he had trained at the 'stone frigate' HMS *St Vincent*. After a brief spell at HMS *Appledore*, he'd joined the escort aircraft carrier HMS *Slinger* (Captain A. N. C. Bingley OBE, RN), on her commissioning. *Slinger* had been constructed in the United States by the Willamette Iron and Steel Corporation, Portland, Oregon. Her commissioning took place on 11 August 1943. Mr Austin F. Flegel, Vice President of the Willamette Steel Corporation, had handed the vessel over to Captain L. D. Whitgrove USN, thereafter Old Glory had been played, before Captain Whitgrove handed over to Captain Bingley, whereupon the steel corporation band had played God Save the King and the commissioning pennant had been broken. A religious service, with singing of 'Eternal Father, strong to save', had completed the ceremony.

It seems possible that Alex had had his fill of big ships when he volunteered for special service. Evidently he realised that service in a COPP could provide a more exciting contribution to the war effort, than could any sea-going command he might be offered. He left Britain well briefed on operating difficulties any COPP party might encounter in the field. He was undeterred and proved before long that he could handle staff officers as well as Japanese coastal defences.

COPP3 had arrived at Hammenheil Camp, Jaffna, Ceylon, on Tuesday 3 October 1944, the day the German Messerschmitt 262 became operational in Europe. Soon after their arrival group photographs were taken. In these Alex, alone among the party appears deeply tanned. He strikes a relaxed, confident pose, pipe in hand, wearing a wide grin. For a man of thirty his face is quite deeply lined, the face one might say, of a man who knows how to work and play hard – and who knows he has a good team – all keen – and that he can count on them. In training he'd made sure they knew that he'd never call on them to do anything he couldn't do himself.

Perhaps to parody the 'professional' attitude of the straight-lace RN officers he was even prepared to talk politics. He made no secret of the fact that he had leanings towards the left – to the Commonwealth Unionist Party, indeed he was keen to be its leader – this was frankly unconventional, at a time when politics was a taboo subject in most ward rooms. But then COPPs were unlike big ships.

*

The account that follows is based on Alex Hughes's diary of the period: written at the time – against orders – in manuscript on foolscap paper and subsequently clipped into a ring-back folder. It is a vivid account conveying the flavour of the period and the views of a perhaps untypical reservist: by anyone's standards an extremely brave and human person. Inevitably it is almost certainly the most detailed contemporary record of any COPP party's operational tour in the Far Eastern theatre. It conveys not only what it felt like to go on an operational sortie, but also the inevitable frustrations of dealing with planners, top brass and the problems of organising day-to-day depot routine between sorties.

*

Arthur Ruberry was to sum up COPP3's Far Eastern Tour, almost fifty years later by saying: 'I don't know why we got the key recces. Alex was a very experienced navigator, and being Royal Naval Reserve, he was very enthusiastic. At Hammenheil Camp he was "well in" with the Commandant of the SOG (Small Operations Group) Colonel H. T. Tollemache RM'.

Perhaps Alex was 'well in' because he never said no to an operation. Any suggestion that anyone else previously had tended to whet his appetite for action. Early on at Hammenheil he met 'Blondie' Hasler of the Bordeaux 'Cockleshell Heroes' raid – the 2i/c and now operating as development officer at the SOG. Hasler, Hughes, Major Maxwell RM and 'Canada' Alcock went to China Bay for discussions with the Dutch

Catalina flying-boat pilots as to whether a folbot canoe could be fitted into a Catalina. It would fit they found, provided a few holes were cut in the aircraft.

Landing in enemy waters near coasts would pose problems: because of the swell and the difficulty of making accurate navigational pin-points. Nor were the pilots keen on operating in the conditions ideal for COPP operations – moonless nights – they would have preferred last light . . . sadly that would increase risk of compromise of the COPP party. One pilot, whose name Alex records as Wundai, an oldish chap by his standards was keen to do the job. He confided he had put down some special parties before, 'but none have ever come back . . . .' Alex decided that this didn't put him off, and that if SEAC HQ were prepared to approve the scheme, he would do it. It was agreed the scheme should be put up for SEAC approval.

At this stage Alex records that Lieutenant D. H. Mackay RN left the camp for Kandy to discuss another op. Lieutenant Freddie Ponsonby RN, CO of COPP8 had already left with his whole party for detached service in Burma. A rumour caused a flap that Alex's party was off there too. Alex checked with Tollemache who shook his head cryptically. He went on to discuss the Catalina experiments and said he thought SEAC would accept their proposals. In fact experiments with folbots and an engineless Catalina and a Sunderland flying boat were conducted in a Scottish loch. With units as secret as COPP it was inevitable that there should be some unknowing re-invention of the wheel.

Alex had another radical notion: why not a fast surface craft, towing a smaller one, or carrying it on davits? Rather like the idea of the Mayo Composite aircraft, one might say. The great thing was that coastal approaches of over 40-miles would no longer be a problem. The all important thing was that the COPP party's time ashore should not be limited by slow 'carrier' vessels. Time ashore was all important if they were to bring back the sort of information the Staff planners wanted.

Whilst awaiting SEAC's answer COPP3 listened to talks by Captain D. C. Hill, and by Majors R. P. Livingstone and D. H. Sidders – both of SBS – on their recent operations. Sidders was particularly graphic: on an operation to blow-up a railway bridge, in northern Sumatra, he'd met up with trains and natives. He'd captured five of the latter; and not wishing to kill them, had fed them chewing gum until the operation was complete. Asked about Japs the natives screwed up their faces disapprovingly – but did precisely the same questioned about the British. Sidders' 'carrier' submarine had been HMS/M *Turbulent*, and she'd sunk a German U-boat on the way back – all in all it sounded a first-class patrol.

Livingstone's party had not reached their objective because of bad surf and had to return home empty-handed. Arthur Ruberry, the COPP3 coxswain had by now returned from sick-bay, and this faced Alex with another problem: Arthur had been his paddler. In his absence Alex had used Sub-Lieutenant A. J. Thomas DSM, RNVR. Both Thomas and the 'swain were both keen types and neither wanted to give the job up. Thomas was very experienced, but Ruberry was a first-class paddler and had never lost Alex. Alex decided therefore, to keep Arthur and hold Thomas as an all-round first-reserve substitute.

All the COPP3 personnel were keen and Alex's diary records that they seemed more worried by a lack of beer or mail from home – than the prospect of meeting Japs.

On Friday 4 October 1944 Alex organised a day spent assembling canoes and discussing where best equipment should be stowed. This was heresy, of course, depot staff decreed that standard practice was the result of operational experience, and must not be deviated from. Alex was independent enough to want to experiment in the hope of increasing operational efficiency. Some small fittings were changed, unofficially and sub-rosa. Alex laid on homing exercises, knowing full well that the appearance of coast land would change radically when darkness fell. He impressed on the personnel that planning and careful advanced preparation – plus complete faith in the method adopted – were essential. He blessed his own navigational experience at night. He knew that anyone in a canoe, experiencing doubts would hesitate, and as a result probably miss a rendezvous.

Next day Alex was completely surprised to find himself discussing the pros and cons of Nationalization and his political aims with Tollemache. Tollemache shared his view that a greater emphasis on spiritual values could help in the present world. It came as quite a surprise.

That night a full-night's exercise enabled Alex to decide which canoe teams would be most reliable for the Catalina operation. He was glad to have Arthur Ruberry back as his paddler, and confided to his diary that he knew precisely where he was with him. He also confided his personal credo:

If it is possible it *is* done – if impossible it *shall* be done . . . .

Meanwhile, still awaiting the elusive call to action, COPP3 personnel devoted themselves to development of canoes and spares. Most of the team had hobbies. M/COPP3, Alan Hood, devoted himself entirely to gardening. By contrast Alex liked to potter: doing small jobs to the tent, writing a little, painting the odd board, or laying a path to the billet door ... no one task was essential, but all were an enjoyable way of passing base-life time.

Come Sunday, once Divisions and prayers were over, he had a stimulating argument with Major Livingstone of SBS on Nationalization: expounding his prescient view that the final choice would be between nationalization and the corporate state.

Tollemache had taken the aircraft trials' report to Kandy. Alex dearly wished he could have taken it himself: he liked to cut corners, do things himself – not through channels – and to prompt snap decisions. To put this out of his mind he diverted COPP3 with an evening of classical gramophone music. Secretly he was by now convinced that future operations must be a duel of wits – not do-or-die business. He'd picked up a disquietening note from a newspaper: the Commonwealth Party was seeking TUC affiliation. Alex hoped this would not mean that Sir Richard Acland and his supporters were in any way prepared to sell out.

Friday 13 October passed with a picnic exploring Delft Island (35 square miles) populated by Tamils and one Belgian Catholic priest; the only European in the place. The residents provided eggs and/or coconuts and Alex made omelettes for the party as COPP personnel played with the residents' children. The Belgian chatted interestingly of how the caste system operated. In a drought, if their well ran dry, the higher castes would wait by the untouchables' well – in the hope one might, in Christian charity, draw water for them. They dare not defile themselves by touching his well.

Back at Hammenheil, the day ended with a showing of the film *Fanny by Gaslight*, with James Mason, Stewart Granger and Phyllis Calvert. Alex's diary notes that it was a change for living in sin not to be given its just reward. He was probably unaware that the book, by Michael Sadlier, had a less happy ending than the film. The other film was about War Savings and Alex found its message trite and over-simplified.

Two days later Tollemache was back from Kandy but none of the naval parties were sent for. Instead COPP3 received TABT booster innoculations and 'Canada' Alcock suffered a bad reaction. The day ended with yet-another flap about a mislaid code book – found eventually.

Then followed a week of periscope ciné-photography in Trincomalee, then back to Hammenheil, then back to Trinco' for aircraft trials. Flight Lieutenant McKeand, a Catalina captain, had done some special service work for SOE. They had a long talk and Alex felt sure he could do the job. McKeand wasn't keen to have holes cut in his aircraft, but suggested a new canoe – one that could be easily constructed locally – and which would *fit* in the Catalina. It seemed promising.

Less encouraging was a disquietening report that Mike Peacock, Freddie Ponsonby's A/COPP in COPP8 was missing believed drowned. But a possibility existed that he could have been caught. There had been surf on the beach concerned, though not as heavy as at Onchaung. The surf problem was a long way from being solved, Alex said in his diary.

A diversion was the circulation of lists offering the chance to sign on for future service. Typically Alex declined with a rider that he might change his mind, depending on where he was and when, if the conditions were right.

By 10 November 1944, after Alex had sat on a Board of Enquiry, he led three, two-man canoes on a night exercise: himself and Arthur Ruberry: 'Canada' Alcock and Turner; and Thomas and Fred Cammidge. They had to be got off the beach in an ML, in foul weather and a heavy swell. When they transhipped to their canoes Alex felt queasy and was sick; Thomas and Cammidge were worse affected and kept on being sick. Alex decided that they had to be got to dry land pronto. He headed for the nearest beach undeterred by much spindrift, heavy swell and surf. By dint of paddling like mad, he and Ruberry got through it and ended up, as Alex put it: high and fairly dry. Finding a sandy spot he waved in 'Canada's' canoe which had the sick canoe in tow. The sick men were loaded into an RAF lorry, and taken to sick-bay for the night. The remaining canoes put to sea again, through the surf and back to base. Next morning Thomas and Cammidge were fit again.

Two days later the camp had to be organised for an expected visit by Lord Mountbatten. Alex was also mulling over the prospect of some leave and surfing at Arugam Bay. He'd practically forgotten about leave: one's duties in a total war, he confided to his diary took away essential liberties and, almost, one's freedom of thought. Fitting back into civilian life, he reckoned, would be difficult . . . one might almost miss the need for security and the restrictions governing one's present life . . . .

On 16 November 1944, Alex considered an ENSA concert poor: too much emphasis on sex and smutty songs. It was enthusiastically received by an audience of some one hundred, probably frustrated marines. A chance for adult education, Alex considered, sadly missed. He vented his spleen by playing Rachmaninoff on the gramophone.

*

Four days later Denis Mackay and Alex attempted a leave trip to Arugam Bay. They left at 0830, in a heavily-laden 15-cwt truck, but punctured after the first hour. This left them with a frustrating stop at Jaffna awaiting another truck, from the camp, with a replacement tyre. With a fresh tyre they drove on, stopping only to eat corned-beef sandwiches at lunchtime. These nauseated them and they may have thought enviously of the rest of the party – proceeding to Colombo by sea. At Kandy, finding they had nowhere to sleep, they filled up and pressed on towards Posselawa, in a heavy downpour. Tired of stopping at every crossroads, they drove in reckless haste up narrow mountain roads, scarcely realising the risks they ran. After a bath, a good dinner and a bed at Posselawa, they made an early start climbing about 4,000 feet in three hours. Alex found the moors at first reminiscent of Scotland, but changed his mind on finding the hills a mass of plantations, decided the scenery had a beauty of its own. At the summit they found Nuwara Eliya – a lovely place, in bright sunlight. Then came rain and the truck began to give trouble outside Bandarwela. By now they had a driver and, when the dashboard caught alight, Alex and Mackay baled out and left him to keep guard. They walked on through the rain finding all garages shut, but managed to ring the Camp Commandant at Dyatalawa Naval Rest Centre, persuading him to send a three-tonner with a tow-rope. It wouldn't pull the 15-cwt truck up the hills. So they gave up and went off in the three-tonner in search of dinner. Instead, finding the RASC prepared to send a break-down truck, they went back with it and recovered their stores. Then they had a bath and dinner, finding it cold at 5,000 feet altitude.

With the truck repaired – a burnt-out coil replaced – next day they were off again. After miles of breath-taking scenery, that no artist could paint, they made it to Arugam Bay . . . for a single day. After that, a rush back to Nalanda, just north of Kandy, brought frustration: Lord Mountbatten's visit had been delayed a week. In due course a demonstration was arranged to show Lord Louis what COPP did. Commander Austin, who represented COPP at Combined Operations HQ, settled lots of problems and Alex left for a fortnight's relaxation away from signals, orders and, as he wrote in the diary, marines.

Alex's fortnight finished almost before it had begun, with the arrival of a despatch rider with a recall signal and orders for COPP3 to relieve COPP8 in Burma. By 12 December, COPP3 stores were again packed on a lorry and sent to Kankesanturai aerodrome. Then Alex rushed around collecting money, getting bills paid, then to the airfield and taking-off, in a Dakota, for Madras. The party were all fit except for

'Canada' Alcock, laid low by a stomach ailment. Alex felt sorry for Mackay, who had seen the party off at KKS (Kankesanturai); he'd been there four months longer than they had. And they were off on a job.

COPP3 landed in Madras, flew to Calcutta, spent the night there and flew off for Chittagong, with Comilla as a staging post. Here their aircraft went unserviceable. When they took-off in another, they left three angry-looking brigadiers on the tarmac, probably wondering why this party of seamen's priority overrode their own. At Chittagong the Naval Officer in Charge staff knew nothing about their coming. Alex scrounged a jeep and screamed about organising transport and sleeping accommodation. He also got 'Canada' into hospital, secretly cursing him for having tried to carry on and say nothing, despite being sick on the way up.

By mid-December things were better. COPP3 was at Rejukhal – a tiny spit of land between Cox's Bazaar and the Naaf River, 45-miles distant from Teknaf. Here an unexpected windfall: they took over all COPP8's stores. Alex set to work getting the place altered to COPP3's ways, once Freddie Ponsonby's COPP8 personnel had left: everyone would mess together, that meant a single cook could cater for the lot. It was typical that Alex should regard this as essential; it was far more usual for COPP officers to mess separately from the ratings and military other ranks – even if they had the same cook. Freddie Ponsonby, in fact, stayed on doing his staff job at NCF 64.

Things began to settle down, though Captain D. C. Hill RN remained NCF 64, Admiral B. C. S. Martin CBE, DSO, Force W, seemed to take over most of the action. Captain W. E. F. Johns RE went off to Teknaf to draw the cigarettes and wine ration. The joint messing arrangements were working well. 'Canada' would be out of hospital in five days. Alex made a note to keep him off booze till he was fully recovered. By now COPP3 had cups, saucers, gin, beer and wine. What else was needed? Alex went on his travels and came back with a truck a telephone and two native boys to cook and wash up.

Swimming practice would toughen the party up; so Alex insisted their day began with all personnel swimming 400-yards across a chaung. It had a current: exactly what they needed. Explosives were used to catch fish; and the boys laid on fish-and-chip suppers. Captain Hill and his Chief-of-Staff, Commander Hughes, RN (no relation to Alex Hughes) might have gone to Colombo and, as a result, 'the war came to a standstill', but Alex was blowed if training should stop.

The party had acquired Jasper, a goose, earmarked for Christmas dinner, but fast becoming one of the family . . . it looked as though no one would be able to face killing him. None the less everyone cut firewood and stockpiled it for Christmas. Just before Christmas COPP3 were briefed for their next – or rather first job – the Catalina job had sunk without a trace. Beyond saying it was a good one, Alex confided no details of it to his diary.

Christmas was celebrated with Jasper smoked in a petrol can, by the Indian cook. He was a skilled culinary artist, before the war he'd worked in a Bombay hotel. COPP3 ate it alfresco, with lots of wine, rum punch and a midnight bathe before coffee. Arthur Ruberry considered their army rum as good as pusser's naval rum. It probably was, they all had blinding headaches and the sunlight seemed far too bright, on the morrow.

They learned the sobering thought that Geoff Richards M/COPP8 had been killed in a fall from a train near to Madras: very bad luck after eighteen months service. He'd been a picturesque chap, with a flaming-red beard and a pet monkey, called Chota. He'd done a parachute course and believed an M/COPP should be as operational as the rest of the party.

In his last 1944 entry Alex commented that the Allied advance along the coast was proceeding fast; with few Jap defenders being encountered. That could mean that the Japs were quitting North Burma, or scheming to cut-off the Allied advance. Either way, there was the prospect that COPP3 might at last find action. All preparations had been undertaken for an anticipated D-Day of 9 January 1945.

SOURCES

Imperial War Museum
Lieutenant-Commander A. I. Hughes DSC, RD, RNR (Retd) archive
COURTNEY, G. B. *The SBS in WW II*, Robert Hale, 1983

CHAPTER TWENTY-SEVEN

COPP3(1): Akyab, Myebon, the Stakes

Events moved faster than Alex Hughes had anticipated: on Saturday 30 December he was summoned by telephone, at 0100, and told to report to Cox's Bazaar – 25-miles away – immediately. On arrival he was asked to do a reconnaissance of Akyab Island, for a landing in four-days' time. He rushed back and started to get gear ready; only to be called back to Force *W* and given details of the set-up – plans and information required.

In order to cover the naval and military aspects of the reconnaissaance, two canoes were embarked on *ML 855*: operational teams to be Alex and Ruberry, for the naval side; and Johns and Cammidge, for the military objectives. Both parties transhipped to their canoes and proceeded to a rock, about a mile from the nearest Jap defensive positions. On beaching Alex thought he saw fresh tracks; he cocked his Tommy gun and scouted around, but no-one was there. He examined the 'tracks' again and decided they were the result of a curious rock formation; not of human origin. They carried out the recce, hauled the canoes onto the rock and camouflaged them and settled down to wait. At high water their rock was only three-feet above water; even so the party contrived, with pieces of driftwood to make their canoes look like rock formations. Thus, without ceremony, 1945 was quietly ushered in. As Alex put it:

No Old Lang Syne, no clock chimes – just darkness and quiet . . . on a rock.

Next day the whole party lay hidden and Alex did a panoramic sketch of the invasion beaches and tried to gather tidal information, concluding that charts and pilot information for the area were hopelessly wrong.

After dark both canoes paddled out and made rendezvous with *ML 855* and were taken back to Teknaf. Alex reported his findings to Force W and was given the job of leading in the assault.

On 2 January 1945 an assault convoy formed up after dark bound for its target: Akyab. It sailed next day. There were reports that the Japs were abandoning the area, but it would be folly to suppose this might be an unopposed landing. Alex and 'Canada' were with the first wave of LCAs (Landing Craft Assault); though not in the same craft. That way, if Alex was hit, 'Canada' could carry on and take over.

Alex knew the order of battle: the spearhead was two waves each of twelve LCAs carrying the 3rd Special Service Brigade (Commandos), followed by the 19th (Bengal) Lancers, in Sherman Tanks; the follow-up waves would be from 74th Brigade (including Oxfordshire and Bucks Regiment), then the 51st and 53rd Brigades and 25th Indian Division.

The force touched down at H-1, 1235. The Commandos rushed the beach, but the Japs were moving fast and were gone. Landing craft were handled well and before long troops, tanks and transport were pouring ashore. They had bomber and fighter cover, as well as destroyer and cruiser escort. Alex Hughes jumped ashore and met up with Alcock. They sounded a passage for the LCTs (Landing Craft Tanks) – which drew more than the LCAs – and marshalled them in. Alex jumped onto the first tank ashore and told the tank commander he was to survey Akyab harbour. Travel by tank seemed only sensible. Four-miles ashore, however, he was told that orders had come through: no one was to enter Akyab, but to form up outside whilst patrols scouted ahead. Disappointed Alcock and Hughes walked and hitch-hiked their way back to the beach and boarded the HQ ship for the night, travelling back on the destroyer HMS *Nepal*.

On their return Force *W* expressed satisfaction at the COPP3 role. Alex met some of the top brass: Admiral Martin; Captain E. W. Bush DSO**, DSC, RN, Chief of Staff; Commander Pumphrey DSO**, DSC, Staff Officer Operations; Lieutenant-Commander Williamson 'N'; Lieutenant-Commander O'Brien Staff Officer Plans; Lieutenant Bremner Forward Observation Officer. Alex noted both Bush and Pumphrey were triple-DSO, plus-DSC types and easy to work with. It was rumoured that Bush had earned his first DSO, as a midshipman, at Gallipoli. Hughes expounded his gospel across: that not everything can be worked out in advance on a plotting board, when dealing with beach assaults: that snap decisions, on half-information, have to be made – and they must be right. He found them charming and prepared to listen.

*

On 6 January Alex was signalled to take three canoes and equipment, to Teknaf and to be ready to operate around 10 January 1945. He found Mackay and his COPP4 party at Teknaf. Furious packing ensued and at last Mackay's and COPP3 stores were all packed up and loaded on to an LCI (Landing Craft Infantry) which sailed for Akyab.

Akyab they found devastated after Japanese occupation: houses had collapsed and jungle was growing in the streets. The harbour was chaotic with sunken ships. COPP3 moved into the midship section of a ship – or rather wreck – alongside the jetty. As her bridge deck was above water, Alex judged it would make a satisfactory, if crowded home. At least till the next move, which would probably be soon.

On 9 January 1945, Mackay and COPP4 were off with four canoes to sound out a river ahead of an assault force. Alex had let him take his canoe, since Mackay's was not assembled. Alex had been warned he'd be doing a job next morning.

*

At 1900 a boat came alongside and asked for Alex. They'd been searching for him all over the harbour. The Special Service Brigadier and the Naval Planners wanted a job done – he was told no details – just shown a chart and asked would he do it. Alex agreed, not knowing what the job was, hoping against hope that he could borrow sufficient equipment. In time in the course of discussion the true nature of the proposed operation emerged. The task was to breech a line of wooden stakes, to clear a passage for landing craft, and in passing to test the softness of the mud in the area, to ascertain whether it was suitable for the passage of troops and vehicles. Though offered specially sharpened saws, Alex opted for plastic explosive, and lead-creep 6-hour delay, time-pencils – all there were. The party would also be carrying twenty-eight 2-lb charges of Nobel 808, each charge fitted with a Cordtex connection, to link it to a Cordtex ring main. The stakes were situated on a shore on the southern tip of the Myebon Peninsula. To preserve the element of surprise there must be no preliminary reconnaissance . . . it promised to be quite a party.

*

On the night of 11-12 January three canoe teams left in *ML 854* and steamed to Hunters Bay, arriving at 2145. The ML anchored three-miles offshore. Alex had wanted to go in closer, but the night was quiet and

ML noises seemed alarmingly loud. The three canoes: Alex and Ruberry; Alcock and Turner; and Johns and Cammidge, had a back-breaking run-in, against the ebb tide. By the time Alex made it ashore his hands were covered in blisters and he'd have been glad to rest up and weep. In fact, he knew there could be no rest or hesitation: their task was to destroy some of the stakes on the beach and so make way for assault landing craft. The party grounded their canoes and made their way over the soft mud that covered the area to where the stakes were situated. The stakes proved to be solid teak, 12-inches in diameter, and covered in barnacles. Probably they were fishing stakes; unquestionably they formed an impenetrable barrier. Working in the dark and unaware that their hands were becoming cut all over they fixed a total of twenty-five charges, connected them up to a Cordtex fuse ring-main; then initiated the time delays.

As the tide had receded they found they had to drag their canoes over 150-yards of mud, with noisy squelching and sucking noises. To Alex it seemed that any moment they'd be coned by a searchlight and a machine gun would open up: they'd have looked pretty stupid: up to their waists in mud . . . . Alex spoke sharply to Alcock and Turner – the last two team members to finish placing charges – in a stage whisper: that the easiest method to cross mud was on hands-and-knees, and that the noise they were making was enough to waken the dead. Turner loyally dropped flat on his face and crawled.

They were back at the ML by 0145, steamed down the river and reported to the Force Commander, Captain M. H. St L. Nott RIN, aboard HMIS *Narbada*. Hughes found himself repeatedly cross-examined (a) about the charges: was he certain they'd go-off? (b) about the mud, and (c) about what he'd seen on the beach – nothing. The party on the bridge were on tenterhooks until 0630, when the first charges were due to go-off. From then on Alex found himself sweating profusely until 0640 when they heard the first of several explosions.

At 0730 Alex boarded *ML-380* and piloted the assault craft in to the beach. It was plain their demolitions had taken out all of twenty-three stakes plenty to get the first waves through. The Japs gave them a hot reception with medium machine-gun fire and mortars; it wasn't like Akyab. The RAF contributed a spectacular bombing attack. And a cruiser, a destroyer and several sloops engaged the enemy with gunfire. The MLs did their bit too. Alex metaphorically took off his hat to them: completely unarmoured they seemed to think nothing of steaming up a river with Jap defences on both sides.

Once back at the wreck there was gear to be cleaned and generally improving the COPP3 billet, whilst awaiting the next job. Alex organised 'wash decks' and the erection of a canvas screen around the 'heads': one of the poop hatches, with a glass scuttle knocked out. COPP3's morale and health couldn't have been better after their successful stakes job. All personnel were terribly bucked about it.

*

On 17 January another interesting job was in prospect. Orders came to leave Akyab with canoes. Off Myebon, they settled in on the assault beach and prepared for a job that night, at Daingbon Chaung.

At 1900 they left aboard *HDML 1275*, with *LCA 44* (Lieutenant Bowdler RINVR) in tow and proceeded up river reaching the Jap-occupied area by darkness. After they had grounded twice on the mud, Alex decided they were wasting time and the party transferred to the LCA. They had one Bren gun, five Tommy guns – one for each canoe – and one Lanchester carbine. The chaungs had never been charted for depth of channel: so they had to feel their way. On sighting a vessel ahead Hughes altered course towards the shore for cover. The other boat was close – about thirty yards – plainly they'd been seen, for it altered to starboard. Hughes countered by steering hard-a-starboard and rammed the other vessel's stern. He'd already ordered: 'Stand to, but no shooting unless attacked.' The other craft was now visible as an armoured sampan, it drew away down the chaung with the four visible members of her crew screaming their heads off. She had guns fore and aft, but no stomach for fight. Her crew had either decided they were an ordinary river craft or too heavily armoured to take on. The LCA watched her go, fully expecting her to return to investigate.

At about 2330 their objective had been reached and the canoes went off to investigate. Mooring the LCA to the wooded bank proved noisy, snapping branches, jungle noises, human voices and footfalls were frankly bad for the nerves . . . even if they indicated the presence of Burmese.

Once the canoes were embarked the LCA let go and proceeded downstream, straight onto a mudbank. Full astern had no effect. Everyone leapt over the side and attempted to shove off from the bank. The jungle was unsuitable for walking and the river was ebbing away fast. After strenuous efforts the vessel swung and drifted off. As she swung away everyone struggled to climb aboard, Alex swam to the stern and clambered up over the screws. Brigadier Campbell Hardy DSO, RM

– who'd bravely insisted on coming – was pulled aboard by the scruff of his neck, glad not to have to swim for it.

They were back alongside HMIS *Narbada*, to give their reports, before a bath and breakfast. Alex confided to his diary that these chaung jobs were wearing as one was on the *qui vive* all the time; ten-hours feeling your way up an unknown enemy river was frankly tiring. Arthur Ruberry afterwards put in a bouquet for the RINVR Burmese crews: 'Those boys certainly knew their chaungs.' They had been 27 miles up Daingbon Chaung.

Later Alex had time to do a tour of the Myebon beach defences. All were thorough and new. He was amazed they'd not been heard on the stakes night. There were trenches and the beach had been heavily mined. The beachmaster, Lieutenant-Commander Kettle and several others had been killed by mines. COPP3 had been pretty lucky all round.

*

A postscript to the stakes affair was a write-up in *SEAC*, the army newspaper. Alex was amused to find the party referred to as a party of seaman volunteers! Plenty of the top brass had heard of the job and plenty of bouquets came their way. The Supreme Commander, himself, commented on the use of a COPP party in a demolition role. Characteristically, Alex Hughes seems to have taken the view that it would have been hard to refuse this duty. Plainly he felt it was an unwritten part of an S/COPP's remit – that he should undertake anything to ensure the success of an amphibious operation.

Base life at the wreck was quite agreeable, though diet was limited. After the chaung sortie they had no fresh food: just tea, sugar, meat-and-veg in tins and dehydrated potatoes. They lived on that for about three weeks, supplemented by the odd tin of fruit or sausages. All water was heavily chlorinated: so that tea was a filthy grey fluid. Clothes had to be washed in the sea. Yet, Hughes admitted, life at the wreck was good. Even so he longed for a little Ritzness: a week in an enormous, soft bed with hot baths, hairdressers and efficient servants would not come amiss . . . still, that would come.

At least under the moon at night the rumble of the guns was far away; though easily heard. There was also a constant stream of relieved and relieving troops, casualties and prisoners. Hughes recounts how a commando tried to tackle an escaping Jap with his bare hands; and in two seconds found himself being throttled; indeed he had to be rescued by other troops, who beat the Jap over the head with a rifle butt. The

Japs certainly knew their Ju-jitsu! Ruberry was sick in Akyab, with a septic foot – browned-off, of course, because he was keen, but there would be other chances for action. Till then there was a sky flooded with soft yellow light and studded with star brilliants. That sometimes seemed more real than the horrors and bestiality of war.

SOURCES
Imperial War Museum
Lieutenant-Commander A. I. Hughes DSC, RD, RNR (Retd) archive
Public Record Office
DEFE2 1116

CHAPTER TWENTY-EIGHT

COPP3(1): Operation *Baboon* and Assistance in Operation *Copyright*

T owards the end of January Lieutenant-Commander Paul W. Clark DSC*, RN, Senior Officer COPP Far East had informed Alex that COPP1 was on its way up to relieve COPP3. Alex took the news calmly and awaited developments. Soon afterwards all COPP3 were back at the wreck, and on 24 January 1945, Lieutenant-Commander P. G. Wild DSC, RNVR, arrived with COPP1 to relieve them.

COPP3 now had to make their way back to Jaffna. Hood and Cockram left in HMIS *Keddah* for Chittagong, to pick up their stores there. 'Canada' and Alex were to fly to Calcutta a day later. Thomas with the rest of COPP3 was to proceed to Calcutta in HMS *Varella*, with the stores. Two-and-a-half hours after leaving Akyab, on 31 January 1945, Hughes and Alcock were living in the Grand Hotel, Calcutta – with sheets and breakfast in bed. Calcutta was good for shopping, they found. At first light Alex flew out of Dum Dum airfield; breakfasted at Vizagapatam; lunched at Bangalore; then to Colombo. As *Varella* would be arriving Calcutta that night, 'Canada' agreed to pick them up and bring them by rail to Colombo. After three pleasant days in Trincomalee, Hughes was back in at Hammenheil Camp. Letters followed him here as did a government announcement of the War Gratuity allowance: 10/- (50 new pence) for every month of service, for ABs: 35/- (£1.75p) for a lieutenant. With seven years service before demobilisation Alex could expect about £160.00. – bad enough, he felt, but an AB or leading hand would draw only about £50.00. Presumably the explanation would be that Great Britain was a poor country now and could afford no more. It was a scandal compared with the Canadian scheme of £7.10s. per month. Alex could imagine a howl of protest, but supposed the government would win in the end.

He'd been warned to stand by for another job. It would be quite fun and they were all ready; it was bound to be a long-distance sortie. In the meanwhile the store was being rebuilt, all boxes were being painted and a store muster was in process.

On 14 February 1945, Alex had a wonderful evening: the Commandant had a guest, Squadron-Leader Campbell-Johnstone, who is Liberal candidate for Salisbury. Discussion began over a drink before dinner and Alex found they agreed on such subjects as Greece and Belgium and the lack of propaganda war in Germany. All this despite the presence of another guest, a dedicated anti-socialist. At the end of the meal the Commandant brought Campbell-Johnstone into the reading room where discussion ensued until mid-night. Alex felt it had really been worthwhile to get down to a real discussion with a common spirit who agreed on principles and not to be involved in political in-fighting and mud-slinging. Earlier Hughes had given a talk on recent operations in the Arakan. A nice life, he felt, as a base wallah in COPP3.

*

By 2 March 1945, Alex was in Trincomalee and had learned that Operation *Baboon* was to be done from HMS/M *Torbay* (Lieutenant-Commander P. W. Norman DSO, DSC, RN). The last three days had been taken up in exercising with the submarine. It was now known the operation would involve going ashore for three nights and two days – with the party hiding-up by day. Whilst their canoes and equipment were not geared to hiding-up, Alex was prepared to try anything once.

There is a cryptic, unexplained note in his diary:

Tomorrow we sail in *Torbay*. Seaton Sircos goes
forward – pay no regard.

By 8 March Alex and his party were aboard *Torbay*, off the Japanese coast. They'd had an uneventful crossing of the Bay of Bengal. Alex had taken periscope photos of the beach whilst the submarine had proceeded submerged along the coast. They were not far from Phuket. At 1939 *Torbay* surfaced with the three canoes on the casing. They were launched three-miles offshore. Captain Johns' canoe experienced difficulty keeping station: it had been adapted to fit a third seat. The third occupant was Flight Lieutenant Norman H. Guthrie DFM, RAuxAF (attached to COPP3): with responsibility for airfield recces. Guthrie had flown in the Battle of Britain, as a sergeant air gunner; later he had retrained as an airborne radar operator, and won his DFM in night fighters, before commissioning.

Soon after the canoes drew away, 'Canada' astern of Hughes, drew level and explained that he could no longer see Johns' canoe. The remaining pair of canoes proceeded in line abreast, but there was no sign of Johnny. The only explanation was that he had passed ahead and gone in to the beach. They all knew the best landing site was opposite and just north of Hin Luk airfield. 'Canada' and Hughes proceeded ashore and did their recces. They could see a few huts; probably coast watchers: their occupants kept emerging and kept wandering about, flashing torches. This made 'Canada' and Hughes feel particularly naked and conspicuous, lying flat on the sand. When one passed close Alex tried to dig himself in, but found the sand too hard and coarse for that. Alex felt he could see more without a torch. He went back to the water's edge and paddled the five-miles back to *Torbay*. Before they had launched the canoes Alex, 'Canada' and Johns had agreed that the number of huts and people onshore, meant that this was not a shore on which to attempt to hide-up: that their best plan was to return to the carrier submarine each morning. Alcock was back just before him. Both canoe crews were exhausted: they'd spent six-and-a-half hours paddling – not counting the one-and-half hours spent crawling about the beach. There was still no sign of Johnny. The submarine moved away, out to sea. When it dived at dawn, the canoe teams turned-in and spent most of the following day sleeping.

Next day at 1930 they surfaced and once again closed the coast. Alcock and Alex were to finish off the northern recce and to search for Johnny, Guthrie and Cammidge. Tonight, suspiciously, there was an absolute blackout on shore. Asdic reported transmissions to their south. That decided the captain that something was wrong. Clearly he couldn't be expected to hazard his boat, so he cancelled the operation, for the immediate present and headed out to sea again. The COPP3 party turned in again. By 0100 next morning *Torbay* headed inshore again in case Johns' canoe should appear. Alex considered Johns' night vision inferior to his own, finding himself alone, Johns could have attempted to close the submarine. In which case the risk would be that boat and canoe had crossed without seeing one another.

An hour later Hughes and Alcock left and carried out a recce of the beach. There were patrols about, very much on their guard. Eluding them with difficulty they regained their canoes and *Torbay*. Still no sign of Johns, Guthrie or Cammidge. They hung on waiting until the presence of an enemy ship necessitated a dive in short order. In barely enough depth of water, caught very close to the coast, *Torbay* was quite unable to take avoiding action, or even go deep. The period of waiting till the unknown enemy vessel cleared the area was tense and scaring.

After a day submerged they returned to the waiting area. Still no sign of Johns' party. It was incredible: there had been no sound of shots, yet *something* had alerted those onshore, that first night and that must be why the Japs had imposed a blackout. Alex could only conclude the trio had gone ashore found an excellent hide and adhered to the original programme. This didn't entirely square with what he knew of Johnny. The alternative was that the canoe could have capsized and all three drowned. A third occupant in the folbot meant that her gunwales would be low in the water, and she could have been swamped. The discovery of their bodies would have been enough to spark off an alarm.

*

Faced with the unthinkable Alex found himself praying that Johnny had been killed outright: COPPs were not regarded with favour by their 'honourable foes'. As in the case of Mike Peacock, he hoped they'd know soon. Although loss of personnel on an operational sortie was an ever-present possibility; he had never considered it a personal one; 'it just can't happen to any of my party . . . .' Realisation was painful and slow when someone just did not come back; it was not like someone being shot in battle and lying slain – when the tragedy would be instantly apparent.

On the surface on return passage back to Ceylon Alex caught up with his diary. He was to learn later that things had gone worse than he had supposed. The whole of the *Copyright* party had gone ashore, further down the coast from HMS/M *Thrasher* (Lieutenant-Commander M. Ainslie DSO, DSC, RN) and none had returned. *Thrasher* had gone back two nights running but no one had shown up.

A *Copyright* party, mostly marines, with Major I. C. C. Mackenzie RE – COPP senior sapper Far East – had also failed to rendezvous. The *Copyright* party also included Major John Maxwell RM – who Alex knew well and liked – 'a white man, always cheerful and a pleasure to work with,' and Flight Lieutenant B. Brown RAF, and four RM other ranks. Alex hoped he'd be able to arrange a rescue party to take the submarine to the Emergency escape rendezvous – pick up some of 'our chaps', or get a few prisoners: one might be enough to tell them what had happened. On 15th the C-in-C signalled that this was exactly what should be done.

On 18 March *Torbay* rendezvoused with *Thrasher*. Alex swam across so Ainslie could tell him all that was known about the missing *Copyright* party. Alex gave him a canoe because he was off to do an agent-ferrying job.

Alex was well aware that the Escape RV sortie did not appeal to Ainslie: he had reservations about it himself. *Torbay* left the area in search of targets, and after two gun actions was attacked by aircraft. Following the proceedings from the control room Alex felt that, although not a claustrophobe, he preferred to be able to see his enemies.

He had plenty of opportunities when *Torbay* did close the Emergency RV. It was a beach, approximately 150-yards long, surrounded by high ground. There were tents on the beach and it was patrolled by sentries. Obviously it was going to be impossible to get anyone across that beach without being seen. The drill was that Alex should paddle ashore, show himself in case any of their chaps could spot him. If he drew enemy fire, 'Canada' lying a little further out to sea, would fire back while Hughes backed out.

Alex approached with trepidation, watching the shore through binoculars. Then moved slowly the length of the beach, a little out to sea, keeping station with a sentry – thirty-yards away – who incredibly didn't see them. It was an impossible task: Hughes had to be visible to 'our chaps', who could be 100-yards away, yet remain invisible to the sentries, who could be as near as ten-yards away. Whilst he would have liked to have shot the sentry and could have done; it would have served little purpose. With ten men he reckoned he could have wiped out the occupants of the five tents on the beach. But inevitably that would have compromised it as an escape rendezvous. Disappointed they paddled stealthily back to their carrier submarine, feathering paddles and keeping a low silhouette.

*

On 23 March 1945 *Torbay* was back in Trincomalee, where Alex found orders he was to move to Kandy by car. The car turned over before it arrived. Alex discovered all his laundry, sent to HMS *Wolfe* was missing. He used the Supremo's authority to get a fresh car and travelling in old, soiled clothes. At Kandy he was met by Tollemache and Hasler, a room had been booked at the Suisse and sandwiches were waiting. Alex appreciated the thought. After a long lie-in, a car took him to address a meeting of planners. Afterwards he was interviewed by General F. A. M. 'Boy' Browning, late Airborne Division, C-in-C Far

Eastern Theatre and General Lampoul, the Director of Intelligence. Alex made his point about a lack of photo-interpretation and intelligence. Subsequently he heard 'bottles' were handed out to those concerned.

Sent for by General Sir Ouvry Roberts CBE, DSO, commanding 34 Corps, who would go in with the next invasion, Alex told his story. The general introduced his staff, took Alex to lunch and explained why Johns and Cammidge had been killed. The beach had been a mass of defences and trenches: obvious to any well-trained photo-interpreter. Guthrie had survived and he and Maxwell's party were prisoners. Alex realised he'd been within eight yards of trenches and 15 yards of gun positions – and had never known. Had he known he'd have been more careful. He offered to go back to confirm defence positions. Circumstances, however, were to prevent this.

*

With the advantage of hindsight, almost fifty years on, it is possible to piece together what happened. Johns, Cammidge and Guthrie were in a heavily-laden, three-man canoe. Alex Hughes's COPP3 had taken over COPP8's stores and were thus in possession of a three-seater. Staff requirements for an airstrip reconnaissance were far-reaching (see Appendix 6). The RAF officer attached to the COPP party for those duties had to be an aircrew officer: Guthrie was a qualified navigator. The *Copyright* party executing similar duties were burdened down with an Abney level and camera. So that John's *Baboon* party would have been similarly laden and, provided they could successfully lie-up on shore, were committed to survey work in broad daylight. As Alex had surmised the three-man canoe *had* lost touch with his own craft; and, despite a calm night, had capsized. In desperation the three-man crew had flashed torches towards where they supposed Hughes and Alcock were.

After wading ashore the party had been shot-up by a Jap or Thai patrol. Johns and Cammidge had been shot dead, though Guthrie had escaped. None of their specialist gear had been captured; which implies they had been unable to salvage it and so were empty-handed. Without equipment they would have been unable to carry out their mission and must have hoped to contact the remainder of COPP3. Guthrie, who had escaped being hit in the exchange of shots, was seen by natives, the following day, whilst passing through a village. The natives gave him food but called the Thai militia. As a prisoner of war, in Thai hands, he was later to meet up with Mackenzie and Maxwell's party.

*

Whilst Alex Hughes regarded Operation *Baboon*, the Phuket operation as a normal COPP beach reconnaissance to be carried out on a dark night, and was opposed to any idea of lying-up on shore till daylight, it seems probable that the *Copyright* leaders – Majors Ian Mackenzie RE and John Maxwell RM – appreciated that this represented something more of an in-depth reconnaissance. Phuket, with good monsoon anchorages, at least one airstrip – possibly with a suitable site for a second – represented a suitable staging post for an attack on Singapore. A thick file of intelligence on Phuket existed, with aerial photographs of defences – but more detailed information would be needed on beaches, coastal defences and Japanese garrisons; as well as airfields, communications and ports, and the extent to which these had been developed during the Japanese occupation. All this information would be necessary before a detailed invasion plan could be formulated. Intelligence had suggested that the Thais might be friendly and Japanese garrisons thinly spread. For these reasons the *Copyright*, combined COPP/SOG party were committed to the calculated risk of daylight work. Had they realised in advance, that they could scarcely avoid contact with the local population, it could have been prudent to include an interpreter in the party.

After periscope reconnaissance offshore, the entire *Copyright* party: Mackenzie, Maxwell, Flight Lieutenant Bertie Brown RAF – a qualified pilot – and three Royal Marine other ranks had landed in three canoes, which they concealed far up the beach. At 2300, on 9 March 1945, Mackenzie had departed with a reconnaissance party that included Brown and Colour Sergeant Smith RM. The remainder of the party stayed with the folbots.

Mackenzie's party were at a previously selected observation 'post by first light. They climbed trees, observed their designated airstrip site and took photos. They went on to another observation post, by 0800 there were local inhabitants all over the area to be covered, their progress had therefore to be slow and they were spotted by a party of three natives, after photographing two large bunker positions on Bang Thao Bay. Soon afterward two patrols, fifteen-strong passed between the party and the sea. They reached a third observation post position and took more photos, reached the strip and collected soil samples.

Experiments to see where folbots could be carried by aircraft, conducted with engineless Consolidated Catalina.

Fairey IIIF, the aircraft that put paid to Geoffrey Galwey's promising career as a Dartmouth cadet.

A military viewpoint of COPP motor transport. (Copyright © Daily Mail/Solo.)

"You'd think they would be satisfied with a ship"

Cocanada – the canal.

Cocanada
1 *Clock Tower*
2 *Police Stn*
3 *Telegraph office*
4 *Flag staff*
5 *Lighthouse (post 1943)*
6 *Bridge*

Cocanada

Two views of a rigged folbot.

Inter-services co-operation: Robin Harbud and Sergeant Cook manhandling a folbot up from below.

X-23 coming alongside after marking the Normandy beaches, on D-Day. Jim Booth (fo'ard), George Honour in the conning position.

Launching party lowering rigged folbot onto carrier-vessel, submarine's ballast tanks.

Then they rested, awaiting nightfall. Night reconnaissance of the strip proved impossible due to the presence of native huts and dogs; and because of Jap patrol activity, along a nearby road. So an hour before midnight, they left their position and headed for the hidden canoes rendezvous point.

The canoe party: Major Maxwell, Corporal R. A Atkinson and Marine B. Brownlie RM, had early on been spotted by an apparently friendly native, later four fisherman had spotted one of the three canoes. The party had placed sentries and kept watch – short of eliminating the natives with silent weapons, it is difficult to think what more could have done.

By 0930 in the morning a motor launch was seen heading straight for their position, with twelve-to-fifteen armed men on board. The launch grounded and armed men sprang ashore and raced up the beach.

SOG standing orders stated that operational parties might fight to regain (or retain?) possession of their boats. Mackenzie's report indicates that he ordered the party to stand-to. The Thais were armed with rifles (probably Japenese Arisaka rifles, with a cumbersome Mauser-type bolt action). This meant that the *Copyright* party, with Thompson and Sten sub-machine guns had superior fire power. The Thais flung themselves flat and there was an exchange of shots, with at least two on each side hit. Deciding that the Thais might be amenable to a patriotic appeal, Major Maxwell dropped his weapon and went forward carrying a Union Flag. The Thai commander ordered him to strip completely and order his party to surrender. At this stage a Thai fired a round, the *Copyright* party fired back and in the confusion the stark-naked Maxwell escaped to rejoin Makenzie and the others.

Experience in the Falklands War indicated that, in a patrol ambush, it is good tactics to shoot any obvious leaders, in the hope of panicking the leaderless party. Not having exercised this option – what else remained to the *Copyright* party? Modern SAS experience in the Gulf, advocates superior fire power combined with conservation of ammunition. A sustained static firefight is likely to result in casualties for both parties. So one can either advance or make a staged withdrawal with some of the party keeping enemy heads down with covering fire.

The *Copyright* party was doubly vulnerable: if they abandoned their boats, they could not leave the island. If they stood firm they would lose men and their boats would almost certainly get shot up. Without an interpreter any further attempt at parley was ruled out. Mackenzie reports that the party split up and made for the emergency rendezvous, probably half the party covering the other half as they moved. Modern SAS experience militates against firing on the move; slows one down. They kept watch at the emergency rendezvous for a canoe from the submarine, but none was seen. In the firefight Mackenzie had sustained a superficial head wound, Colour Sergeant Smith had a more serious one and a tendency to throw fits. For the next five days the party slept in the jungle still attempting to carry out their mission, avoiding Jap sentries and Thai troops. As their tinned food was in a câche near their original landing point and so, for the most part, they starved or ate berries. Every night sentries were posted and watch kept.

The following day Major Maxwell, Corporal Atkinson and Marine Brownlie set out for Laem Son Bay, hoping to steal a canoe and return to their câche of tinned food. Mackenzie and Flight Lieutenant Brown made a similar coastal search to the east. Maxwell's party were unlucky. They found a canoe but no paddles. Maxwell was captured and in an ambush with a Jap patrol Brownlie was killed outright and Corporal Atkinson evaded. Smith, who had been unable to move from the last hide, had by now been captured.

For a further four days the remainder of the *Copyright* party – with Atkinson – held out, retiring to the jungle by day and by night watching for the return of the others. A second emergency rendezvous was kept without success. A Jap barge, crewed by three men was observed mooring offshore and it was decided to attempt to capture it after dark. Sadly it changed moorings. By now the period without food was beginning to tell on the party, who felt weaker and were breaking out in jungle sores. They headed north, hoping to swim the straits to the mainland. Mackenzie had decided they must have food and a day's sleep before the swim was attempted. They turned inland in search of a native hut, food and a lie-up. They found a hut and bought food, were even allowed to hide in the family air-raid shelter by day. The following morning – the nineteenth since the *Copyright* party had landed – they were brought a message in English, from a Thai district officer. Mackenzie attempted to persuade him to help them to get to Rangoon. The District Officer, fearful of the Japanese, dared not do this; though he did ensure they were made prisoners of the Thai Navy. All so treated survived and eventually reached Bangkok; unlike Maxwell and Smith, who were taken to Singapore and executed.

*

In a report dated 24 April 1945, Major Ian Mackenzie – a New Zealander, despite his Scots names – after his return from prisoner-of-war captivity, revealed the story of Johns and Cammidge. It had been told to him by Guthrie who had been taken prisoner, probably whilst they were both in captivity. Luckily, before the firefight *Copyright* personnel had destroyed an Abney level, samples and a camera before their capture. Although none divulged information under interrogation a rider to the report stated that Phuket Island was to be considered completely compromised. Members of the *Copyright* party had attended the Emergency rendezvous, their failure to contact the *Torbay* rescue party was ascribed to insufficiently precise definition of its location. There could have been only thirty yards between evaders and rescuers. The inference is that they waited on different beaches but that they were probably only a few hundred yards apart.

It was suggested more attention be given to recognition at (Emergency RV) and that canoes should return to their carrier having dropped the reconnaissance party. One suspects COPP3 would not have agreed on this last point. This point was modified by a suggestion that canoes should only return when the recovery point is not more than two miles out, and the homing conditions good. COPP3 members managed greater distances in subsequent operations.

Appendix 4 contains the cover story provided for Operation *Baboon* personnel, which is no doubt similar to that deployed by the *Copyright* personnel and Guthrie. Appendix 3: Notes on how to take a prisoner – gives a remarkably similar procedure to that the Thais attempted with Major Maxwell.

As other writers have pointed out the dropping of the atomic bomb rendered unnecessary an opposed landing on Phuket. This does not, of course, take from the sacrifice, endurance and dogged determination to hold on of the *Copyright* party. After the war Major Mackenzie and Corporal Atkinson were rewarded, for their good services during a reconnaissance behind enemy lines, by mentions in despatches. Flight Lieutenant Bertie Brown was awarded an MBE. It seems hard that neither Maxwell nor Smith was accorded a posthumous mention.

SOURCES

Imperial War Museum
Lieutenant-Commander A. I. Hughes DSC, RD, RNR (Retd) archive

Public Record Office
DEFE2 95 Operations *Baboon, Copyright, Blackcock, Bruteforce, Barbaric, Bristle*
DEFE2 780 Histories and accounts of CCO's Representative Washington, No.
    10 Allied Commando and SOG, in SEAC 1942–46
MCNAB, Andy DCM, MM, *Bravo Two-Zero*, Bantam Press, 1993.

CHAPTER TWENTY-NINE

COPP3: Operation *Confidence*

On 5 April 1945, on leave in Bombay, just after lunch Alex was walking downstairs after lunch, when his foot turned over, there was an audible crack and he found himself in RNA Hospital with one leg encased in plaster: the diagnosis was a fractured foot. The doctor said it must be kept like that for all of six-weeks. So, like it or not, he'd get some rest.

Up to a point he had no complaints: the hospital was a grand place, the sisters and nurses all charming. The food was good and patients even got the odd drink in the evening. For the first time in months he could really relax and – apart from the foot – began to feel better. It wasn't long before the war caught up with him. The surgeon was first class, but the DADMS (Deputy Director of Medical Services) wanted Alex transferred to the army hospital; so he could carry on being debriefed. The surgeon wouldn't hear of it. He said the officers concerned could come here, and he'd give them the necessary facilities – privacy and so forth. Alex didn't want to move, but was prepared to talk about it.

By 15 April he was allowed out for the first time, now sporting a new plaster cast, with an iron heel attached. He could now move about but only slowly, and in great discomfort.

By 6 May 1945 he was back at Hammenheil – a painful step in the right direction – having returned from the RAF hospital at Kankansanturai. The bone joint, they told him, hadn't joined. There was a distinct possibility it never would; and that he'd be left with a weak foot. He didn't worry, simply carried on cutting down on superfluous stores and organising a stores' muster. The team, fresh back from leave, were all in good spirits.

Reliefs had arrived for Johns and Cammidge: Captain John Ashford RE and sapper-Sergeant Lomas. Straightaway he started getting them trained in the ways of COPP, and particularly COPP3. They seemed to be good material he noted in his diary. Denis Mackay left that day to be hospitalised, a very sick man.

Two weeks later Alex was in Ceylon, at the Galle Face Hôtel, after a temporary absence to work for 34 Corps in Bombay and be flown back. Then, almost a week later, back to Hammenheil glad to be back, with plenty of work and only short distances to walk.

When he found the Commonwealth Society had applied for his release he decided he didn't really mind; but equally was prepared to carry on with the war. The news from Europe he found terrific; so much so that he felt there was no need for celebration. He felt they had waited so long for good news and it had been such a hard struggle; that there could only be heart-felt relief that at least part of the war was over . . . . Now one could address oneself to the serious problems of rebuilding the peace. In fact, in Galle, a lovely place with a fort with huge grass-covered ramparts, he'd celebrated Wesak – the Bhuddhist Christmas – celebrated decorously with glasses of coconut milk and bananas, and many expressions of happy Wesak, in congenial company, by now knowing he'd been allocated another assignment – the best yet.

On 4 June 1945 Alex was at sea in HMS/M *Seadog*, reflecting that if one really wanted to experience discomfort: one should go to sea – in the tropics – as a supernumerary in an S-Class submarine. The S-Class was much smaller than the T-Class. There were eight of them on this trip, living and sleeping in a space measuring 8 × 6-feet (including bunk space). And there was nowhere else: the alleyway outside was the boat's main thoroughfare and could not be blocked, or used for anything else. The only other unoccupied space on board was the bridge and its use was extremely limited. After three days Alex couldn't imagine what seventeen-or so days aboard would be like, but guessed it would be a relief to go ashore and get on with the operation. This time at least he'd had a firm briefing requirement from Lieutenant-Colonel Richardson, Chief of Planning (A). A briefing begun in Delhi's Pered{iniija Gardens and finished aboard the Depot ship *Wolfe*.

*

There had been a couple of flaps before sailing. The operation was planned for *Thrasher*, but she'd developed a faulty motor. Captain 'S', 'Jackie' Slaughter, had asked Alex in and explained matters: he knew Alex's preference would be for Mike Ainslie in *Thrasher* – an old hand at the game. Equally he knew that Ashley Hobson – though new to such work – would do his utmost, despite the confined interior of *Seadog*.

Then just before they sailed, one of the planners discovered that the fleet were off on a strike, at the same time as the projected Operation *Confidence* . . . and the coast might have been alerted. Arguably both jobs were top priority . . . . Alex was glad in the end, when the Supremo washed out the other job:

The fleet stays in, while COPP3 goes to sea . . .!

That had his vote. The fact that the job was important made it more fun from his point of view. It could be quite a long job: he estimated four days: the task was to find three good beaches for landing troops and vehicles – out of a possible six beaches. The crucial factor – as it had been in Normandy – would be bearing capacity. The party had an ample supply of condoms for bringing back samples – they could have been made for the job – and prodders to test bearing capacities. It wasn't a case of Dig for Victory, but rather Dig another sample for Freedom. Captain Ashford and Joe Lomas had been left behind; a policy decision dictated that only naval reconnaissance should be made on this trip.

By 6 June 1945 – exactly one year after the Normandy D-Day landings the party started getting their gear ready. Their passage had been sometimes on the surface, with dives each time aircraft were spotted. Attaching fighting knives to their swim suits and checking pistols, prodders, Tommy guns, ammunition, escape kits, in the cramped space below, Alan Hood, who had been an actor began to quote Shakespeare. Then switched to Abraham Lincoln's Gettysburg address, 19 November 1863 – perhaps the greatest speech ever made – the following extract:

> 'But in a larger sense, we cannot dedicate – we cannot consecrate – we cannot hallow – this ground. The brave men, living or dead, who struggled here have consecrated it, far above our power to add or detract. The world will little note nor long remember what we say here. It is for us the living, rather, to be dedicated here to the unfinished work which they who fought here have so far nobly advanced. It is for us to be dedicated to the great task remaining before us – that from these honored dead we take increased devotion to that cause for which they gave the last full measure of devotion – that we here highly resolve that these dead shall not have died in vain – that this nation, under God, shall have a new birth of freedom – and that government of the people, for the people, shall not perish from the earth.'

Alex could have added that tomorrow's battle for freedom would be against cartels, monopolies and political apathy. Action, despite those stirring words of Lincoln would not come that day.

Two days later *Seadog* was in a position off the Aroa Islands, she made her way through a minefield and dived, but too late to do any recce that night. It proved just as well – a gale, known locally as a Sumatra sprang up – a Force 7 wind blew for three hours, there was heavy rain and lightning. They turned in but sleep was elusive.

Next morning *Seadog* crept slowly in to the beach, Alex took photos through the periscope and observed the target for next night. The inshore waters were crowded with sampans and junks, passing both ways. Some so close it seemed impossible they could not see the periscope slide in and out of the water. At 1300, having seen all there was to be seen, *Seadog* submerged and lay on the bottom; all fans and air-conditioning switched off, the atmosphere thickened and the special forces party simply sweated and sweated. By 1900 even a short walk left them panting and the effort of donning a swimsuit and equipment needed a rest every few moments.

When *Seadog* surfaced the night was black and there was nothing to be seen. Her position was fixed by radar, and the canoes were got up on the casing. Tonight three canoes would be going close inshore, with a link-canoe to home on for the return.

At 2115 the four canoes found a sandy spit which lay off the beach – their first objective. They'd been steering blind and guessing what to allow for tidal set . . . but it had worked. They split up, the link-canoe (Sub-Lieutenant A. J. Thomas DSM*, RNVR, and Sapper Cockram) anchored. The remaining canoes: Alex and Arthur Ruberry; Alcock and Turner; Hood and Sowter fanned out to recce their respective stretches of beach.

Alex went over the side and swam ashore, then moved up the beach alone, leaving Ruberry with the canoe to wait for him offshore. Alex moved up the beach taking the gradient, then crawled up it methodically filling his 'rubber goods' with samples of mud and sand. Suddenly he observed that a light he'd seen reflected out to sea came from a man with a torch, not far from where he was working. Alex retreated a bit but the torch-holder came on and Alex knew he had to deal with him. As Arthur Ruberry later put it: 'Alex used his knife to finish-off the man with the torch.'

Alex completed his work in that sector and made his way back to the canoe, undeterred by moving lights at the back of the beach, where there could be tents. The night was dark, he saw nothing of Alcock or Hood, he didn't even spot Ruberry in the canoe till he was within ten-yards of it. The rendezvous was timed for 2300, so Alex got down to his tasks on the spit. Passage to the link-canoe was tricky, with a large junk bearing down on them, they had to do a swift side-step. When it seemed that might work, the junk put her helm down and altered towards them. It almost rammed them, as they struggled to keep out of its way and passed on down the coast. As they approached the link-canoe, its silhouette looked all wrong, rather like a sampan. Alex cocked his Tommy gun and they circled the craft, ready to open fire, then stage-whispering 'Tommy'. The instant he answered, Alex engaged the safety catch, sighed with relief, dropped anchor and prepared to wait for the other two folbots. Tommy, keeping watch through binoculars, whispered that a crowd of fishing boats was coming through. They up-anchored and waited to see better before deciding which way to jump. Tommy prudently streaked away and Alex found his canoe suddenly in the midst of a mass of about sixty large tree trunks, floating upright in the water, with about 15-feet sticking out of it. It was a nightmare experience. They cleared this floating menace with difficulty. It was now 0130, and 15-minutes after the final time for canoes to RV with the link. There was nothing for it but to set course for *Seadog*. They knew she'd be transmitting on RG, but were unable to pick it up. It was getting critical: time for the submarine RV was between 0145 and 0230. At 0230 there was still no sign but they heard an ominous grenade explosion on shore. Thomas had a bongle and transmissions were started in the hope *Seadog*'s asdic might pick them up. They rested their paddles, lit cigarettes and gave a final signal. To their relief *Seadog*'s conning tower suddenly loomed out of the darkness. Alex embarked gloomily, his relief tempered by the news that nothing had been sighted of the other two canoes.

Seadog hunted, surfaced until dawn, going in close to the shore, but nothing could be seen. A large ship passed by forcing them to submerge. They listened carefully for the double grenade signal that those onshore would be going to the daylight rendezvous . . . but it never came.

Alex was bitterly disappointed but hoped that the two canoes crews – having failed to contact link or carrier submarine – would have gone back inshore, destroyed their canoes and made off inland. There was a comparatively safe area, 30-miles inland where guerrillas might be contacted; probably a better bet than the daylight rendezvous, with all the junk traffic about. His estimation was that Canada and Turner, with all their experience would cope with the situation. Hood and Sowter had less operational experience; he hoped they would.

Alex conferred with the captain of *Seadog* and agreed the remainder of the operation should be cancelled. Ashley, he knew, would not relish staying longer in shallow, coastal waters he couldn't fight in: and he had given the COPP3 party every chance. *Seadog* proceeded north, out

through the minefield, then north at top speed. On their return passage a junk was sighted and engaged in a gun action. Someone told the
story of the junkmaster who being taken below, aboard a submarine that
had boarded and sunk his junk exclaimed: 'Just my luck – another S-
boat!'

In a rider to his patrol report on reaching Colombo, dated 16 June
1945, Alex regretted the four missing personnel, but added a cautiously
optimistic note that there had been no sounds of firing or any struggle.
That every man had jungle-green battledress and escape kits and had
been briefed on escaping. If they had succeeded in destroying their
folbots the operation should not have been compromised.

At Kandy he was ordered to fly to Delhi, where his reports and action
were approved; the final view was that the operation had not been
compromised. Alex talked with Admiral Douglas Pennant and Dr
Bernal, the expert on mud- and sand-bearing capacities. The beach
intelligence he had brought back was judged of great value. As at that
time Operation *Zipper:* a landing in force on the Morib beaches was
planned, this is not surprising. Because of the Nagasaki and Hiroshima
atomic bombs, this was not necessary. *Zipper* took place as an
unopposed landing. It is generally accounted a shambles: a popular jest
at the time was that it was called Operation *Zipper* because nothing about
it was buttoned-up.

Whilst Alex was no doubt sorry not to have completed this, his last
operation: his last note in that day's narrative was a political one.
Briefly that, whilst Commonwealth Socialists might disagree with the
progressives of that day: their differences were likely only to be ones
of degree.

*

On 28 June 1945, his thirty-first birthday, Alex took his Wren girlfriend,
Joan, dancing at the Silver Fawn – Colombo's sole night club – popularly
known as the Silver Prawn. When they came out both got soaked by
a tropical downpour.

*

What of COPP3's four escapers? Probably a whole book could be
written on this subject. Certainly Lieutenant-Commander Ian Ernest
'Canada' Alcock RCNVR produced a magazine article on the subject.
He may have drawn on his own report on regaining civilisation,

dated 6 November 1945, in which an ingenious typist wrote bugle for bongle. Alcock had swum ashore and carried out his tasks, similar to those allocated Alex Hughes. With the deadline running out, delayed by an unexpected junk close inshore, he had attempted to find Hood, away to the south, before attempting independently to contact *Seadog*. Unable to use RG receiver he'd blinked a shaded blue torch in the approximate direction. Faced with a choice of attempting to paddle west to Sumatra (in Japanese hands); or 1,700 miles to Australia (he had a small sail for the folbot); or escape inland: Alcock chose inland escape. After daybreak he and Turner threw over-board most of their equipment, the Tommy gun and items too heavy to carry. They changed into jungle-green battledress, cut the folbot into small pieces and proceeded inland. They met up with pro-Allied Javanese and eventually with Hood and Sowter. After many privations, Alcock, naked, footsore, bleeding and filthy had made contact with 'Reed' – in reality Lieutenant-Colonel Claude Fenner, who had parachuted into Negri Sembilan three-weeks before, to liaise with the Malayan Peoples' Anti-Jap Army. 'Canada' gave him the positions of Hood, Sowter and Turner. Fenner (the late Tan Sri Sir Claude Fenner) promised to have them picked up; forty-eight-hours later they were safe in hospital. Colonel Fenner told Alcock that it was 23 August 1945 and that the war had been over eight days. At this Canada collapsed. Happily he recovered and lived to become a prospector back in his native Canada.

Alcock, Hood, Sowter and Turner were all awarded mentions in despatches for their escape. On the subject of decorations, after Operation *Confidence* Alex Hughes found he'd been awarded a DSC and two mentions, many of the team also got mentions, among them Thomas and Arthur Ruberry, who won two. Alex was to say of his service in COPP3, that he had the satisfaction of having lived a full exciting and satisfying existence for twelve months. Probably all COPP3 surviving members – even the jungle escapers – would have agreed.

SOURCES
Imperial War Museum
Lieutenant-Commander A. I. Hughes DSC, RD, RNR (Retd) archive

Public Record Office
DEFE2 95 Operations *Baboon, Copyright, Blackcock, Bruteforce, Barbaric, Bristle*

EXTRACT DEFE2 780

Morib

On the night of 9/10 June a recconnaissance of one of the Morib beaches was carried out. Four canoes carrying eight all ranks, were launched from the submarine for the task. It was discovered by the leader of the party [Lieutenant Alex Hughes DSC, RNR] at the time the canoes were due to return to the submarine that two of them were missing. They failed to RV with the 'link' canoe which was fitted with 'bongle' for homing to the submarine. On return to the submarine it was found that they had not homed direct to her, by means of their RG equipment . Before the S/COPP returned to the submarine a thorough search was carried out and the next day the submarine kept the prearranged daylight RV, but in neither case was there any sign of the missing canoes. In view of the risk of compromise the S/COPP and the CO of the Submarine decided to cancel the remainder of the reconnaissance and return to base.

It has since been learned that the occupants of the missing canoes succeeded in getting ashore further south and joining up with some guerrilla forces, and have now returned safely.

The information gained included: -

a) An accurate cross section of the beach including beach gradient at selected points.

b) The bearing surfaces of the beach including details of the runnels above water level.

c) Details of underwater runnels and of a spit off the beach, including the heights of tide and rates observed on the edge of the spit.

d) Samples of surface above and below water level.

e) A periscope photograph showing the beach silhouette.

f) information about enemy coast watchers.

As a result of the above information, plans were made for the landing of 34 Corps on the MORIB beaches between PORT DICKSON and CAPE RACHADO. The remaining members of COPP3 were to have been used for marking the channel and guiding the assault craft. This was later cancelled in view of the situation.

CHAPTER THIRTY

Far East Final Operations

On 18 July 1945 Alex Hughes learned that he had been awarded a DSC, and a mention, as he put it 'for past jobs.'. 'Canada' Alcock had also got a DSC and Turner a mention. Two days later after a good night out with Peter Wild and others, he confided to his diary –

> The thought that I may not do another recce is an appalling one – still in my prime in the COPP sense and with a team that isn't in the least browned-off or operationally unfit. But perhaps that is the way to end it.

It is plain that, having conducted a postmortem on Operation *Lightning* he would have quite liked to have gone back. But he did not: he considered he'd had a good year and he made a clean break. He also decided to make a break with the single life and married Joan, the attractive girl he had taken dancing on 28 June, at the 'Silver Prawn'.

They were married in St Andrew's Kirk, Kullopoijya, Ceylon: all his COPP and many other COPPists attended. The bride wore a beautiful dress and carried an impressive bouquet. Alex wore immaculate tropical whites, with sword and regulation buckskin shoes. His DSC ribbon lent distinction to his tunic. Thus Alex Hughes – and COPP3(1) pass from the story, with a certain style.

*

COPP1 it will be remembered had provided D-Day pilotage markers on 6 June 1944, under Lyne. In the Far East a re-commissioned COPP1(1) operated with Lieutenant Peter Grenville Wild DSC, RNVR as S/COPP. Wild, who had won his decoration for work in Sicily and Italy, had also taken part in the Normandy Recces and pilotage, for which he had won a mention in despatches.

In the course of a short, SEAC commission lasting from 24 January

1945 to 14 February 1945, COPP1(1) mounted no less than seven operations, all save one were led by her S/COPP in person. COPP1 personnel were attached to the SOG (Small Operations Group) under Colonel H. T. Tollemache RM, and based at Hammenheil, Jaffna, Northern Ceylon. They operated in the Arakan area under direct control by General Lomax of 26 Indian Division. Lomax personally gave his orders before each operation and after their operations interviewed all personnel individually.

In the first Wild led a team of two officers and one rating on a reconnaissance of beaches in the Myebon area. Their aim was to find beaches suitable for landing infantry and guns. They found they were only suitable for infantry. It was the same story, a day later, when Wild led a similar team on the same sort of mission. The result was identical. A day later Wild, in a single canoe, with a rating paddler, provided pilotage marking for the beach reconnoitred on 25 January 1945.

31 January to 3 February 1945, Wild led a larger team of two officers and 2 ratings to reconnoitre three beaches for landing infantry in the region of Dalet Chaung. Two beaches only proved satisfactory. In passing Chaungs are inland water ways, muddy-bottomed and frequently overgrown with slimy mangrove roots; many had tidal ranges of thirty feet!

This is what Peter Wild had to say about operating in chaungs:

> One found with experience that a little moonlight gave best operating conditions for making a foray up a chaung. The trees on either side of the narrow channel came down to the water's edge and gave good cover – with good dark shadows to hide under. Jap craft mainly used diesel engines and one could hear them miles away, giving you plenty of warning of their presence. Apart from that the high rise and fall of tides meant that the mangroves would dry out – quite noisily – sounding exactly as if their branches and twigs were being trodden upon. Fortunately Jap sentries' night vision was not good: so that a sentry would often stand clear of trees, or even sit still and rattle the bolt of his rifle, rather than enter the undergrowth and do a search. Along the banks of chaungs we found a number of foxholes, at strategic points: each had an entrance hole – facing front – but never an escape hole at the back! Japs in small craft we encountered in chaungs would often stop, perhaps fifteen yards from us, discuss what we might be, and then pass on. We would freeze and lie flat in the canoe, and every time it worked! If one had to move in a moonlit situation, the trick was to do it *very* slowly . . . and gradually. To a person with bad night vision, that way the movement would be imperceptible.

On 9 March 1945 the COPP1 E/COPP, Captain Jack Crane RE, plus three ratings went to reconnoitre a beach for vehicles in the region of Ru Wya Chaung: it proved satisfactory. Two days later Wild took a three-canoe team there on a similar mission, again it proved satisfactory. On 14 February 1945, Wild and two officers and one rating returned to lead in the assault. If this group of seven operations sound a shade repetitive and uniformly successful it should be remembered that such performances could only be achieved by rigorous training, ruthless discipline and repeated practices.

Peter Wild worked out a rationale for chaung operations. There was no point in hazarding two officers in a single canoe: the best composition for a party was three canoes. Canoe No. 1 should be the naval officer and a petty officer; Canoe No. 2 a naval officer and sapper sergeant; Canoe No. 3 the sapper captain and a petty officer. The best combination of carrier vessels was, he felt probably a Fairmile ML and a Harbour Defence Motor Launch (Royal Indian Navy). The sorties were not to be 'butcher and bolt' forays; all tidal data and soundings must be obtained. Colonel Tollemache RM of the SOG suggested a chaung questionnaire; but Wild's operation orders rendered this superfluous. If beaches had no mangrove their bearing capacity must be noted – how much a man sunk in was a good start – hard, rice paddy could be quite a good landing surface; mangrove swamps were to be avoided.

*

Probably the most notable operation for General Lomax that Wild laid on, was a chaung recce in preparation for a landing by the Green Howards. Wild remembers that the General said that he would understand if he declined. Lomax said that he had already asked an American unit, similar to COPP, which had been driven back by heavy enemy fire. Wild said he'd have a try. His party was fired upon but suffered no casualties – and completed the job satisfactorily. Lomax was delighted.

Subsequently Peter Wild took over the post of Senior Officer COPP Far East from, Paul Clark, who by now was seriously ill; Wild held this appointment from around June 1945: he seems an obvious choice. Peter had been the first RNVR officer to become an S/COPP and under his command, COPP1 had acquitted itself well. At the end of the war he and his COPP were at Bombay, learning how to land in layers of mud and in big surf: all of which they expected to encounter in reconnoitring the Malayan beaches which were to be the next strategic invasion site.

COPP1 in the course of their operations under Peter Wild – though often fired on – they lost not one man.

*

A re-commissioned COPP4(1) – no longer under Neville McHarg – but under Lieutenant Denis Handcock Mackay DSC, RN, was attached to the SOG from 31 December 1944 to 14 March 1945. During which time five successful missions were executed – all of them in the Arakan area. All were led by Mackay.

On the night of 18/19 January 1945, Mackay led a team of five officers and three other ranks to make naval and military reconnaissance of the beach and seaward approach to Akyab.

Lieutenant Terry Burke RNVR served as A/COPP4(1), under Dennis Mackay, after a brief period with Peter Wild in COPP1(1). His descriptions are particularly vivid. There was little attempt to keep the COPP teams informed as to the general strategic picture. As 2i/c it fell to him to take over the team and supervise training routines when Mackay had to be at headquarters. At Akyab he was happy to join the poker school presided over by Alex Hughes. COPPists did not talk shop – they all suffered a form of security paranoia. It was popularly believed that the Japs would extort *any* information from anyone captured . . . so there was no point in knowing about any other party's operations. All one needed was the limited objectives of one's next operation.

On the night of 11/12 February – Operation *11* – a reconnaissance was mounted from Ramree, its objectives the Myebon and Sethkaw River area. Mackay was in command of the carrier vessel. Three canoes were involved. Canoe No. 1 carried Captain J. W. Crane, and Sergeant E. Cooke RE: Canoe No.2 Terry Burke and AB Nicholls; Canoe No.3 Sub-Lieutenant Ronald 'Angel' Gambrill RNVR and Petty Officer A. Briggs – searching for landing areas.

It was probably on this sortie that Burke and Nicholls, at the top of the tide, found a landing place, secured their canoe to trees and went on foot to investigate the hinterland where they could hear vehicle noises and shouted orders. In a large paddy they observed Japs pulling out southwards, with heavy equipment. This was good news. On their return to their canoe, they found the tidal chaung, water level had dropped six-to-eight feet and their canoe was suspended by her painter and stern line. This contrary to the tidal predictions of their briefing. It was quite a problem.

On 17/18 January Mackay was back again with a team of three

officers and three other ranks to reconnoitre the River Gangan, Akyab. On 19/20 January Mackay led a naval and military reconnaissance of Daingbon Chaung.

On 9/10 February Mackay led a six-strong team for a naval and military recce of the Sethkaw River. Marking a chaung to guide in assault craft with one officer and two other ranks, on the night of 15/16 February 1945.

Towards the end of their operational tour COPP4(1) found their cloak-and-dagger chaung reconnaissances hampered by HMS *White Bear* – a requisitioned yacht, previously used for submarine training, in Scottish waters – which to their embarrassment, spent all its time patrolling and surveying chaungs in broad daylight.

On 10 July 1945, *The London Gazette* carried a note of the award of a bar to the DSC, to Denis Mackay, of Nelson, New Zealand. The same edition carried a note of a mention in despatches to Peter Grenville Wild DSC, RNVR. Considering the last mentioned Lomax operation alone: one cannot help feeling as do some former COPPists – that a DSO might have been more appropriate.

*

COPP9 had provided personnel for X-craft D-Day marking in Normandy. A reconstituted COPP9(1), under Lieutenant J. Morison RN, was sent to the Mediterranean, to Ischia. Then back to the Depot and out to Ceylon. They left Ceylon on Christmas day 1944. They were sent up to Akyab and completed ten audacious operations in the Arakan, between March and April 1945, most of them from MLs: generally leapfrogging up chaungs. On 8 March Morison led a recce up Sabyin Chaung, searching for landing places. It was very dark, but the team of two officers and one other rank did get to within one mile of the beach.

On 15 March Morison and two officers reconnoitred a wire boom and the defences to Lamu beaches. On 18 March with a similar team, a reconnaissance of a doubtful beach at Zani had to be cancelled. On 19 March a swim reconnaissance of a bar across chaung beaches for a landing at Tanlwe.

On 21 March their luck ran out it seems, investigating beaches and a suspected boom, reported by American OSS, Morison's party was fired on and unable to approach the beaches. On 29 March the same team was surveying and piloting craft up to FMA (Forward Maintenance Area), Tanlwe Chaung area. On 31 March Morison took the complete

COPP9 team on a daylight recce to see how far craft could proceed up Upper Tanlwe.

On 1 April Captain Gates and three officers and a single other rank made a recce of Taungup Jetty and roads. This was a recce made in co-operation with V-Force, for a proposed lie-up of eight days in Jap territory.

Morison and his complete team were unlucky at the same venue, next night. Attempting to recce the steamer route they were shot-up by a 75mm gun and unable to complete their recce. The same night Lieutenant Hartnett RNVR made a recce of Mon Bauk Chaung and landed a detached party to lie-up eight nights in enemy territory.

On the night of 6/7 April. Morison, two officers and five ratings reconnoitred Taungup Chaungs, cutting wire booms, and reconnoitring jetties and roadstead. Thereafter lying-up one night in enemy territory.

COPP9's last operation involved the whole team, plus one officer and one other rank from 82 West African Divisional Signals. The operation involved a lie-up of four nights in Jap territory and enabled them to reconnoitre the inland-water route from Rat Island to Sandoway Natkan. For these operations, not surprisingly, Morison received the award of a DSC. COPP9(1) was among the first British personnel to enter Rangoon. In late December 1945 the COPP returned to the UK soon afterwards and was disbanded. Nigel Willmott's memo to Earl Mountbatten of Burma claims that they took a prisoner on one of their chaung forays.

*

Final operations in the Far East had proved the efficacy of at least three of Nigel Willmott's dictums. First that a lieutenant commander – as Senior Officer COPP Far East – helped to co-ordinate S/COPPs' requirements at highest levels. Secondly that teams should be retired after operational tours: in the same way as Bomber Command aircrews. Thirdly that the letters COPP must be used to designate absolute priority.

*

The advent of the atomic bomb ceased COPP activities in the Far East. Whilst those dropped on Hiroshima and Nagasaki caused a total of 152,000 civilian casualties and any civilian casualties in wartime are to be deplored; a single air raid by 279 American Superfortresses on Tokyo, devastated a quarter of the city and caused twenty percent more casualties. It is said that the crucial factor for the Japanese was that, whilst the privileged with deep shelters could survive conventional air attacks, nobody had deep shelters that would withstand atomic attack. The alternative to atomic warfare could have been a land invasion of the Japanese mainland.

Studies executed by the General Staff allowed for a probable 1,000,000 Allied casualties in making a formal invasion of Japan from the sea. And in any event, it is known that plans existed, for all Allied prisoners-of-war in Japanese hands to be liquidated, should this happen.

Prior to any projected land invasion, COPP would inevitably have been required to make beach reconniassances. Given that the Isle of Wight is a mere 147 square miles in area – but has some sixty miles of coastline: and Japan is 142,727 square miles in area – it is not difficult to imagine the scale of the task involved, nor to envisage the scale of casualties which could have been suffered by COPP personnel in the process of surveying that coastline, guarded by a formidable and ruthless foe.

SOURCES:
FOOT, M. R. D. *SOE Special Operations Executive 1940–46*, published by BBC, 1984.

WARNER, Philip *World War II, The Untold Story*, The Bodley Head, 1988 (Coronet Books Edition, 1988).

PRO DEFE2 780

PRO DEFE2 1116

LADD, James *SBS The Invisible Raiders*, David and Charles, 1983.

Testimony of surviving participants

Daily Telegraph, obituary of Peter Wild, 17 February 1995.

CHAPTER THIRTY-ONE

Depot and Development

T he command set-up at COPP Depot, Sandy Point, Hayling Island was always flexible. Nigel Willmott was, of course, the original CO; Nicholas Hastings, the original First Lieutenant; Geoffrey Galwey was responsible for victualling, stores and administration, and did his share of recruiting. Rollo Mangnall and Peter Wild in time were both First Lieutenants. When Willmott was absent making reconnaissances off Normandy, Ralph Stanbury, recently returned from the Mediterranean, took over as Depot CO in his absence. When Nigel went sick, just before D-Day – as has been seen – Paul Clark took over as S/COPP1 and Nicholas Hastings, recently promoted, was Depot CO. Military training was in the hands of Basil Eckhard for many months, until he handed over to Major Logan Scott-Bowden. Later Majors Ian Mackenzie and John Basil Griffith were at times Senior Military Officer COPP.

Development went on almost continuously at the Hayling Island COPP Depot. Every procedure, piece of equipment – including canoes – was constantly reassessed, improved and practised with to achieve greater efficiency on operations. To avoid repetition, however, it will be sufficient to pick out a few.

Here was tested the prototype Mark III canoes, powered by a small Britannia motor, running in a telescopic well. Sadly it proved a reluctant starter. There was even an electric-powered Mark III. Its batteries were so heavy it proved impossible to launch from a submarine without damage. Here too was developed the Bongle (or bong stick), hand-powered and infallible; the hand-cranked triphammer, whose signals were readily picked up by a submarine's asdic. This meant that a carrier submarine could wait off-shore *submerged* . . . and still pick-up signals from a folbot. Duggie Kent played his part in its development.

A sounding device, without a lead-line to tangle the operators limbs was also pioneeered here. It involved a trace on a U-tube, but it never got beyond development stage.

Many experimental devices among them a special compact, short-handled model mine-detectors and self-heating soup were received and tested. Donald Campbell's 'Pogo stick' has already been mentioned. There is a canard that one of the Wrens was given a tin of the soup, which she passed on to the family where she was billeted. Somehow the essential precaution of piercing the can before heating was omitted and a fine mist of tomato soup is said to have emerged under pressure as a result.

In reading the day-to-day records of the Depot, the author was amazed to find the name of one of his friends: there is a note that on Sunday 7 May 1944: Captain J. L. Milverton RE visited COPP HQ and made experiments with E/COPP6 [probably Captain D. E. Hunter RE] with Cordtex net as a means of exploding anti-personnel mines by sympathetic explosions. No doubt both were aware that certain types of mine – the German S-mine – for example were immune to sympathetic detonation. The British type V mine had a 'spider' cover intended to prevent sympathetic detonation; no doubt the Germans were working on similar devices. When the author was working on *Operations Most Secret*, reprinted Crécy Books 1994, John Milverton had explained to him what COPP stood for – at precisely the time he needed to know. On another occasion he did mention Cordtex net, but – perhaps motivated by wartime secrecy – never admitted any personal connection with COPP.*

*

Not all development happened at Sandy Point. Tests with flying boats were undertaken at Oban, as they were in the Far East. RAF interest had arisen, because of the necessity to put RAF officers ashore to survey airfield sites. Tests proved inconclusive: a Mark II** canoe could be more readily embarked through the bulbous waist gun turrets of a Consolidated Catalina, than aboard the larger Short Sunderland. The RAF did not favour landings on moonlit nights near to defended shores. In practice submarines or MLs were never superseded as carrier vessels. It was suggested instead that COPPists

* Prior to his retirement to the West Country, the late John Milverton was Churchwarden, part-time organist in the parish where the author lived. In addition his family provided more than half the church choir.

could be parachuted in with their canoes, on moonlit nights. They would be retrieved in daylight – by the 'Jerk of Jesus'. A process similar to picking up messages from the ground by a an army co-operation Lysander – where a hook is lowered from the aircraft, to pick up a line stretched between 'goalposts'. There is no trace that this was ever used on operations.

*

There were occasional 'scares' about the possibility of a German raid on the COPP Depot. Bill Tebb on guard duty, took no chances whatever – loosing-off with his Sten gun at the sound of any movement on the foreshore – just in case it might be an enemy raider. This led to a general alarm being sounded. Happily the culprits always proved to be crabs . . . to Bill's disappointment.

SOURCES
GALWEY, Geoffrey V, *Geoff's Opus.*
Conversations with COPP personnel

CHAPTER THIRTY-TWO

The COPP Association

Emblem of the COPP Association

'An informal association of COPPists and associates . . . .'
COPP was always a very exclusive bunch: many applicants
who applied were turned away. Nigel Willmott always
strove for quality not quantity, many *were* called and few were chosen;
so the operational parties never comprised more than about 150 brave
souls, all told.

Through the good offices of Norman Jennings, M/COPP7, a Savile
Row cutter an informal COPP association of COPPist and associates
was formed. On Jennings' death the work was taken over by Nick
Goodyear: a dagger-and-dolphin emblem designed and a tie manufactured. Several of their reunions have been held in Cambridge. Nick
Goodyear is happily married to Sheila, the Wren he met while training
in Roedean, HMS *Vernon*, in 1942. Geoffrey Galwey attended from the
earliest, when the party was liable to end with a cold dip – although there
was no longer any need for hardening.

Sadly, since the end of the war a great many prominent members
have died far-too-early deaths, and sometimes unnecessary
deaths: Lieutenant-Commander Freddie Ponsonby RN (in command
HMS *Sole Bay*) was accidently drowned in Setubal, Portugal, in
October 1950, when a car drove off a quay. Many others lived
respected and died regretted: Geoffrey Lyne, who was captured
by the Vichy French in the pre-Torch recces: Bruce Ogden Smith,
who trod the Normandy shore on New Year's Eve 1944; Rollo
Mangnall, Alex Hughes, Robin and 'Kitten' Harbud and many
others. In 1992, Nigel Willmott himself, died aged 82-years. And
while these pages were being written, Peter Wild died in February
1995. He was so modest about his war that his obituary surprised
even close friends. He had operational experience in the Mediter-

ranean, Normandy and the Far East: even more operational experience than Nigel Willmott.

During the war, of course, they were all young. Nigel was 33-years old at the time of the Normandy reconnaissance. Scott-Bowden was 24-years old then: a major and accounted one of the older spirits in the bunch.

Many went on to achieve successes: Logan Scott-Bowden left the army as a major-general, having trod the Normandy beaches on D-Day, for the *fifth* time – then, feeling he'd done his bit for COPP, he reverted to orthodox soldiering. Geoffrey Hall became an admiral and Hydrographer of the Navy. Alec Colson is now the Reverend Alec Colson and always glad to give a blessing before the ex-COPPists sit down to dine. Ruari McLean became a freelance typographer and book designer, living in the Isle of Mull. Commander Ralph Stanbury after distinguished postwar service – including navigating a cruiser in the Korean War – was Sir Bernard Lovell's Personal Assistant during the Apollo Moon missions. Ronnie Williamson went from corporal to captain in fourteen months, postwar became a company director, and now lives in Edinburgh. Several COPPists now live near the Depot or Portsmouth. One lives near to Tighnabruich. Some have returned to Commonwealth countries. It is chastening to note that even the fresh-faced midshipmen RNVR – with carmine collar patches on the lapels of their khaki battledress are now retirement age . . . if they survive. Even so, recent reunions have been well-attended.

No official history of COPP has been written: when contacted the Naval Historian sadly confirmed this to be the case. In 1958 *The Secret Invaders* appeared: it is not claimed as a history – it appeared long before the archives of COPP and COHQ were released to the Public Record Office – but it was written with the help of some of the participants. One of its authors, Michael Pearson, was an RNVR officer: M/COPP with the re-constituted COPP1(1), in the Far East. Since then some of the association members have felt that a history should be produced – Nigel Willmott among them. This book is the result.

The author will be very happy to put any COPPist readers, interested in the COPP Association in touch with Nick Goodyear. Nowadays former COPPists are spread all over the globe – not surprisingly – since those who trained at the Hayling Island Sailing Club, COPP Depot included personnel from Australia, Canada, New Zealand and South Africa, as well as all parts of the British Isles.

As a symbol of the close collaboration between naval and military in the COPP operational parties, in action and, of course, during training which went on between operations: the late Lieutenant-Commander Freddie Ponsonby RN, wrote the following poem – *Cast off your cares* – in it the words: 'To hell with the pips and the lace . . .' epitomise the spirit of an operational COPP party in an operational theatre, where all ranks worked together -

Cast off your cares

Hurrah for an open space
Away from the piles of bumph.
To hell with the pips and lace
The stupid red tape and guff.
Away from domestic worries,
The follies of petty strife,
The panics and daily flurries.
My God this is just the life!

Hurrah for an open space
Away from the signals wet
Penned by some morbid face
Whose loss wouldn't cause us regret.
Oh! To be rid of the battles,
Where interference is rife.
To hell with the tongue that prattles
My God this is just the life!

Hurrah for an open space
And the jungle land as well.
It may be a thorning place
But it's heaven compared to hell.
I'm game for the thickest of thick,
Armed with a fighting knife,
For I'm rid of a mental sick.
My God this is just the life!

(Written during three-weeks jungle warfare course in Ceylon, June 1944, run by COPPs 8 and 4, between operations).

CHAPTER THIRTY-THREE

Postscritum

By the end of 1943 most Force Commanders insisted on COPP assistance before proceeding with amphibious offensives. It was also common knowledge that Captains (S) were insisting that submarine commanding officers in their flotillas, co-operating with special forces personnel – for the safety of their vessels and crews – adopted COPP methods for landing and recovery and rendezvous etc.

Postwar COPP were disbanded around 1946. Royal Marine Commandos took on SBS work, which by now was deemed to include a reconnaissance element. Nowadays HMS *Dryad* maintains a watching brief. Improved radar and Decca Navigation Systems now available, mean that much of the assault pilotage aspects of COPP no longer remain. At least one distinguished COPPist, contacted by the author, is convinced beach reconnaissance can only be properly done by Royal Navy officer navigators. He did prove they could do it very well.

In 1949 *Survey by Starlight*, a true story of reconnaissance work in the Mediterranean, by Ralph Neville (Stanbury) was published by Hodder and Stoughton. Selfridges had a window display with a folbot and a model in a COPP swimsuit. It was displayed during a very hot July and may have failed to boost sales as it should. Ralph Stanbury used noms de plume for the characters and the exact nature of COPP was not spelled out.

Indeed, COPP remained properly secret until around 1954 – when its existence was 'blown' by the American press.

*

COPP reunions have been held in recent years, chiefly due to the initiative of Nick Goodyear. Most have been held at Cambridge with some at the Hayling Island Sailing Club – which was pleased to make Nigel Willmott an honorary life member.

After Prue pre-deceased him Nigel Willmott married Pamela, another
Hayling Island Wren. She had been at one of the Northney camps.
Ronnie Williamson, ex-COPP5, was Nigel's best man. Through the
good offices of ex-Sergeant Toby Haythorne (ex No. 1 Commando)
Ronnie was able to arrange for a cake decorated with intricate sugar
confectionery representations of the Special Boat Section, COPP and
Combined Operations; a difficult, painstaking process, requiring
twenty-four hours between the application of separate colours. It was
a masterpiece. Nigel – having saved Roger Courtney's life on the Rhodes
recce – was perfectly entitled to display the SBS emblem.

*

In recent years Nigel Clogstoun-Willmott's love of sailing did not
diminish – he often sailed with Ronnie, 'Blondie' Hasler and Peter Wild
– but his health had started to deteriorate. His very last meal in England
was at the Rag: the Army and Navy Club, Pall Mall, in the company of
Logan Scott-Bowden. Captain Willmott RN (Retd) and Major-General
Scott-Bowden met in the bar. Soldier and sailor had a few glasses
together, toasting one another.

Then they sat down to one of Nigel's favourite meals: game soup,
Dover sole, Stilton-and-port. It was typical of Nigel that every dish
chosen should be quintessentially British. They may have reflected that
48-years before, instead of sharing a table they'd shared an X-Craft.

Both men enjoyed their meal and chatted amicably: but it was clear
that Nigel's once acute mathematical brain could no longer add up and
subtract: he could remember his daughter's date of birth, but not work
out how old she was. In all other respects Nigel was his wonderful,
charming self.

They ended their evening in the main anteroom where one might
obtain the best vintage port. Nigel was supremely happy and no-one
could have told that he was a very sick man.

*

Nigel travelled back to Cyprus, where he had lived for five years. He
died there in hospital on 26 June 1992: he was 82-years of age. He was
buried in the Military Cemetery at Dhekilia Garrison. Local regulations
meant that neither his retired rank, nor his decorations could be
inscribed on his headstone; nor yet the words 'Father of COPP', as he
would have wished. Someone even suggested that no-one these days

had heard of COPP. Nigel had never sought fame – was used to regulations – though frequently outspokenly critical of those he found 'damn stupid. So probably he understood.

Memorial services were held for Captain Nigel Clogstoun-Willmott DSO, DSC* RN (Retd), 'Father of COPP', at Cyprus on 31 July 1992, and at Palmerston Street Church, Edinburgh, on 21 November 1992. The Edinburgh service was well-attended by former COPPists, friends and relations. Two serving members of the Royal Marines Special Boat Squadron represented serving naval personnel . . . naturally *they* had heard of COPP . . . . Security required that they be anonymous: Nigel would have understood that.

SOURCE:

Major-General Logan Scott-Bowden CBE, DSO, MC* at 1993 reunion, at Cambridge.

Appendix 1

CHRONOLOGY

1940
Apr/May   Norwegian campaigns

1941
28 Mar   Beginning of 18 months gap in the development of COPP

1942
late Mar   Op *Cordite* – Rhodes recce
27/28 Mar   Battle of Matapan
28 Mar   Op *Chariot* – St Nazaire, HMS *Campbeltown*, Commando raid
11/12 Apr   Op *JV* – Montanaro's folbot limpet attack on merchantman in Boulogne harbour
21/22 Apr   Op *Abercombie* – Le Hardelot, Lord Lovat leads Commando raid
24 Apr   British Evacuation of Greece begins
19 Aug   Operation *Jubilee* – Dieppe raid
9 Sep   British land on Vichy French Madagascar
mid Sep   *Party Inhuman* assembles – development of COPP resumed
6 Oct   Vichy forces in Madagascar surrender
6/7 Oct   *Party Inhuman* provide pilotage markers for Op *Torch* – invasion of North Africa
7 Nov   Op *Torch* – invasion of North Africa
early Dec   COPP placed on an official basis
7 Dec   Op *Frankton* – Hasler's Bordeaux limpet raid

1943
10 Jul   Op *Husky* – invasion of Sicily, COPP3, COPP4, COPP5, COPP6, COPP ME 1 and 2
9 Sep   Op *Avalanche* – Salerno Beachhead, COPP5 and SBS
20/25 Oct   Op *Provident* – Akyab recce, Burma, COPP7
Oct/Nov   Projected Op *Buccaneer* (Andamans) planned but not executed, COPP8
Dec   Op *Bunkum* – Mayu Peninsula, Burma, COPP8

25/26 Dec	Op *Bell Push Able* – Normandy coast, COPP1
28/29 Dec	Op *Bell Push Baker* – Normandy coast, COPP2
31 Dec–Jan 44	Op *KJH* – Normandy coast, COPP1, COPP6

1944

17/21 Jan	Op *Postage Able* – Normandy coast, COPP2
22 Jan	Op *Shingle* – Allied landing at Anzio, COPP10, SBS and COPP ME
23 May	US 5th Army breaks out from Anzio
23/26 Apr	Special operation COPP8, N. Sumatra recce
1 Jun/30 Dec	COPP10 active in Mediterranean and Adriatic
6 Jun	Op *Neptune*/Op *Overlord* – D-Day landings, COPP1, COPP9
17 Jun	Op *Brassard* – Allied amphibious landings on Elba: previous recces made by COPP10
17/24 Aug	Op *Frippery*, COPP7 and 8 Sumatra recce for projected Op *Culverin*
16/19 Oct	Op *David* – Ondaw, Onchaung and Elizabeth Island, Burma, COPP8
Dec–Apr 45	Arakan and Chaung operations by Far East COPP(1), COPP3(1), COPP4(1) and COPP9(1) preparatory for Rangoon offensive

1945

3 Jan	3rd Commando Brigade enters Akyab, Burma
11/12 Jan	The Stakes, Myebon, Burma, COPP3(1)
18 Jan	Assault on Myebon, Kangaw, Burma, COPP3(1)
8/9 Mar	Op *Baboon* – Phuket recce, Thailand, COPP3(1)
8–27 Mar	Op *Copyright* – Phuket recce, COPP3(1)/SOG
23/24 Mar	Op *Plunder*/Op *Varsity* – Allied crossings of the River Rhine, COPP5(1)
9 Apr	British offensive against Rangoon begins
13 Apr	Op *Roast* – Lake Commachio Bridgehead, Italy, COPP2(1)
18 Apr	COPP7(1) make Elbe recce near Luneburg
25 Apr	Russian and US troops link up at Torgau on the River Elbe
3 May	Rangoon surrenders
8 May	VE Day in Britain
9 Jun	Op *Confidence* – Morib Beaches recce, Malaya, COPP3(1)
6 Aug	Atomic bomb dropped on Hiroshima
14 Aug	Japan surrenders
15 Aug	VJ Day in Britain
9 Sep	Op *Zipper* – unopposed landing on Malayan peninsula

Appendix 2

PRO DEFE2 1116

Ref: C.R.4204/43
Combined Operations Headquarters,
14, Richmond Terrace,
Whitehall, S.W.1.

MOST SECRET

2nd August, 1943.

Allied Force Headquarters, North Africa
Commander-in-Chief, Mediterranean
Commander-in-Chief, India
Commander-in-Chief, Eastern Fleet
Commander-in-Chief, Middle East
Commander-in-Chief, Levant
Chief of Staff to the Supreme Allied Commander
    (Designate)
Commander-in-Chief, Portsmouth

    Copies to: Admiral (Submarines)
               Officer Commanding, Combined
               Operations Pilotage Party Depot.

    As a result of experience gained in recent operations in
the Mediterranean, it has been decided that, in future prior
to undertaking Combined Operations, one or more Combined
Operations Pilotage Party Units, as necessary, will be placed
at the disposal of Commanders-in-Chief. It is therefore
thought advisable to state briefly the composition of a
Combined Operations Pilotage Party Unit (hereinafter referred
to as C.O.P.P.Unit), what it can do, how it is achieved and
some of the administrative problems involved.

    2. A C.O.P.P. Unit complete, consists of 11 personnel, of
which 4 are Naval Officers and 1 are Military Officer (Royal
Engineers). The remainder are ratings of which 3 are Seamen, 1
an engine mechanic, 1 a Corporal Special Boat Section, and 1
Royal Engineer Draughtsman, together with specially developed
stores and craft.

3. As the problems involved are mostly navigational, the Commanding Officer is invariably a Lieutenant Commander or Lieutenant (Navigational) or (Hydrographic) specialist.

4. This is more particularly summarised as follows:-

Operational   (a) 1 Lieutenant (N) or (N) Specialists R.N., Senior Officer, Combined Operations Pilotage Party.

(b) 1 Lieutenant, R.N.V.R. (ex.Beach Parties) – Assistant to above.

(c) 1 Captain, Royal Engineers, for military reconnaisance ashore.

Duties at   (d) 1 Lieutenant, R.N.V.R. for Maintenance
Base   duties.

(e) 1 Midshipman, R.N.V.R.

In addition the operational officers have specially selected paddler guard ratings attached to them, though for the more important navigational duties, they would require the supervision of an officer.

5. The Officer Commanding, C.O.P.P. can be relied upon for complete daylight persicope reconnaissance sketches and navigational pilotage directions for an assault. In most units this can also be done by the Assistant Commanding Officer and the military officer. As a specimen of the type of sketch and sailing direction produced, each C.O.P.P. Unit will carry for the information of their operational authority a specimen of sketches and sailing directions prepared for themselves on an exercise during training.

C.C.O.'s C.R. 4204/43 of 2nd August 1943

6. All operational officers, however, have been fully trained in swimming, beach gradients, beach surfaces, obstacles, exits and defences, though their specialist qualifications themselves indicate for which they are bst suited. The Base Officers are regarded as first line reserves for operations, though their training naturally is not so thorough.

7. Beach reconnaissance is properly divided into four progressive categories.

(a) Approach by submarine to the assault beach are for the purpose of sketching the general coastal silhouette and conspicuous leading marks by day and night periscope reconnaissance.

(b) Approach by canoe to the beach in darkness to complete
the silhouette night aspect and take soundings as requisite
beyond the swimmer's depth.

(c) Approach by swimmer on to the beach to obtain beach
gradients and texture.

(d) Military reconnaissance of the beach for exits, wire
obstructions, etc.

It will be appreciated that risk of compromise increases
generally speaking with each successive approach and it is
considered that the Officer Commanding, C.O.P.P. Unit, should
be given a clear directive as to which of (a), (b), (c) or (d)
should be undertaken.

8. By C.O.P.P. methods, each officer could produce a 120
yards beach gradient in 30 to 45 minutes. Also, by close
observation, a valuable estimate of the potentialities of the
beach would be obtained.

9. A successful beach reconnaissance requires a minimum
of five hours darkness.

10. The craft used by C.O.P.P. is the canoe Mark 1**,
which has been evolved as a result of considerable operational
experience. It is seaworthy in wind up to force 4, but a
C.O.P.P. Unit cannot be expected to obtain satisfactory beach
reconnaissance in any but fine weather, i.e., wind not over
force 2.

11. C.O.P.P. have trained and operated entirely with
submarines and no other form of carrier has been employed to
date. In fact, the Mark 1** canoe is designed to pass through
a submarine's $29^1/_2$" fore-hatch.

12. Whenever possible, every C.O.P.P. Unit will have
studied their operational area at the Inter-Services
Topographical Department at Oxford and will possess all
available information, such as photographs of models, charts,
General Staff Service maps, Inter Service Intelligence Section
reports, and air reconnaissance photographs.

13. C.O.P.P. Units abroad are kept up to date as far as
possible as regards technique and development and new
instruments and stores can be flown out when perfected for
operational use, if available.

14. In addition to producing pilotage directions and
sketches for the use of landing craft officers, C.O.P.P.
personnel are trained and available to act as pilots and
markers on D.Day.

15. Piloting would normally be done by the Navigational or Hydrographic officer and possibly by the Assistant Commanding Officer, if more than usually skilled in navigation; marking could be done by the Assistant Commanding Officer, Maintenance Officer and military officers using ratings as paddler guards.

16. The technique for which C.O.P.P. teams are trained is as follows. A submarine carrying pilots and markers proceeds as close inshore as possible and launches the canoe. The markers paddle inshore and anchor in the agreed position. Alternatively, they may take up a position on a convenient island or on the assault beaches as requisite. It is desirable that pilots should take markers in a dummy run on D-1 to familiarise him with landmarks for his fix. The markers are then in a position to display the R.G. lantern for the guidance of landing craft.

17. After the markers leave, the submarine retires to her beacon position.

18. The leader of the first flight, usually a Motor Launch, can then proceed alongside the submarine, pick up the pilot, take up her position in the flight, and proceed to the assault beach on the I.R. ray from the markers, using her R.G. receiver. Transferring of pilot to Motor Launch from a submarine should be practised in harbour and at sea both in daylight and darkness.

19. As markers may have to proceed ashore after the assault and work under the orders of the Principal Beach Master, it is most important they should know the password for their beach in order to avoid risk of being shot.

20. Appendix "A" is a copy of a letter of authority which is given to each officer in charge of a Unit and incorporates the requirements as regards administrative problems such as facilities required, access to Commander-in-Chief and Force Commanders and direct communication with C.C.O.

(Signed) Louis Mountbatten
Chief of Combined Operations.

APPENDIX "A" to C.C.O.'s C.R. 4204/43 of 2nd August

INSTRUCTION TO THE OFFICER IN CHARGE OF
A C.O.P.P. UNIT

You are placed in charge of C.O.P.P. Unit No ---
comprising the following Combined Operations personnel:-

            4 Naval Officers
            1 Military Officer
            5 Naval Other Ranks
            2 Military Other Ranks

2.   These instructions should be produced as your
authority, should such be questioned.

3.   On arrival on the station you will be under the
orders of the Naval Commander-in-Chief, or such other
Authority as he may decide. If the usual practice is followed,
you will be placed under one of the Captains (S).

4.   Your normal method of communication should be through
the Authority under whose orders you are placed. In order,
however, that the general organisation, development and
training of C.O.P.P. Units may proceed to the best advantage,
you should keep the Chief of Combined Operations informed on
matters of detail concerning training, development, stores and
personnel, i.e. those questions not directly concerning
operations. If by signal, this should be done by requesting
the Authority under whose orders you are to forward a message
in the following form:-

        "Following for Chief of Combined Operations from
        C.O.P.P._____."

        If requirements are forwarded by letter and action is
required to be taken, the letter should normally be addressed
to the Authority mentioned, with a copy to the Chief of
Combined Operations. This will enable the Chief of Combined
Operations to take preliminary action, if it is necessary, but
definite action can only be taken by the Chief of Combined
Operations when the requirements are forwarded through the
normal service channels.

5.   In Enclosure 1 is given a full list of facilities
which experience has shown are required by a C.O.P.P. Unit.
Enclosure 2 is a copy of an Admiralty Letter M/P.D. (Q) 4036/
43 of 4th January, 1943, addressed to the Commander-on-Chief,
Mediterranean.

6.   You will receive from the Officer-in-Charge, C.O.P.P.
Depot, a contingent fund of £60.0.0d in British bank notes. A

strict account of all expenditure is to be kept and rendered in due course to the Director of Navy Accounts at the Admiralty. The object of the fund is to enable you to purchase stores and provide facilities not readily available form Services sources. Replacement of accounts expended may be obtained from the Local Accountant Officer.

MOST SECRET

ENCLOSURE No.1 to APPENDIX "A" to C.C.O.P.'s
C.R. 4204/43 of 2nd August, 1943

Being mainly self-contained as regards stores and normal maintenance, the following minimum facilities are required at your operational base.

(a) Canoe assembly space with single work bench; floor to be 25 ft. by 25 ft. minimum, or two such spaces 25 ft. by 16 ft. with door in short sides.

(b) Two store rooms 25 ft. by 12 ft.

(c) Drawing and General office 25 ft. by 12 ft. with safe, steel cabinet and telephone.

(d) Occasional lathe and battery charging facilities.

(e) Secure printing facilities for Perrogallic, etc. paper.

(f) Occasional working party.

(g) Permanent 15 cwt. truck and driver.

(h) Facilities for drawing or replacing special Army and R.A.F. stores locally.

NOTE
(a), (b) and (c) should be adjacent and secure, a guard being required.

2.   It is desirable for security reasons that personnel should be lodged and messed away from other personnel, preferably near operational base, which need not be actually at the water's edge.

3.   Additional ration scale has been found necessary during training periods and may be demanded, quoting K.R. & A.I. Art. 1825, para 4.

4.   A 3 or 6 ton lorry and a large motor boat or landing craft is required during coastal exercises.

5.   The maximum possible amount of coastal and physical training, including day and night harbour launching exercises from an allocated submarine should be given before proceeding on an operation. An allocation of Exercise Areas and adequate communications will be required for this.

MOST SECRET

ENCLOSURE No. 2 to APPENDIX "A" to C.C.O.'s
C.R. 4204/43 of 2nd August 1943

        With reference to Admiralty Message 2008/1, I am to inform you that Party C.O.P.P. No. 3 and Party C.O.P.P. No. 4 are mainly self-contained as regards stores and normal maintenance, but it may be necessary to send a few items by air after the parties have left.

        The following facilities are required in addition to those given in Admiralty Message 2008/1.

        (a) Occasional working parties.

        (b) Facilities for drawing or replacing special Army and R.A.F. Stores locally.

        (c) Contingent fund £50. each party for local purchase of stores.

        (d) A three or six ton lorry and a large motor boat or landing craft during exercises.

3.   Additional ration scale has been found necessary during training periods.

4.   This is the first occasion on which this requirement has been undertaken under anything but perfect weather conditions and some of the gear supplied has therefore not been tested under conditions likely to be met in February. Although some of the parties have previous experience, it is essential, in order to ensure physical fitness, that a minimum of 16 days' training should be given.

5.   It has been found that the Senior Officers of parties must be kept as clear as possible of day to day administrative questions, as they will be fully occupied in training. It is therefore recommended that they should have direct access to a senior officer at the base, who would be responsible for ensuring that urgent requirements, working parties and transport are met. This also avoids the necessity of explaining their requirements to a number of authorities before supply can be made.

6.   Close communications between the Senior Officers of the parties and the Force Commander is most necessary, and it is desirable that they should be able to signal to him direct or through the Senior Officer referred to in para. 5 and also to their Administrative Authority in the United Kingdom regarding developments and general administration.

BY COMMAND OF THEIR LORDSHIPS

CHART OF RECONNAISSANCES IN
SALERNO BAY ~ 30 & 31 AUG

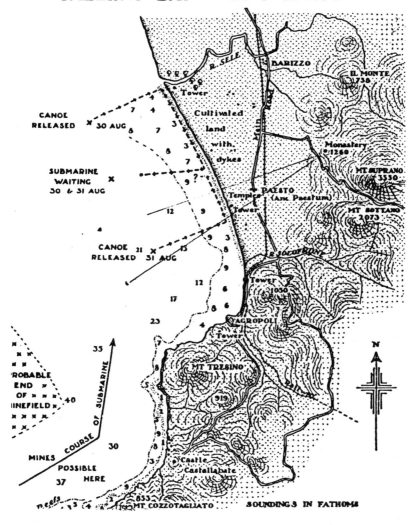

Crown Copyright: reproduced with permission of Controller HM Stationery Office.

Appendix 3

PRO DEFE2 970

```
DEFE2 970    SBU SPECIAL BOAT UNIT
             principally at Hammanheil
```

Operation CONCERT

TAKING A PRISONER

  If possible individual enemy will be stalked and knocked out
from behind. If they make any noise they will be shot
immediately by Sergt Tuck with a Welrod. But (exercise)
friendly attitude entering hut. If an enemy is knocked out he
will be immediately stripped of all his clothes and
belongings. He will be gagged and blindfolded with his hands
tied behind him, his sight being eliminated to prevent any
chance of his trying to escape. If he recovers sufficiently he
shall walk, if not, he shall be carried by a fit person
detailed at that time. Lt Ryan will be resonsbile for the
prisoner and belongings delivered back at headquarters.

FIGHTING

Party will not fight save to regain possession or get back
their canoes or to attack as small post after selecting a
Burman.

Appendix 4

PRO DEFE2 970

Operation BABOON

COVER STORY

1. If captured delay as long as possible then grudgingly give the following information. Take a long time to tell how the arrangements in Trincomalee were made and you were kept in the dark.

2.

(a) You volunteered for special service - were assembled with others of all services in Trincomalee where you were given some training in canoe work, briefing for the operation was given in the submarine. There were 7 or 8 other parties sent out, and although you weren't told where they went, you believe they were doing similar jobs in Sumatra, Burma and Malaya.

(b) Your job was to get on the airfield and see what kind of planes were there and how many. Then if you could, see how many men were about and how many guns were mounted.

(c) There was no priority about the job and you only did it as part of the submarine's normal patrol in the area. All the briefing was vague and there weren't any specific questions.

(d) There is no local escape plan or emergecy RV, you were to get over to Indo-China, if return to the submarine was impossible, and then try to contact any guerillas.

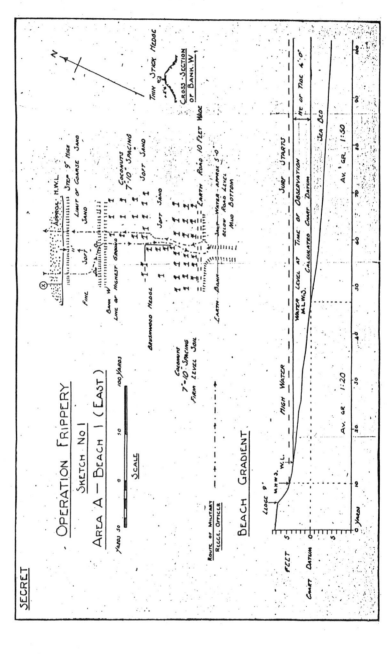

OPERATION FRIPPERY

SKETCH No 1

AREA 'A' — BEACH 1 (EAST)

Crown Copyright: reproduced with permission of Controller HM Stationery Office.

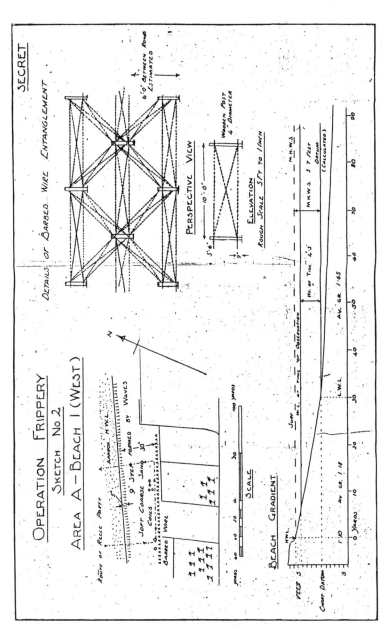

Crown Copyright: reproduced with permission of Controller HM Stationery Office.

Appendix 5

AIR INTELLIGENCE QUESTIONNAIRE OPERATION CONFIDENCE

NOTES

The following require answers supported where possible by photographic evidence:

1.   (a) Is the site generally in your opinion an easy, medium, difficult engineer task for an airfield construction group?

        (b) Is it good, fair or bad from an air operational point of view if constructed?

2.   (a) Type and depth of surface soil?

        (b) Type of subsoil 6"-9 min. depth. and W.M. Bring back samples of (a) and (b) if possible inspect any open cuts or wells to estimate sub-soil at greater depth.

3.   If site soil requires other ingredients to stabilise it, are any of these available locally that you can spot? If possible bring back samples.

4.   What is the general nature of airfield surface? e.g. cultivated, fallow, level, undulating, very irregular etc? Is there rock outcrop?

5.   What is the general drainage? Will it drain naturally i.e. has it a cross fall? Any natural drainage lines nearby?

6.   Nature of vegetation on site? If trees present try to identify them and give rough idea of height and girth.

7.   Nature of clearable obstructions in approaches in terms of 6 above.

8.   What is the bearing and gradient of any permanent obstructions within <u>10°</u> approach funnel.

9.   Are there any major obstructions in the circuit area, with approximate bearing and gradient.

10.   Any major engineer difficulties to preparation of taxiways and aprons up to 1, 2, 3 or 4 squadrons of (a) fighters, (b) medium bombers, (c) transports?

11.   Any major difficulties for approach roads.

*   *   *

The following general engineer points if possible are required:

1.   Any information re Water Supply in the Island.

2.   Regarding nature of existing roads.

3.   Classification of bridges.

4.   Suitability of timber for construction purposes.

The following guide for maximum and minimum standards may be useful:

	<u>Max</u>	<u>Min</u>
Length of runway	2000 yards	1200 yards
Length of overruns	200 ,,	100 ,,
Width of strip	250 ,,	150 ,,
Approach Gradient	1/50	1/30
Funnel angle	15°	10°

*   *   *

<u>Air Ministry Bulletin dated 9 April 1946: RAF Museum File 2065A</u>

<u>Additional Member in the Military Division of the Most Excellent Order of the British Empire</u>

<u>Flight Lieutenant Bertie Brown (122365), Royal Air Force Volunteer Reserve</u>. Flight Lieutenant Brown was a member of a party engaged on a special operation behind the Japanese lines.

He completed his mission and was at large in enemy territory for
seventeen days without food, evading enemy search parties. On at
least two occasions Flight Lieutenant Brown fought his way out
of difficult situations. Throughout these hazardous
circumstances he showed great bravery and determination. It was
only lack of food and sickness that forced him to take shelter
in a village where his presence was betrayed to the Thai
authorities and he was taken prisoner. The whole operation was
carried out under imminent danger of capture and involved night
marches through the jungle. After the fifth day the party had no
food. They grew daily weaker and suffered from jungle sores in
addition to wounds and sickness.

Courtesy RAF Museum, Hendon

Appendix 6

List of COPP operational parties showing recommissions

COPP1　　　Lt-Cdr N C Willmott, DSO, DSC*, RN (1)
　　　　　　Training and development: *Party Inhuman* (Op *Torch*); LCP(N) and
　　　　　　X-craft Normandy recces 1943–44

COPP1　　　Lt-Cdr P W Clark, DSC*, RN
　　　　　　Normandy pilotage

COPP/ME1　Lt P R G Smith, DSC, RN
　　　　　　Sicily recce: evaded to Malta

COPP/ME2　Lt P de C De Kock, MBE, DSC, SANF
　　　　　　Lost on Sicily recce

COPP/ME　 S-Lt K G Patterson, RANVR
　　　　　　Evaded following Anzio recce, eventually made POW/repatriated

COPP2　　　Lt-Cdr F M Berncastle, DSC*, RN
　　　　　　Specialist, hydrographic tautwire surveys 1943–44

COPP3　　　Lt N M J Teacher, DSO, RN
　　　　　　Sicily 1943

COPP4　　　Lt N T McHarg, DSO, RN
　　　　　　Sicily 1943

COPP 5　　 Lt R N Stanbury, DSC, RN
　　　　　　Sicily, Italy, Salerno 1943

COPP6　　　Lt D W Amer, DSC, RNR
　　　　　　Sicily, Normandy 1943–44, South of France (abortive)

COPP7　　　Lt G P D Hall, DSC, RN
　　　　　　Arakan, Sumatra 1943–44

COPP8　　　Lt F W Ponsonby, DSC, RN
　　　　　　Arakan, Sumatra 1943–44, Andamans (abortive)

COPP9　　　Lt L G Lyne, DSC, RN
　　　　　　Party Inhuman (Op *Torch*); Normandy X-craft 1943–44

COPP10　　 Lt-Cdr J S Townson, DSC, RN
　　　　　　Anzio, Italy, Yugoslavia, Dalmatia, Aegean 1944

COPP1(1)　 Lt P G Wild, DSC, RNVR
　　　　　　Arakan, Siam, Malaya 1945

COPP2(1)	Lt R H Fyson, DSC, RN
	Corsica, Adriatic, Yugoslavia, South of France 1944–45
COPP3(1)	Lt A I Hughes, DSC, RNR
	Arakan, Siam, Malaya 1945
COPP4(1)	Lt D H Mackay, DSC, RN
	Arakan 1944
COPP9(1)	Lt J Morison, DSC, RN
	South of France (abortive), Arakan 1944–45
COPP6(1)	Lt D G Kay, RN
	Mediterranean, SEAC – too late to be operational 1944–45
COPP5(1)	Lt A H Winship, SANF(V)
	Rhine crossing 1945
COPP7(1)	Lt J R Hashim, RN
	Elbe crossing 1945
COPP5(2)	Lt A G Hamilton, RN
	SEAC – too late to be operational 1945

(1) = Indicates 2nd Commission
(2) = Indicates 3rd Commission

Appendix 7

List of operational parties with dates for leaving and return to Hayling Island depot (where applicable):

		Left UK	Returned
COPP1	Lt-Cdr N C Willmott, DSO, DSC*, RN (1)	31.10.43	28.6.44
COPP1	Lt-Cdr P W Clark, DSC*, RN (2) (Normandy)		
COPP/ME1	Lt P R G Smith, DSC, RN (Med – ex Malta)		
COPP/ME2	Lt P de C De Kock, MBE, DSC, SANF (Med – ex Malta)		
COPP/ME	S-Lt K G Patterson, RANVR (Med – ex Ischia) (Anzio)		
COPP2	Lt-Cdr F M Berncastle, DSC* (Normandy/Med)		
COPP3	Lt N M J Teacher, DSO, RN (Med)	8.1.43	31.7.43
COPP4	Lt N T McHarg, DSO, RN (Med)	8.1.43	31.7.43
COPP5	Lt R N Stanbury, DSC, RN (Med)	26.5.43	14.10.43
COPP6	Lt D W Amer, DSC, RNR (Med)	26.4.43	8.10.43
COPP7	Lt G P D Hall, DSC, RN (SEAC)	16.6.43	7.1.45
COPP8	Lt F W Ponsonby, RN (SEAC)	27.9.43	26.3.45
COPP9	Lt L G Lyne, DSC, RN (Normandy)	30.11.43	28.6.44
COPP10	Lt-Cdr J S Townson, DSC, RN (Med)	1.11.43	12.12.44
COPP1(1)	Lt P G Wild, DSC, RNVR (SEAC)	5.11.44	30.10.45
COPP2(1)	Lt R H Fyson, DSC, RN (Med)	23.4.44	26.6.45
COPP3(1)	Lt A I Hughes, DSC, RNR (SEAC)	17.7.44	30.10.45
COPP4(1)	Lt D H Mackay, DSC, RN (SEAC)	23.3.44	11.6.45
COPP9(1)	Lt J Morison, DSC, RN (Med)	25.7.44	7.9.44
COPP9(1)	Lt J Morison, DSC, RN (SEAC)	5.11.44	30.10.45
COPP6(1)	Lt D G Kay, RN (Med/SEAC)	12.2.45	30.10.45
COPP5(1)	Lt A H Winship, DSC, SANF(V) (Rhine)	20.3.45	25.3.45
COPP7(1)	Lt J R Hashim, RN (Elbe)	25.4.45	2.5.45
COPP5(2)	Lt A G Hamilton, RN (SEAC)	24.4.45	30.10.45

(1) = Indicates 2nd Commission
(2) = Indicates 3rd Commission

Appendix 8

List of Gallantry awards to COPP personnel commemorated on the commemorative tablet at Hayling Island Sailing Club

Note: dates shown in figures relate to *London Gazette* entries.

Disinguished Service Order
Willmott, Herbert Nigel Clogstoun, RN
    Lt MiD Norwegian coast, April/June 1940, 26.9.40
    Lt-Cdr DSO Rhodes recce with Capt R J Courtney, 3.1.41
    Lt-Cdr DSC Op *Torch*, Beach recce, N Africa, 1942, 16.3.43
    Lt-Cdr COPP1 MiD* LCP(L) 190 Op *KJH*, 15.2.44
    Lt-Cdr COPP1 DSC* NC Force Juno, Op *Bigot*, 4.4.44
Sinclair, George Sutherland, RNR
    Lt DSO COPP4 Sp Op Med, Sicily, 1943
McHarg, Neville Townley, RN
    Lt DSO COPP4 Sp Op Med, Sicily, 1943
    (Later Captain RN, OBE postwar)
Scott-Bowden, Logan, RE
    Major MC Normandy recce, Op *KJH* (MC* subsequently), Dec/Jan 1944
    Major DSO Normandy recce, Op *Bell Push Able*, Jan 1944
    (Later Major-General, CBE postwar)

Order of the British Empire, Member of the British Empire
    Colson, Alexander Francis Lionel, RE
    Capt MiD COPP8 Op *David*, Arakan, Oct 44, 22.3.45
    Capt MBE COPP8 Op *Frippery*, Sumatra, Aug 44, 22.3.45
Lucas, Alfred William Tindall, RE
    Capt MBE Op *Frippery*, N Sumatra, Aug 1944
McGuire, James
    AB COPP ME 2
    BEM Op *Torch*; escape from enemy hands (picked up by Vichy French trawler) N Africa 1942

Distinguished Service Cross

Willmott, Herbert Nigel Clogstoun, DSC* RN
  (See above)

Kent, Douglas Thomas, DSC* RNVR
  T/S-Lt DSC Beachmaster Commando raid Le Hardelot, 1942
  Lt DSC* COPP5 Sicily/Italy, May 1943, 7.12.43

Stanbury, Ralph Neville, RN
  Lt DSC Sicily/Italy, May 1943, 7.12.43

Amcr, Donald Wolfenden, RNR
  Lt MiD *Party Inhuman*, Op *Torch*, N Africa, 1942
  Lt DSC COPP6 Sicily, 7.12.43
  Lt MiD* LCA(N) Op *Neptune*, Normandy, June 1944

Wild, Peter Grenville, RNVR
  Lt DSC Italy/Sicily, 7.12.43
  Lt MiD *X-23* Op *Neptune*, Normandy, June 1944
  MiD* COPP1 Arakan, Nov 44/March 45, 10.7.45

Hall, Geoffrey Penrose Dickinson, RN
  Lt DSC COPP7 Arakan coast, Oct 1943
  Lt MiD COPP7 Op *Frippery*, N Sumatra, Aug 1944
  (later Rear Admiral and Hydrographer of the Navy)
  (CB postwar)

McLean, John David Ruari, RNVR
  MiD: Liaison Officer French submarine *Rubis*, 7.12.43
  Croix de Guerre
  Lt DSC COPP7 Arakan, Oct 1943
  Lt MiD* COPP7 Op *Frippery*, N Sumatra, Aug 1944
  (CBE postwar)

Clark, Paul Wilson, RN*
  Lt-Cdr DSC COPP1 Op *Neptune*, Normandy, June 1944
  Lt-Cdr DSC* COPP1 Ops Arakan coast, Nov 1944/Mar 1945, 10.7.45

Lyne, Lionel Geoffrey, RN
  Lt DSC *X-23* Op *Neptune*, Normandy 1944
  Lt MiD HMS *Courier* mineseeping Elbe, Weser, Mar/June 1945
  (A/Cmdr OBE Queen's Habour Master, Port Said, Suez ops, 13.6.57)

Harbud, Robin Frederick Andrew, RNVR
  T/S-Lt DSC COPP1 Op *Neptune*, Normandy, 1944, 14.11.44

Talbot, George Richard, RNVR
  Lt DSC COPP10 Ops Aegean, 1944

Smith, Peter Roger Gilmour, RN
  Lt DSC COPP ME1, paddled Sicily to Malta, 4.5.43

Brand, David, RNVR
  Lt DSC COPP ME1, paddled Sicily to Malta, 4.5.43

Mackay, Denis Handcock, RN
  Lt DSC COPP4 Ops Arakan coast, Nov 1943/Mar 1945, 10.7.45

Hughes, Alexander Ian, RNR
  Lt DSC COPP3 Ops Arakan coast, Nov 1944/Mar 1945, 10.7.45
  Lt MiD COPP3 Op *Baboon*, Phuket, Siam, 10.7.45
  Lt MiD COPP3 Beach recce Morib, Malaya, June 45, 23.10.45

Alcock, Ian Ernest, RCNVR
  T/Lt DSC COPP3 Op *Baboon*, Phuket, Siam, Mar 1945
  T/Lt MiD COPP3 Op *Confidence*, Morib, Malaya, June 1945
Fyson, Richard Hugh, RN
  Lt DSC COPP2 recce Lake Commachio, Mar/Apr 1945
Dawson, Bryan, RNVR
  Lt DSC COPP2 recce Lake Commachio, Mar/Apr 1945
Townson, John Stover, RN
  Lt later Cdr DSC COPP10 Ops in Aegean, 1944
  (OBE postwar)
Morison, John, RN
  Lt DSC COPP9 Ops Arakan coast, Mar/Apr 1945

Military Cross

Courtney, Roger James, KRRC
  Capt MC Rhodes recce with Nigel Willmott, 21.10.41
Matterson, Peter D, RE
  Capt MC COPP5 Salerno, Italy
Scott-Bowden, Logan, RE
  (See above)
Gates, Ronald Henry Charles, RE
  Capt MC COPP9 Far East recce ops

Mention in Despatches

Hastings, Nicholas Patrick Comyns, RNVR
  Lt-Cdr DSC HMS *Prince Charles* Op *Archery* (Vaagso)
  Lt-Cdr MiD *Party Inhuman*, Op *Torch*, N Africa, 1942
Amer, Donald Wolfenden, RNR (two mentions)
  (See above)
Cooper, Noel Wilson, RNVR
  Lt MiD *Party Inhuman*, Op *Torch*, N Africa, 1942
Eckhard, Basil Newton, The Buffs
  Capt MiD *Party Inhuman*, Op *Torch*, N Africa, 1942
  Capt King's Commendation
Moorhouse, Leslie Hugh, RNR
  Lt-Cdr (Retd) MiD *Party Inhuman*, Op *Torch*, N Africa, 1942
Willmott, Herbert Nigel Clogstun, RN (two mentions)
  (See above)
Hunter, D C, RE
  Capt MiD COPP6 Sicily/Italy, 1943
Hall, Geoffrey Penrose Dickinson, RN
  (See above)
Maclean, John David Ruari, RNVR (two mentions)
  (See above)
Booth, John Charles Macaulay, RNVR
  Lt MiD *X-23* COPP9 Op *Neptune*, June 1944
Wild, Peter Grenville, RNVR
  (See above)

Peacock, John Michael, RN (two mentions)
>   T/A/Lt MiD COPP8 Recce Burma, Dec 1943/Sumatra Apr 1944
>   T/A/Lt MiD* COPP8 Op *David*, Arakan, Oct 1944

Pond, Stanley Victor
>   Elect Mech 4 MiD COPP8 Burma, Dec 1943/Sumatra, Apr 1944

Ponsonby, Fredeick William, RN
>   Lt MiD COPP8 Op *David*, Arakan, Oct 1944

Richards, Geoffrey, RNVR
>   T/A/Lt MiD COPP8 Op *David*, Arakan, Oct 1944

Gascoigne, Robert Amos (two mentions)
>   T/A/PO MiD Ops Burma, Dec 1943/Sumatra, Apr 1944
>   T/A/PO MiD, MiD* COPP8 Op *David*, Arakan, Oct 1944

Neil, James G
>   A/L/Sea MiD COPP8 Op *David*, Arakan, Oct 1944

Parker, Leslie Norman
>   Elect Mech 4 HMS *Tabins* COPP10 Sulet Islands, Aug 1944

Briggs, Arthur
>   PO MiD COPP3 Arakan coast, Nov 1944/Mar 1944, 10.7.45

Ruberry, Arthur Symons (two mentions)
>   T/S/Sea MiD COPP3 Arakan coast, Nov 1944/Mar 1945, 10.7.45
>   T/L/Sea MiD COPP3 Op *Confidence*, Morib, June 1945, 23.10.45

Starn, Harold Charles
>   T/L/Sea COPP4 Ops Arakan coast, Nov 1944/Mar 1945, 10.7.45

Hughes, Alexander Ian, RNR
>   (See above)

Stanley, Alfred E, RNVR
>   T/Lt COPP10 Aegean ops, 1944

Burke, Terence Martin, RNVR
>   Lt MiD COPP4 Ops Arakan coast, Mar/April 1945

Cumberland, Crawford, Royal Scots
>   Sgt MiD COPP8 Op *David*, Arakan, Oct 1944, 22.3.45

Stewart, John Michael
>   L/Sea MiD COPP1 Ops Arakan coast, Mar/Apr 1945

Hatton, Thomas
>   L/Sea MiD COPP9 Arakan coast, Mar/Apr 1945

Morrison, A A, RE
>   L/Cpl MiD COPP7 Op *Frippery*, N Sumatra, Aug 1944

Preedy, Richard F, RE
>   Capt COPP9 Ops Far East, 1945

Colson, Alexander Francis Lionel, RE
>   (See above)

Alcock, Ian Ernest, RCNVR
>   (See above)

Hood, Alan Martin, RNVR
>   S-Lt MiD COPP3 Op *Confidence*, Morib, Jun 1945, 15.5.46

Turner, Thomas Harry
>   AB MiD COPP3 Op *Baboon*, Phuket, Siam, Mar 1945, 15.5.46

Sowter, Alan Tregarthen
>   AB MiD COPP3 Op *Confidence*, Morib, Jun 1945, 15.5.46

DSM

Thomas, Alfred James DSM
    Stwd MiD HMS *Salvia* Greek withdrawal, April 1941
    Stwd DSM HMS *Salvia* Crete withdrawal, 1941
    T/A/L/Sea DSM* COPP5 Sicily/Italy, May 1943, 7.12.43
    T/S-Lt RNVR MiD* COPP5 Morib, Malaya, June 1945, 23.10.45
Main, Caruth
    L/Sea DSM COPP4 recce Sicily/Italy, May 1943, 7.12.43
Phillips, Frederick William
    L/Sea DSM COPP6 recce Sicily/Italy, May 1943, 7.12.43
Bowden, John Henry
    AB DSM COPP6 Recce Sicily landings, 1943, 7.12.43
Reilly, Thomas
    A/PO DSM COPP4 Recce Sicily/Italy, May 1943, 7.12.43
Harding, Eric William
    L/Sea DSM COPP10 Ops Adriatic Aegean coast
Kennedy, Lawrence
    T/A/PO DSM COPP7 Op *Frippery*, N Sumatra, Aug 1944
Turner, Thomas Harry
    T/A/L/Sea DSM COPP3 Op *Baboon*, Phuket, Siam, Mar 1945, 10.7.45

DCM, MM

Ogden-Smith, Bruce Walter, HAC and E Surrey Regt
    Sergt MM COPP1 Normandy recce, Op *KJH*, Dec/Jan 1944
    Sergt DCM COPP1 Normandy recce, Op *Bell Push Able*, Jan 1945

Note: This makes a total of over 90 decorations for gallantry, including MiDs. Where known, decorations in previous service have been included, but not included in this total.

Appendix 9

Personnel in COPP parties

Note: It is extremely difficult to put together a finite list of personnel in COPP parties. Not least because, as each COPP returned to base it was disbanded – then reconstituted with the *same* number. So that there were never more than ten COPP parties.

Service numbers, where known, have been included: ratings' numbers have proved meaningful to COPPists who have seen the list in draft. In principle all Combined Operations ratings should have been given new (Combined Operations) numbers – as with Jack Phillis – but *London Gazette* entries, for gallantry awards, indicate that this official policy was not always implemented.

3-Day Recce of the Island of Rhodes
Lt N C Willmott, RN
Maj R J A Courtney, KRRC
J M H Shepherd, Cpl, MM, RASC

Party Inhuman – pre-Op *Torch*
Lt-Cdr N C Willmott, DSO, RN
Lt D W Amer, RNR
Lt L G Lyne, RN
Lt F W Hayden, RN
Lt N W Cooper, RNVR
Lt P D Thomas, RNR
Lt N P C Hastings, DSC, RNVR
Lt J C Tongue, DSO, RNVR
Lt N T McHarg, RN
Lt N J M Teacher, DSO, RN
Lt T E Edwards, RN
Lt G Sinclair, DSC, RNVR
Lt-Cdr L H Moorhouse, RNR
Lt G M H Drummond, RN
Lt J S Townson, RN
Sub-Lt K F Gwynne, RNVR
Lt I H Harris, RNVR

Lt R M Mangnall, DSC, RNVR

SBS Personnel
Capt G B Courtney, QORWK
Capt R P Livingstone, Royal Ulster Rifles
Capt B N Eckhard, The Buffs
Lt P A Ayton, Argyll and Sutherland Highlanders
Lt J P Foot, Dorsetshires

COPP1 – Naval Party 750
Lt-Cdr N C Willmott, DSC, RN (S/COPP)
Lt N P C Hastings, DSC, RNVR (A/COPP)
Lt G V Galwey, RNVR (M/COPP)
R F A Harbud, Midshipman, RNVR (AM/COPP)
Maj L. Scott-Bowden, RE (E/COPP)
B W Ogden-Smith, Cpl, East Surrey Regt & HAC (6826651)

COPP1 (1) Far East Recommission – Naval Party 750
Lt-Cdr Peter Wild, RNVR
Sub-Lt R F Harbud, RNVR
Sub-Lt M Pearson, RNVR
Sub-Lt David White
Maj Jack Crane, RE
Cooke, Sergt
Fish, PO
Richey, Cpl, SBS

COPP Depot Personnel
A Briggs, PO (P/JX 144952)
R C Hunter, Sailmaker (P/JX 113055)
O Olufsen, Shipwright 4th Class (P/MX 79106)
J Phillis, PO Writer (P/MX 60866CO)
C W Fish, Elect A 5th Class (P/MX 99097)
F I Wilkens, L/Stores Asst (P/MX 59960)
N E Pelley, L/Stores Asst (P/DX 241)
W Spence, Shipwright 4th Class (P/MX 78621)
H E Canning, Sailmaker's Mate (P/JX 156440)
A Prior, AB (P/JX 159124)
R R M Rourke, AB (P/JX 261965)
W Tebb, AB (D/JX 145150)
R M W Kedge, Spr RE (1949872)

COPP2 – Naval Party (700 or 701)
Lt R H Fyson, RN (S/COPP)
Lt B Dawson, RNVR (A/COPP)
Sub-Lt J A Younger (M/COPP)
Sub-Lt A H Wallwork, SANFV (AM/COPP)
Capt D R Freeman, RE (E/COPP)

C Irvine, L/Sea (Coxwain Paddler/Leadsman to S/COPP)
S T Davies, EM (Gear maintenace and reserve paddler)
B A Gillingham, AB (Leadsman and paddler)
J B Cox, AB (Leadsman and paddler)
H. Blackmoor, RE, SBS (Paddler/asst to E/COPP, armourer)
D G Bromfiled, L/Cpl, RE (Draughtsman and storekeeper)
Hunt, Spr (Orderly and general duties)
plus the following:
J Smith, Cpl, RE
Lt Dawson, RNVR
Lt J. R. Hashim

COPP/Middle East 1
Lt P R G Smith, RN
Lt A Hart, RNVR
Lt D Brand, RNVR
Sub-Lt E. Folder, RNVR
Austin, Pte, SBS

COPP/MIDDLE EAST 2
Lt De V P de C Kock, SANF, MBE, DSC
Lt G Davies, RNVR
Sub-Lt A H Crossley, SANF
J McGuire, AB
Budd, Pte, SBS

COPP/Middle East (unnumbered)
Sub-Lt K G Patterson, RANVR
Gordon Lockhead, AB

COPP3
Lt-Cdr N J M Teacher, DSO, RN*
Lt N W Cooper, RNVR*
Capt G W Burbidge, RCE*
C Main, L/Sea**
Loasby, L/Sergt, SBS
Harris, AB

* Lost in Sicily reconnaissances
** Caruth Main lost following D-Day, Normandy landings

plus:
D M Hutton, Writer (P/MX 106002)
J W Walker, Spr, RE (1949872 to rejoin COPP3 on its return)

COPP3 (1) (Recommission) – Naval Party 775 – Far East
Lt A I Hughes, RNR (S/COPP)
Lt A I Alcock, RCNVR (A/COPP)

Sub-Lt A Hood, RNVR (M/COPP)
Sub-Lt A J Thomas, DSM, RNVR (AM/COPP)
Capt W E F Johns, RE* (E/COPP)
A S Ruberry, L/Sea (Coxswain, Hughes's paddler)
F Cammidge, Sergt, RE*
A White, L/EM (party electrician)
T Turner, AB (Alcock's paddler)
A T Sowter, AB (Hood's paddler)
J Young, L/Cpl, RE (party draughtsman)
R Cockram, Spr, RE (Storesman/Officer's batman)
* Both killed, in action at Phuket, replaced by:
Capt J Ashford, RE (E/COPP)
J Lomas, Sergt, RE

COPP4 – Naval Party 770 (PRO DEFE2 1101)
Lt N T McHarg, DSO, RN (S/COPP)
Lt G D Sinclair, DSO, DSC, RNR (A/COPP)
Lt R B Mangall, DSC, RNVR (M/COPP)
Capt N E C Rice, RE (E/COPP)
C Main, L/Sea (P/JX 131567)
J Reilly, L/Sea (A/JX 154647)
P J Harris, AB (P/JX 270894)
J B Seagust, AB (P/JX 162854)
P Hallet, SA (P/MX 105735)
P J Palmer, EM (P/MX 99618)
J E Hinkley, RE (2162287)

COPP4 (1) Far East Recommission – Naval Party 755
Lt D H Mackay, RN (S/COPP)
Lt T M Burke, RNVR (M/COPP)
Sub-Lt Wickenden, RNVR (A/COPP)
1. Capt J B Griffith, RE (E/COPP)
2. Capt W Kingston, RE (E/COPP)
Davidson, Sergt, RE
H C Starn, L/Sea
Kerr, Sean, Elect. Mech 5th class
A B Nicholls, AB
E J Oram, AB
Truner, Draughtsman, RE
Adamson, Pte, Pioneer Corps

COPP5 – Naval Party 730 (Sicily, Italy, Salerno recces)
Lt R N Stanbury, DSC, RN (S/COPP)
Lt D T Kent, DSC, RNVR (A/COPP)
Lt M T T Simpson, RNVR (M/COPP)
Midshipman, P S Sykes, RNVR (AM/COPP)
Lt P D Matterson, RE (E/COPP)
A J Thomas, DSM, A/L/Sea (P/SR 38974)

A B Nicholls, Ord Sea (FX90901)
J Hatton, Ord Sea (P/JX 323641)
N H Goodyear, EM, 5th Class (C/MX 97527)
R A Williamson, Cpl, R Scots and SBS (5959801)
J R Smith, Spr, RE (1953343)

COPP5 (1) First Recommission Rhine Crossings
Lt A Harvey Winship, SANF(V)
Lt Alastair Gavin Hamilton, RN
Capt Richard Francis Preedy, RE
Young, PO
Armstrong, AB

COPP5 (2) Second Recommission (Italy and SEAC)
Lt Alastair Gavin Hamilton, RN (S/COPP)
(personnel otherwise as First recommission)

COPP6 – Naval Party 725 (Sicily, Normandy and S of France)
Lt D W Amer, RNR (S/COPP)
Lt P G Wild, RNVR (A/COPP)
Sub-Lt A G Sayce, RNVR* (M/COPP)
Midshipman J G Watson, RNVR (AM/COPP)
Capt D C Hunter, RE (E/COPP)
F Phillips, A/L/Sea (P/JX 216631)
V F P Manning, A/L/Sea* (P/JX 198429)
J Bowden, AB (P/JX 153781)
R Cook, Cpl, SBS (5508855)
J Plummer, Spr, RE (1952963)

* Sayce and Manning killed in Sicily landings – Commonwealth War Graves
Commission state no known graves.

COPP6 (1) Recommission – Italy, Ceylon
Lt David Glassford Kay, RN
Lt 'Bill' Reid, RNVR
Sub-Lt 'Jack' Watson, RNVR
Sub-Lt Chisholm, RNVR
Capt 'Johnny' Johnson, RE
Phillips, PO
Baxter, AB
(Plus 3 others)

COPP7 – Naval Party 735 (Arakan, Sumatra (SEAC))
Lt G P D Hall, RN (S/COPP)
Lt J D R Maclean, RNVR (A/COPP)
Lt N H Jennings, RNVR (M/COPP)
Midshipman P G R Gimson (AM/COPP)
Capt A W T Lucas, RE (E/COPP)

D T Owen, Cpl, SBS (595801)
J B Nichol, L/Sea (P/JX 153628)
L. Kennedy, AB (P/SSX 28553)
E Alexander, EM, Class 5 (C/MX 95153)
Witham, AB
A A Morrison, Draughtsman, RE (3768553)

COPP7 (1) Recommission (Elbe Crossing)
Lt John R Hashim, RN
Lt Alastair Henderson, RN
Sub-Lt P Gimson, RNVR
Sub-Lt John Turner, RNVR
Maj J B Griffith, RE
Young, PO
John Bowden, L/Sea, DSM
Francis McNally, Company Sergt-Maj
Gale, Sergt

COPP8 – Naval Party 740 Arakan, Sumatra, Andamans (SEAC)
Lt F Ponsonby, RN (S/COPP)
Lt M. Peacock, RNVR (A/COPP)
(later) Sub-Lt R W Gambrill, RNVR (A/COPP)
Lt G Richards, RNVR (M/COPP)
Capt A F L Colson, RE (E/COPP)
P Crafer, Later Lt G F v N Kuyper, SANF (V) (AM/COPP)
R Gascoigne, PO
J C Neil, L/Sea
S V Pond, EM
R R M Rourke, AB
C Cumberland, Sgt, Royal Scots, SBS
Duffy, Spr/L/Cpl, Draughtsman, RE

COPP9 (Mediterranean and Far East)
Lt John Morison, RN
Lt John Charles Macaulay Booth, RNVR
Lt Hartnett, RNVR
Capt R H C Gates, MC, RE
Harold Charles, Starn, PO
James McGuire, PO
Thomas Hatton, L/Sea
W. Tebb, L/Sea
Jack Powell, Sergt
L/Cpl, Draughtsman, RE
Batman, Spr

COPP10 Anzio, Italy, Yugoslavia, Dalmatia, Aegean
Lt (N) J S Townson, RN (S/COPP)
Lt A E Stanley, RNVR (A/COPP)

Lt G R Talbot, RNVR (M/COPP)
Sub-Lt J H Maynard, RNVR (AM/COPP)
Capt J C Lamb, Commando, SBS, RE (E/COPP)
L S Parker, PO Elect
G H Lamont, Sergt, Commando, SBS, Royal Scots
W Harding, L/Sea
Duncan Brown, AB
J Carter, AB
H E McCarey, Spr, Draughtsman, RE

Appendix 10

ROLL OF HONOUR

1 On COPP Operations

Lt-Cdr N J M Teacher, DSO	COPP3: Sicily recce
Capt G W Burbidge, RCE	COPP3: Sicily recce
Lt N W Cooper, RNVR	COPP3: Sicily recce
Lt P de C DE Kock, MBE, DSC, SANF	COPP2: (Middle East): Sicily recce
Lt A F Crossley, SANF(V)	COPP2 (Middle East): Sicily recce
Sub-Lt A G Sayce, RNVR	COPP6: Invasion of Sicily
L/Sea V F P Manning	COPP6: Invasion of Sicily
Capt W E F Johns, MC, RE	COPP3(2): Phuket recce
Sergt F Cammidge, RE	COPP3(2): Phuket recce

2 On Operation *Provident* (armed recce Oyster Island) by COPP7

L/Sea A B Sayers (crew member LCP 360) drowned following collision with ML 438, after operation, returning to Cocanada.

3 Following Normandy D-Day Landings (at sea)

L/Sea C Main, DSM	ex-COPP3

4 Killed in cross-fire Greek civil war 1944

L/Sea W Harding	COPP10

5 On Combined COPP1(2)/SOG Operation *Copyright*: Phuket

Maj J Maxwell, RM	(PoW) executed by Japs
C/Sergt E R Smith, RM	(PoW) executed by Japs
Mne B Brownlie, RM	killed in action by Japs

As COPP records at the Public Record Office are incomplete, it is not possible to compile a list of those killed after return to General Service.

Appendix 11

CANOES

Mark I** – COPP favourite: proofed canvas and proofed linen over a wooden frame.

Mark II** – Plywood deck and hull bottom, used by the RMBPD on the Bordeaux raid, had canvas sides.

Mark III – 2-man rigid canoe, moulded plywood, three sections. Foe'ard and aft sections filled with table-tennis balls for buoyancy. It took four men to lift it.

Mark IV – Powered by a 4 horse power, two-stroke engine.

Mark VIII – Four-seater, motor propelled, developed from Mark III.

Select Bibliography

Anonymous. *The Royal Marines,* The Admiralty account of their achievement. London HMSO, 1944.

Curtis, Rupert. *Chronicles of D-Day.* Privately printed.

Courtney, B G, MBE, MC. *SBS in World War II.* Robert Hale, 1983.

Davie, Michael, ed. *The Diaries of Evelyn Waugh.* Weidenfeld and Nicolson, 1976; Penguin Books Edition, 1979.

Eckhard, Basil. *Party Inhuman Log,* an unpublished contemporary diary, 1942.

Galwey, Geoffrey, V. *Geoff's Opus,* a record of survival, one way or the other. Privately printed.

Jewell, N L A. *Secret Mission Submarine.* Ziff Davies, New York, 1979.

Ladd, James. *Commandos and Rangers of World War II.* Macdonald and Jane's, 1978.

——. *SBS: The Invisible Raiders.* Arms and Armour Press, 1983; David & Charles, 1989.

McNab, Andy (pseud.). *Bravo Two–Zero.* Bantam Press, 1993.

Macksie, Kenneth. *Commando Strike,* the story of Amphibious Raiding in World War II. Leo Cooper in association with Secker and Warburg Ltd, 1985.

Miller, Russell. *Nothing Less than Victory,* an Oral History of D-Day. Michael Joseph, 1993.

Mitchell, Pamela. *The Tip of the Spear:* The Midget Submarines. Richard Netherwood, 1993.

Neville (Stanbury), Ralph. *Survey by Starlight.* Hodder, 1949.

Pearson, Michael and Strutton, Bill. *The Secret Invaders.* Hodder, 1958.

Seymour, William. *British Special Forces.* Sidgwick and Jackson, 1985; Grafton Books, 1986.

Public Record Office
Naval Staff Histories Submarines
ADM234/52 1, 2 and 3.
DEFE2 and WO series.

Historical
DEFE2 1111 COPP Reports, History (fragmentary).
DEFE2 1116 COPP Progress Reports 1–135.
DEFE2 1152 Lists some personnel of some COPPs.

DEFE2 1214 Awards and Medals for COPP Personnel – includes COPP numbers involved Sicily and Italy; India; Europe

Far East
DEFE2 1101 COPP Allocation of personnel.
DEFE2 780 Histories and accounts of Chief of Combined Operations Representative Washington, No 10 Inter-Allied Commando and SOG (Small Operations Group) in South East Asia 1942–46.
DEFE 1158 DCO India; monthly bulletins (includes Op *Gosling*).

Training Manual, Peripheral Interest
DEFE2 748 COPP Depot Training Book.
DEFE2 1008 COXE: Programme of trials 1943; Torridge House, West Devon – last entry, 23 Dec 1943.
DEFE2 842 Folbot 'Historical' file; there are other folbot files.
DEFE2 1192 COPP Recce by an aircraft.

Special Boat Section *et al*
DEFE2 740 Special Boat Service.
WO218 103 No. 2 Special Boat Section.
ADM202 311 No. 2 Special Boat Section, *War Diary 1943–44:* CO R J Courtney, MC.
DEFE2 970 SBU (Special Boat Unit) – principally refers Hammenheil.

Operations
DEFE2 Operational codes names, by no means exhaustive.
DEFE2 588 Operation *Torch* Beach Recce.
DEFE2 95 Operations *Copyright* and *Baboon*.
WO203 4317 Operation *Culverin*.
WO203 3006 Planning for Operation *Culverin*.
WO203 2174 Intelligence Java and Sumatra.
WO203 1670 Intelligence Phuket.
DEFE2 291 Sicily, Operation *Husky*: notes/memos.
DEFE2 295 Sicily, Operation *Husky*: Basil Henriques refers beach reconnaissance, including wave velocity method of estimating gradients.
DEFE2 296 Sicily, Operation *Husky*: report on signals.
DEFE2 297 Sicily, Operation *Husky*: lessons learnt (RAF).
DEFE2 298 Sicily, Operation *Husky*: diary of events includes typed copy of letter from HMK George VI to WSC.

Related Topics
DEFE2 1232 Research on Beach Recce: post D-Day.
DEFE2 1148 Disposal of beach- and underwater-obstacles.
DEFE2 783 Destruction of minefields.
DEFE2 275 Operation *Anteroom* – beach recce Bay of Mont St Michel: 1 MTB plus surfboats for landing recce party: military personnel approx. 15 (all ranks) COPP (sic). No evidence included that this was more than projected.
DEFE2 754 Combined Ops HQ Bulletins X/17 M.C. Beach Tester a/k/o Malcolm Campbell's 'Pogo stick'.

Eulogy

PART I

We have gathered here today in Palmerston Place Church in Edinburgh, from Cyprus to the Isle of Mull, from Devon and Cornwall to Mallaig, from high ranks to low, to remember with gratitude, and with not a little wonder, the life of Nigel Clogstoun-Willmott, Captain in the Royal Navy. Five times in World War II, Nigel's acts of bravery were officially recognised by the award of 1 DSO, 2 DSCs and 2 Mentions in Dispatches.

Nigel was born in Simla in 1910 and died in Paphos, Cyprus, just before his eighty-second birthday. Fortunately, three excellent tributes have been published about this remarkable Naval Officer, both at home and abroad. So I feel free to concentrate on Nigel's most outstanding achievements, starting with his naval career.

In World War II, Nigel invented, pioneered and gradually perfected the complex professional techniques for reconnoitring beaches and for leading in invasions, mainly using submarines and canoes. As a Lieutenant-Commander RN he was ordered by Lord Louis Mountbatten with maximum speed to select, equip and to train what became known as COPPs – Combined Operations Pilotage Parties and was given the Top Priority of the War.

Nigel was therefore free to *select* the specialists he needed from the Navy, the Royal Engineers and the Commando Special Boat Section. But just as vital, Nigel could *commandeer* the finest equipment available – and could even redesign it (or design it from scratch) *exactly as he wanted*. As a result COPPs were so efficient in all invasions, and even in major river crossings, that Nigel's ideas probably saved thousands of lives and certainly shortened the War.

But the end of hostilities did not signal the end of his brainchild. His original concept lives on in the elite Special Boat Squadron of the Royal Marine Commandos. All their members are hand picked from the Royal Marine Commandos before being rigorously trained. Some of Nigel's original equipment is still in use, though much of it has been vastly improved.

It is now over 51 years since Nigel saved the life of the CO of the original SBS, whilst carrying out the first beach reconnaissance of the war. At this Remembrance Service, Coppists have assembled from all over britain. Also present is Ron Youngman, General Secretary of The Commando Association, accompanied by many Scottish Commandos, who knew Nigel personally. From the Royal Navy, and representing the Flag Officer Scotland and Northern Ireland, we have Captain Duncan J Ellin, OBE, Naval Regional Officer. Finally, although security prevents me from mentioning names, you have my personal assurance that the *modern* SBS is very adequately represented. Nigel has been fittingly remembered.

I owe it to you to mention that the music for the Introit was played exactly one month ago to celebrate Trafalgar Day, a very important day in Nigel's calendar. As we sing the next hymn, let us all remember, with gratitude and with due humility, the incalculable debt which Britain, and indeed the wider world, owed to Nigel in World War II. Let us sing together Hymn 480 – a great favourite of Nigel's – 'Glorious things of Thee are spoken', to the tune of the Austrian National Anthem.

PART II

From Nigel the Naval Officer, I now turn to Nigel the man. In Nigel, we have a man of sterling qualities. He was intensely loyal – to his family, to his friends, to his country and to his ideals. He had a penetrating inventive genius. The Commandos admired his charisma, his zest for life, his enormous courage and his disarming modesty. His sensitivity and his wry sense of humour made him many friends. Though the list of his qualities is endless, it does perhaps explain why a man of 81, who died thousands of miles away, should attract hundreds of letters of sympathy and dozens of telephone calls.

All who passed through COPP Depot will remember with affection the elegant Leading Wren, Prudence Wright. Towards the end of the war, when Nigel had left COPPs, Prue and Nigel were happily married. They had three children, all of them present today – Jonathan, Teresa and Serena. Throughout his life Nigel was always genuinely concerned and caring about his family and his grandchildren. He was especially pleased when his grandson Kit was born, because the *family* name would be preserved for a further generation. Indeed, the compelling reason for his last visit to the UK, only a month before he died, was to attend Serena's wedding.

In his retirement, his love of the sea continued. In his 10-ton ketch, he enjoyed cruising between the Bay of Biscay and the Butt of Lewis. Up to the age of 76, Nigel sailed his ketch up and down the west of Scotland single-handed, a feat of navigation and seamanship which won the admiration of all the locals.

It took another ex-Wren, Pamela, to lure Nigel ashore and back to civilisation. Ten years ago they were married in this Church and at once found themselves in a really welcoming congregation. Pamela was the perfect foil for Nigel, bringing laughter and gaiety into his life. Together they attracted friends, like snowballs running downhill out of control. Five years later, before settling in Cyprus, they threw a party in the New Club. Only 65 friends were able to attend. History repeated itself in Cyprus, where they took the island by storm.

On Nigel's last visit to Britain, he accomplished much in spite of failing health. He visited all his family. Serena's wedding gave him great joy, as did his dinner at the Club in London with his old COPP friend Scotty (Major-General Logan Scott-Bowden, DSO, MC). With all his missions accomplished, Nigel returned to Cyprus, where he died in hospital on 2nd June.

Nigel possessed many of the qualities that we all admire. I would suggest that those of us who knew him well can best keep his memory fresh by taking even *one* of these qualities and trying to emulate his high standard.

Ronnie Williamson

Index